Winter India

Winter India

Eliza Ruhamah Scidmore

GYAN

Published by

Gyan Publishing House
5, Ansari Road
Daryaganj, New Delhi-110002
Phone: 011-47034999, 9811692060
E-mail: books@gyanbooks.com

Distribution Network
gyanbooks.com
India, USA, Canada, UK, Australia, France

ISBN: 978-81-212-8374-8 (PB)
First Published, 1903

2nd Impression 2023

Printed at: Gyan Press, Delhi.

WINTER INDIA
Author: ELIZA RUHAMAH SCIDMORE

Winter India

THE SACRED BO-TREE AND THE DIAMOND THRONE, BUDDHA-GAYA.

THE CENTER OF THE UNIVERSE AND THE VERANDA OF KNOWLEDGE.

Winter India

By

Eliza Ruhamah Scidmore

Author of "Jinrikisha Days in Japan," "Java: The Garden of the East, and "China: The Long-Lived Empire"

New York
The Century Co.
1903

CONTENTS

LIST OF ILLUSTRATIONS

INTRODUCTION

IT can hardly be said with literalness that one enjoys India. I had not expected to enjoy it, and it proved itself, despite its color and picturesqueness, quite as melancholy and depressing a country as I had thought it would be; but so absorbingly interesting, so packed with problems, so replete with miracles accomplished by alien rule, so ripe with possibilities, that one soon overlooked the unnecessary hardships and discomforts of travel—travel as plain and primitive as in the Klondike, or as if the country had been conquered only within this decade.

The surprises, the contrasts, and the contradictions administer perpetual shock and mental stimulus, and the unexpected continually confronts one. Never have I suffered with cold as in India. Not a snake did I see or hear of in the cold-weather, tourist season, save in zoölogical gardens or snake-charmers' baskets, and the tigers were likewise caged.

There are so many Indias that no one person can know them all, and the Winter India which the tourist sees during the cold-weather weeks is not the real one which the Anglo-Indian knows the year around. The military man, the civilian officer, the missionary, planter, and merchant has each his own India and view-point; and the British visitor, who is passed from home to home by the endless chain of Anglo-Indian hospitality, sees and thinks differently from the other tourists who suffer the drear hotels, the dak banglas, and the railway-station rooms.

The worst hotels in the world are those of India, and a British traveler has truthfully written: "You will enjoy your traveling in India if you have so many friends there that you need never put foot in a hotel. If you have not, you had better go somewhere else." Each winter the peninsula holds a growing number of surprised and resentful tourists, who, whether they land at Bombay or Calcutta, usually conclude that the shortest route across India is the best one. One month or six weeks is the average stay; and very few tourists ever go to the hills for the summer and come back to the plains for a second cold-weather season of travel. The average tourist sacrifices itineraries without compunction, and lives to warn away aged and invalid tourists and to convince those with weak lungs and impaired digestions that death waits in Indian hotels.

The glamour of the East does not often or for long enthrall one while touring Hindustan. Later it asserts itself, reveals its haunting charm; and then, be it months or years afterward, he "hears the East a-callin'." He forgets the ice in the bath-tubs at Agra and Delhi, the bitterly cold nights in drafty, dusty, springless cars, and in visions he sees only "the sunshine an' the palm-trees an' the tinkly temple bells," the brilliantly costumed people, and the miracles of architecture scattered so lavishly from end to end of the empire.

A new India for the tourist will date from the great durbar at Delhi in 1903, and India, which has been a winter preserve for visiting English, will be virtually discovered and opened to a wider clientele, made as possible and fit for luxurious travel as Egypt. Equally this day of cheap travel and cheap living will vanish as completely as on the Nile.

For one to announce that he will spend a winter in India is hardly more definite or precise than to say that he will winter in Europe. India is a very large country,—several large countries,—since it equals in area and population all of Europe outside of Russia; and one travels the nineteen hundred miles of its extent from south to north through as many political divisions as there are great divisions of Europe, and differing as greatly in climate, physical features, and inhabitants. The Spaniard does not differ more from the Laplander than the sooty Tamil from the blue-eyed Afridi, the weak Bengali from the fighting Rajput or the fierce Sikh. Besides the thirteen provinces under British rule, there are six hundred and fifty native states; but only two hundred of them are of great importance, since native states range in size from Hyderabad, the size of Italy, to single villages in Kathiawar and tiny valleys in the Himalayan foot-hills, empires two miles square.

The census of 1901 gave a total of 294,360,356 inhabitants—five times as many Hindus as Mohammedans, and one hundred and nine times as many natives as English. The fourteen distinct races follow eight forms of religious belief, and speak some two hundred and forty languages and three hundred dialects; all legislative acts are published in English, Persian, Bengali, and Hindustani—and then only one man in ten can read. The permanence of British rule and the safety of British interests lie in this diversity of race, language, government, and religion. In division is strength, in discord is stability, since their race hatreds, jealousies, animosities, and antipathies would never permit a native leader to be acceptable to all the native malcontents, and patriotism or any national spirit is as lacking as the sense of those words, and of even the word for gratitude. With no common language or religion, no national feeling, in this congress of nations, one may paraphrase a certain interrogative and exclaim: "The Indians! Who are they?"

One fifth of the human race dwells between the Himalayas and the ocean; the records of their civilization go back for three thousand years, and history has been written upon history on those plains. Rice—two hundred and ninety-five kinds of rice, called by as many names in as many tongues—and pulse are the staple food of this great agricultural people, drought and famine the lot of some state or province each year, with plague and cholera seldom absent. Two great famines and the continual ravages of the bubonic pest greatly reduced the population during the last decade of the past century, the decrease in the native states being many times greater than in the British provinces. Increased areas of irrigation and cultivation have made it possible for the increasing millions to live—to half live, according to European standards, for the Indian coolie or agricultural worker is lowest in the scale of living and wages and in standard of comfort of any Asiatic. Great calamities and scourges afford the only relief from over-population,—a population in which the women are in deficit to the number of six millions, and their illiteracy so great that only one woman in one hundred and sixty can read.

All these diverse races and peoples are picturesque to look upon, with their graceful draperies of brilliant colors and the myriad forms of turbans; but they are not an attractive, a winning, a sympathetic, or a lovable people. They are as antipathetic and devoid of charm as the Chinese, as callous, as deficient in sympathy and the sense of pity as those next neighbors of theirs in Asia, and as impossible for the Occidental to fathom or comprehend,—an irresistible, inexplicable, unintelligible repulsion controlling one. India vexes one sadly because of the irrational, illogical turns of the Indian mind and character, the strange *impasses* in the Indian brain, the contradictions of traits; and, because of the many things he cannot account for or reach solution of, he quits the country baffled and in irritation—forever the great gulf yawning between the Occidental and the Asiatic. "East is East, and West is West."

Not one of the innumerable tongues that he hears spoken by the common people in the bazaars falls musically on the ear, and beyond the numerals and a few utility words he is little tempted to dabble even with Urdu, the camp language, the lingua franca of the upper part of the peninsula. *Jao!* (Begone!) is the first word he learns and most constantly uses, the last syllable uttered on leaving.

From the babel of tongues, with no common alphabet, has come a confusion of spelling, and the modern or Hunterian method, although officially adopted by the government in 1880, does not enjoy general acceptance and use in India. Sir William Hunter gave years to investigating and recording local usages, to transliterating from Sanskrit and the vernacular the geographic names of the peninsula, and the publication of his great *Gazetteer* should have ended the confusion of nomenclature. Many of his departures were too radical for the older Anglo-Indians to accept—*bangla* was not the same as bungalow to them, *kuli* did not represent coolie, nor *pankha* the cooling punka; and five, eleven, and seventy-two ways of spelling a single place-name continue in common use—three distinct systems of spelling and local usage still prevailing, often in determined opposition to the Hunterian method. The first American authority, which is followed in this volume, does not wholly accept Sir William Hunter's decisions. The new method will ultimately prevail, but with another generation.

WINTER INDIA

WINTER INDIA

CHAPTER I

ON INDIA'S CORAL STRAND

THE monkeys built a bridge for Rama to cross to Ceylon, and sections of the causeway by which Adam traversed the Palk Strait remain as evidence of his good fortune on tour; but for us there was the worst of many bad "B. I." boats, and a night of never to be forgotten misery, disgust, and discomfort on the Gulf of Manaar's deceptive waters. Of all dream nights in the tropics, none matched that night on which we coursed slowly along the south shore of Ceylon, from Colombo westward. Enormous stars pulsed in an intense indigo sky, the moon rose and, streaming across a summer sea, made a heaven above, beneath, and far around us. In the midst of this silvery world floated the odorous, untidy coasting steamer, from whose decks we instinctively lifted our skirts by day, and across which by dark sped myriads of enormous brown roaches. The dark boxes of cabins rustled with these fleeing insects when a light was brought, and we retreated to spend the night in deck chairs.

Some cross current in that pent-up pocket of Manaar makes it a rival of the English Channel for nausea; but at daylight the ship anchored in shallow, gray-green waters seven miles off the low-lying coast of the Indian peninsula—"India's coral strand"—and for two hours it rocked there more fully to complete the misery of two hundred coolie passengers, heaped together on the forward deck like so much cargo. It was slow work disembarking these limp folk, who fell prone in every stage and attitude of misery fore and aft on the reeling tender. A greasy bench was reserved for us amidships, fairly touching the boilers, and, after inhaling steam and engine grease for an hour, we reached the snow-white beach. Inky-black cargo coolies in red and white draperies filed up and down the sandy shore and the narrow pier of Tuticorin, and there was local color to spare; color, too, in the Custom-house, where an aldermanic black official, with an exaggerated sausage of a turban linked around his caste-marked brow, received us with unctuous gravity, listened to our declaration that we had neither spirits, ammunition, nor firearms, and let us go with our unopened luggage, free to wander at will from that furthest end of the empire to the uttermost mountain wall, without official interference or question, welcome without passport or permit, free from espionage and annoyance: a liberty of entrance, a courteously opened door, that covers the American tourist with chagrin as he contrasts it with the landing at any of his own ports.

Tuticorin's white walls and houses, white sand

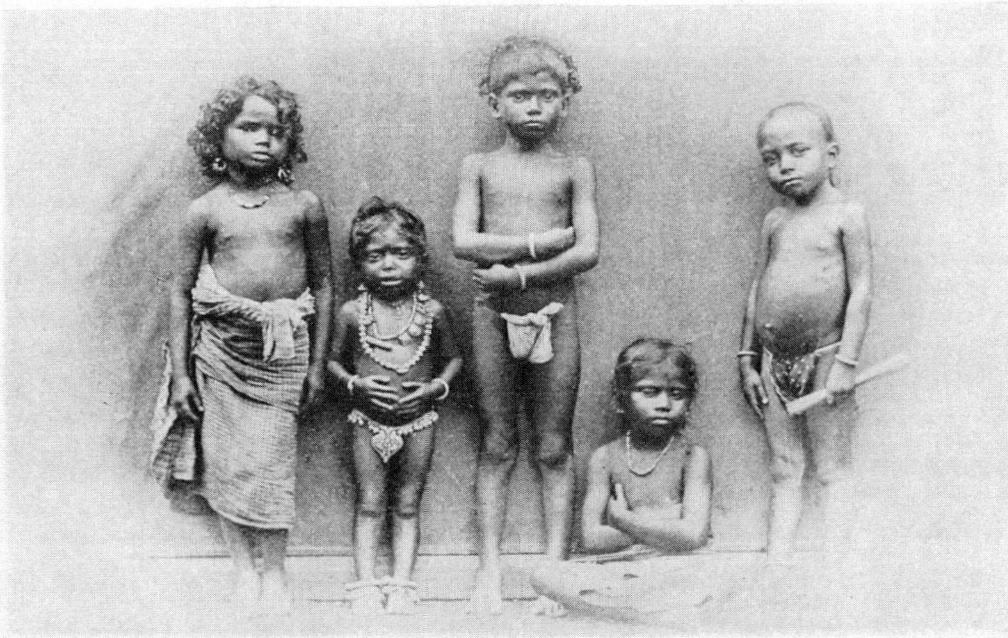

TAMIL CHILDREN.

streets, and the paling turquoise sky were background only for the stage processions and groups of the blackest people on earth. Heavens! how black they were! How very black! When Marco Polo came to the Malabar coast, he said: "The children that are born here are black enough, but the blacker they are, the more they are thought of, so that they become as black as devils."

The Tamil people, ebony black, inky black, sooty black, tall and spare to emaciation, lilted past us on the thin, spindle legs of storks. A mountain of red peppers was heaped in one white square, and scores of the blackest Tamil women, in pepper-red draperies and much silver jewelry, slowly walked and worked around its edges. It was too theatrical, too barefacedly a color tableau set to catch the tourist eye, and I was convinced that it lasted only for that half-hour. The primitive hotel facing the railway station was but a loge looking upon the white roadway of a stage, where a specially engaged troupe of tall Tamils and noble white sacred bullocks paraded for our delight. When the train came in there was bedlam drama at the station's street door; then all the black troupe made exit and melted away to distance and shade; there was an interval, an entr'acte, and we went over and behind the scenes for a while.

The station-master was black, the telegraph operator was shades blacker, and an uncut emerald, swinging from the upper rim of one ear, held me with a great fascination while he skimmed the handful of despatches. First and last, and all of the time, in Indian travel, one telegraphs, and then sends more telegrams ahead, to any and every person connected with his future movements. One telegraphs to dak banglas, to station rooms and hotels, that he is coming; to station-masters that he shall want sleeping accommodation on certain trains; to local guides to secure their services; to high priests, magistrates, commissioners, and commandants that he wishes to see certain temples or sacred treasuries of jewels; and—the government telegraphs being moderate in price—one may "wire" away as recklessly as an American railway president for a comparative trifle.

The Tuticorin station walls were hung with notices and framed regulations, and there was posted a formidable black list of fines and punishments judicially awarded; the offender and his offense paraded to all who travel. Pattu This and Moolie That were fined "for letting their cattle stray and be killed on the track"; another had been caught "riding on the trucks without a ticket"—presumably some passengers, having tickets, do ride on the trucks. They run the Indian railways for the good of the stockholders evidently, and receivers of unhappy railways in America might learn lessons of economy in this land of want, for this is only a periodical advertisement which I cut from a Calcutta paper:

EAST INDIAN RAILWAY

Tenders for the right of picking cinders from ashpits and pumping engines during the twelve months ending 31st March ——

TENDERS will be received at the office of the Controller of Stores, East Indian Railway, Calcutta, up to noon of Thursday, the 14th February ——, for the right of picking cinders from ashes removed from ashpits and pumping engines throughout the line during the twelve months from 1st April —— to 31st March ——.

Form of tender, embodying full particulars, can be had on payment of Re. 1 to the Company's Chief Paymaster, Calcutta, or to the Store-keepers at Asansol, Jamalpur, Dinajpur, Allahabad and Cawnpore, to whom applications, with remittance, should be addressed. Applicants are also referred to the hand-bills posted at railway stations.

All other payments, including a deposit of Rs. 100 as earnest money, will have to be made direct to the Company's Chief Paymaster in Calcutta, whose receipt alone will be recognized, and no payment in respect thereof will be received in the Store Department. Hoondees and stamps will not be accepted.

The Company will nct be bound to accept the highest, or any, tender, and reserves the right to accept any tender in part only.

By order,
J. OATES,
Controller of Stores.

CALCUTTA.

We had heard much of the luxury of Indian railway travel, of the roomy compartment and dressing-room that came to the holder of a first-class ticket without extra charge. We found that the roomy compartment was destined for four people, and contained two long leather-covered seats, or couches, along the side of the car, with two hanging berths that could be dropped at night. The seats had no springs and no backs, unless one chose to lean against the single, rattling window-pane, that lifted by a strap like a carriage window. The cast-iron fittings in the dressing-room were ruder and more primitive than those of any American emigrant car, and when the train began its deliberate progress, we found that the body of the car swung so low, so nearly rested on the trucks, that we were jolted and shaken and deafened, as if in a coal-car, and covered with the dust of the road-bed. Nothing different or better was found, save once, in any part of India. When night came, a feeble oil-lamp was introduced through the roof, that made it possible to distinguish outlines and large objects, but not to read.

The train jogged along northward through a flat, cultivated country, with aloe and thorn hedges inclosing the tracks. After the rank greenness of Ceylon, these dusty fields of the dry season seemed poor and sterile. The train halted near mud villages, and the station platforms were covered with lean and leisurely black folks in red and white cotton draperies, standing at ease, their foreheads so dotted and striped with red, white, and ocher caste-marks, those ciphers, crests, and hall-marks of their creed, that they looked like so many painted red Indians of our West on the war-path. There was the usual station bedlam when the train drew up in darkness at Madura, and we followed a Tamil leader out to blacker darkness across the tracks to the dak bangla. The coolie who carried the bearer's tin trunk on his head stumbled over tree roots and finally struck a branch overhead. There was a crash, a bang, and a wreck of Tamil property, and then a flood of Tamil language, as David, our venerable traveling servant, poured out his wrath on the whining offender, who had been bruised and dented a little himself.

The dak bangla was Spartan in its simplicity, the government providing only beds, chairs, tables, and bath-tubs, the stern necessities of comfort in a hot climate. The stillness was as intense as the darkness all night, and after the *chota hazri* (little breakfast) of the Indian dawn we drove three miles across awakening Madura—a city of low, white houses, with green cocoa-palms and broad banana leaves the only strong color notes. The white houses were dusted and clouded with the red earth surrounding them, all dilapidated and in need of repair, of fall cleaning and whitewash. All Madura was awakening at that dewy hour,—tousled folks who came to the doors, yawned like alligators, stretched their leans arms in air, and scratched their heads vigorously. Men lounged face down on charpoys, or string-beds, or lolled on the high shelves built in the alcoves beside the house doors, and chatted with neighbors who had also spent the night in the open; babies sprawled on the warm red earth, and pious women traced religious symbols in white chalk on the red thresholds. Every door had its sect-mark, its religious symbol and monogram, as much as the foreheads of the people. Every blank wall, too, was plastered over with flat manure cakes, the common and universal fuel of the country, which one sees in process of manufacture and use from end to end of the empire; a fuel whose rank smoke can be detected in everything one eats and drinks in India, from the earliest tea and toast of the morning to the final rice pudding and coffee at night; a fuel whose use deprives the fields of their natural enrichment and adds to the general poverty; a fuel whose manufacture—the gathering, kneading, and shaping into flat cakes to be slapped against a wall to dry—is such ignoble work that rarely any but women are employed in the unending task.

After these early morning sights in the streets, the fantastic Teppa Kulam was a bit of fairyland, a great tank inclosed in a striped red and white stone parapet, with a dazzling marble platform in its center upholding the most fanciful little white coroneted temple, the glorified pavilion of a confectioner's dreams, four mites of lesser pavilions reflected from each corner of the platform. We drove down shady lanes, past the elephant stables, to the garden of the English judge to see the great banian tree, whose main trunk, over seventy feet in circumference, is surrounded by a hundred lesser trunks and newly rooted filaments—a leafy hall of columns, measuring one hundred and eighty feet across.

We went to the spacious Moorish and Hindu seventeenth-century palace of the great ruler, Tirumala Nayak, and after a small boy of the neighborhood had taken us in charge and scolded, stamped his foot, and pushed an old gray-haired sweeper about, that abject being produced the keys and admitted us to cool, shadowy halls and council-chambers with richly carved and paneled ceilings, to the king's bedchamber, where a carved and gilded bed once swung by chains from latticed ceilings, and down whose chains the clever thief slid to steal the crown jewels; and from the terraced roof where the prime minister used to dwell we saw the whole,

THE GREAT GOPURA, MADURA TEMPLE.

flat-roofed city with the great gopuras, or temple gateways, standing like so many Gibraltars in its midst.

These gopuras loom and dwindle away toward the sky in such a way as to make all things seem toys, and the people pygmies. One such monument would be architectural fame for any city, but Madura's rich shrine is protected by nine such soaring, pyramidal sky-scrapers, the four in the outer wall nine stories in height. These most ornamental of defensive constructions begin with door-posts of single stones, sixty feet in height, and rise, course upon course, carved with rows of gods and goddesses, peacocks, bulls, elephants, horses, lions, and a bewildering entanglement of symbolical ornament all colored and gilded, diminishing with distance until the stone trisul at the top, two hundred and fifty feet in air, looks like the finest jeweler's work. This great shrine of Shiva and his fish-eyed consort is a labyrinth where one easily wanders a whole morning. The anteroom or vestibule of the temple is a long hall or choltry, an open pavilion divided by four rows of most elaborately carved columns, where the king used to receive the annual visits of Shiva—a miserable little black image. Neither kings nor idols occupied it then, but a legion of shopkeepers were gathered there, who vaunted their goods and pushed their wares upon us with fury and zeal—cloth, cotton, lace, brass, glass, perfumes, incense, and fruits. One spectacled merchant was casting up his accounts in a ledger made of strips of talipot palm leaves, an orthodox fashion as old as writing.

Others pressed upon us pieces of filmy, gold-bordered Madras muslins, eight yards of which are required for a turban or a woman's sari. There were none of the ancient India muslins, those "floating mists," or "webs of the air," of which one has heard but never sees in this day of Manchester piece goods, steam-mills, and spindles.

Our Tamil servant, being a Christian, would not enter the heathen temple, so consigned us to a high-caste Brahman draped superbly in a white sheet, and striped between his eyebrows with the frowning mark of Shiva. Inside the temple compound, every forehead was freshly painted, breasts and arms striped and smeared with other hall-marks of piety. The black images were streaming with oil and butter, garlanded with chains of marigolds, and surrounded by abject worshipers. In that temple one may fully realize what heathenism and idolatry really are. One meets there the India of the Sunday-school books, and is appalled with the seeming hopelessness of the missionary's task, of the impossibility of ever making any impression upon such a people, of coping with such superstition. Yet the American Mission in Madura is one of the largest and most successful in India, and in this southern presidency one fifth of the people are Christians. Whole villages even are Christian, Syrian, Nestorian, and early Jesuit missionaries having labored there since the third and fourth centuries.

We could look down dark temple corridors to darker shrines, where faint lights glimmered and the highest-caste Brahmans were tending the images of Shiva and Minakshi. Every May these idols are paraded in state to another part of the temple, and the gold and silver chariots and palanquins, the jeweled elephant trappings, and all the treasury of gems belonging to the shrine are brought to light. The Madura temple jewels are among the finest in southern India, and one sees them by special permit, and afterward pays a fee for the cleansing of the jewels. Despite the rupees and rupees that pour in during the cold-weather season of tourists' defilement, no one has ever seen the famous sapphires and big pearls when they were not greasy and gummed over from much tourist and Brahman handling. Other famous treasures are a ruby-covered scepter, three feet long; several pairs of golden shoes and gauntlets coated with rubies; and a head-dress fringed with tallow-drop emeralds.

The famous Hall of a Thousand Columns does not contain nearly that many columns or carved pillars, and, despite the miracle of stone-worker's art lavished on them, and Fergusson's praises, it was disappointing. The tank in the heart of the labyrinth, a water court or quadrangle, was most picturesque with the crowds descending the steps to purify themselves in the water, where broken reflections of the great gopuras wavered across the thick and oily liquid. Sacred elephants came shuffling across sunny courts, their bells, swinging by long ropes over their embroidered trappings, clanging an alarum. Having returned from the river with the gold lotas filled with water for the daily bath of the goddess, they stood at ease in a shady hall, swinging their painted trunks and shifting their weight from one foot to the other. At the word of command, the hugest of them tossed his trunk in salute, made a court courtesy, and, nosing the ground, picked up the tiniest silver three-anna piece. The elephants flicked their flanks with fly-brushes of green twigs as they stood guard benignly over the hall where jewelers were hammering, welding, and carving gold and silver ornaments. Veiled women sat around a merchant of cheaper gauds, who, with a small prentice boy, cracked or filed off the old bracelets and soldered on the new.

It was then ten o'clock in the morning, the heat was terrific, the sun blinding, and we had spent five busy hours abroad. The dak bangla was an asylum of coolness and shade, and after a bountiful tiffin the keeper presented his account-book, we entered the items, added up the bill, and settled our score with the British government in India. The keeper bowed profoundly, and wished the "ladyships" a good health, when a fee had gone his way; and then, in strict order of social precedence, the cook and the coolie, the sweeper, the water-carrier, and what not, presented themselves, bowing, at different doors. They rubbed their palms upward across their faces, extended them to us, wobbling their fingers as if gathering grains of rice, and whined: "Prissint! Prissint! Memsahib!" We gave to each one, and, without stopping to bow or to thank us, each one looked greedily into the other's palm and went away loudly wrangling—a first encounter with the most cringing, graceless, shameless tribe of alms-seekers in all the world.

DETAIL OF GOPURA, MADURA TEMPLE

CHAPTER II

TRICHINOPOLI AND TANJORE

WE rumbled and jolted along all that hot afternoon over a monotonous, dry brown plain of parched fields and thorn hedges. There was uproar in the forward part of the train as it left Dindigal station, a hundred voices clamored and shrieked, and a hundred heads hung from the windows of the third-class cars. The train halted, men leaped from it and ran back, while all on the station platform ran up the track toward a small object beside the rails. The station-master came on toward the train, holding fast to a lean little black imp, who was struggling to release himself and fairly bursting with wrath. An excited woman, wailing and declaiming with uncovered face, leaned from a forward car window, talking to an excited group on the ground. At last, an oily babu came to tell us that the small boy had "had a dispute with his mother," and, not wishing to leave Dindigal, had jumped out of the window. "His fearful mother had thought him killed," said the babu, but at sight of the lost heir her fear gave way to fury. She raved and ranted like an Indian Bernhardt as she leaned from the window, unveiled, talking to the station officers; and the small boy talked back to everybody, until he was suddenly lifted by the back, like a kitten, and handed through the window to "his fearful mother's" arms. "Because of his youth they will not arrest him," said the babu; and, from the shrieks that came from that compartment, there was no need for the law to add aught to the chastisement of the barefaced, nose-ringed mother.

We were in the heart of the tobacco country, and Trichinopoli in these modern days is as much a synonym for cheroots as Dindigal. Samuel Daniel, the local guide, who claimed us in the darkness of Trichinopoli station, had the advertisement of his own cigar factory on the back of his card, and everywhere we saw and smelled the local cheroot. We slept in the travelers' rooms in the Trichinopoli station, after dining at a table trailed over with bougainvillea vines and set with glasses of great double hibiscus. Trains rumbled by all night, the mosquitos sang a deafening chorus, and at sunrise we sped across another city of dirty white houses, whose inhabitants were just waking and scratching, and whose Brahman families were marking the door-sills and themselves for the day, the houses' toilet as necessary as their own.

The rock of Trichinopoli, exactly as it looked in old geography pictures, loomed ahead; and after a few turns in the narrow streets we came to the carved entrance of the staircase, tunneled up through the solid rock to temples on the side and summit. Two elephants went past on their way to the river to fill the sacred water-vessels, and we started to climb the two hundred and ninety steps worn slippery with the tread of generations of barefooted worshipers and painted with the perpendicular red and white stripes of Shiva. Our elderly, pompous guide was voluble, measured, and minute, and permitted no trifling nor omissions. Samuel Daniel talked like Samuel Johnson, using the grandiloquent, polysyllabic literary language of the eighteenth century. We had engaged him to show us the sights, and he did it thoroughly. "Here is the place where many hundreds of people were crushed to death in the dark of the afternoon of a festival in 1849," he said. Since then, the British government has cut windows in the rock, placed lamps, and forbidden climbing after four o'clock. At one landing we found a group of little boys sitting before a greasy, black image of Ganesha, the elephant-headed god, receiving instruction from a Brahman teacher; at another landing a high priest stood statuesque in yellow robes, the sacred white Brahman thread and bead on his neck, his forehead smeared with ashes; and at last we came out to the air at a small shrine on an outer shelf of the rock, where we had a far-reaching view of the level plain. After one more tunnel staircase we gained the open summit, climbed a last pinnacle, and found ourselves two hundred and thirty-six feet above the city, that lay like a relief-map at our feet, the fortress-like gopuras of the Srirangam temples rising from green groves southward. A little temple to Ganesha crowns the rock, the goal of the breathless pilgrimage. Half-way down the staircase, we were deafened by the flutes and flageolets of the priests and flag-bearers toiling up with water-jars just brought from the river. The sacred elephants at the foot of the stairs saluted us with lifted fore feet and waving trunks, rubbing their foreheads as they begged, plainly demanding a "prissint," after the custom of the country.

It was a short drive of three miles down to the temple of Vishnu at Srirangam, on an island in the dry bed of the Kaveri. This, the largest temple in southern India, is on a magnificent scale, its fifteen gopuras so many marvels of architecture; the greatest of them falling short of its intended three hundred feet by the interruption of building during the French and English wars of the eighteenth century, when the French intrenched themselves at Srirangam and mounted cannon on the gopuras. The outer, inclosing wall of the temple measures three thousand feet each way, and within that lies a first quadrangle of bazaars. A second gopura admits to a quadrangle where the three thousand high-caste Brahmans of the temple dwell. We drove on through a third and a fourth gopura, in one passage disputing right of way with a temple elephant, who backed out before our brougham, and, with the courtesy of a well-bred creature, swept his trunk and lifted a fore foot in apology. The last gateway had great teak doors, and the doctor of the temple and director of the Srirangam government hospital met us there; also the council of priests and five huge elephants, their foreheads striped with the same yellow and white tridents of Vishnu as their piously frescoed keepers. We saw the famous Hall of the Horse Columns, where single blocks of granite are as intricately carved as wood or ivory, and we saw the other curiosities of the stone-cutter's art, serried columns displaying the many incarnations of Vishnu. We saw, too, the Hall of a Thousand Columns—nine hundred odd shabby, whitewashed pillars only—and from the roof we were given a glimpse of the golden cupola covering the shrine of the sacred image—the identical image brought by Rama in the age of fable, and which grew fast to the ground when left for a moment. They were then preparing for the great mela or festival of early December, when forty thousand pilgrims assemble, crowds spending day and night in the temple for three weeks.

We were shown to a last pavilion, given armchairs before a table, the five elephants were stationed in line across the entrance, and fierce-foreheaded Brahmans multiplied. Strings of keys clanged on the table, five clumsy wooden chests were lugged in, five padlocks yielded to blows and wrenches, and the table was heaped with riches; the feast of jewels was spread, and a flood of color and light illuminated the shadowy pavilion. Gold armor and ornaments and utensils incrusted with jewels were heaped on the table and handed us to examine, until one wondered if any more rubies, emeralds, sapphires, diamonds, or pearls were left in southern India. Gold helmets, crowns, breastplates, gauntlets, brassards, belts, necklaces, bracelets, anklets, were sown with rubies of thumb-nail size, with sapphires and diamonds seeded between, and fringed with pearls and uncut emeralds. Plain gold salvers, water-bottles, gourds, and bowls had neither value nor interest in our eyes after the play of gems. Even the Prince of Wales's gold salver, inscribed "Dec. 11th, 1875," to commemorate his visit to the temple, seemed dull and commonplace. Far better was the gold breastplate fringed with tallow-drop emeralds, which he also gave as a souvenir of his visit to this great shrine of Vishnu. There were several Vishnu tridents in diamonds, and jeweled feathers trembling with diamond fringes; turban ornaments in which jeweled birds held great drops of rubies and emeralds in their beaks; a jeweled umbrella-stick with an inch-long sapphire for its ferrule, a crust of rubies for its handle, and a fringe of tinkling bo-leaves edged with pearls. Four great wings of head-ornaments covered with jewels had been given by a pious beggar, who had gathered more than fifty thousand rupees in alms to spend for such gifts to the gods and gauds for the temple, his stones better cut and set and of better quality than any others in the treasury. Strings and strings of pearls—pearls strung alone or alternating with balls of emerald, ruby, or carved gold—slipped through our hands to weariness. Our eyes were sated with splendor and color when, as a climax, they produced a fine bit of gold carving, representing a religious procession, the idol in the state chair cut from a large ruby, the tiny face, the drapery, and the many ornaments most cleverly done.

It was a characteristic and a picturesque scene

INDIAN LOTAS.

there under the mandapan, the riches of India laid out on a dirty cotton table-cover!—the wise elephants a contrast in good manners to the horde of noisy and excited Brahmans. Although it had required the intervention of three officials to permit us to see the jewels, and each chest is locked with five keys and sealed with five seals of that many Brahman keepers, thefts are frequent, and fifty thousand rupees' worth of jewels vanished at one time. The police kept their eyes on each of the priestly band, the elephants blinked and watched too; and when we had offered our rupees to clean the jewels, the Brahmans set up an approving shout, dropped garlands of marigolds around our necks, and presented us with fragrant lemons. We rose to go, and the most gaudily painted and blackest old Brahman of them all pushed forward, shouting: "I want my photograph now. You have it in that box. You took it an hour ago. I am Venketerama Iyenzar, revenue inspector of Srirangam. Send it to me by the post." And with the elephants trumpeting and nosing for two-anna pieces in the dust, we drove away to the silk and silver and muslin shops of "Trichi," as one soon learns to call it. There the tahsildar spied our brougham, and, descending from his bullock-cart, paid us a visit at the silk merchant's shop front—the courteous, gracious old tahsildar, a fine product of two civilizations.

Samuel Daniel, our guide with the tobacco factory attached, was radiant with the success of the whole morning. Elated from his converse with Brahmans, doctors, and tahsildar, he dropped so much architectural and historical information about Chidambram, Conjeveram, and Mahabalipur, that we said: "Why, you must have read Fergusson?"

"Yes, your ladyship. I have the book. Ten rupees."

"Then you had better go with us as guide."

"Yes, your ladyship," and he went and made our way so plain, so smooth and interesting, that we compared all other guides in India with him to their detriment.

A Catholic priest in cool white robes tiffined also at the station, and told of some of the great successes in mission work in the south; how whole villages have become Christian when the priest permits them to retain their caste. "It is among our converts, or in places where we have worked before them, that your Protestant missionaries have most success," he said.

From the rock of Trichinopoli we had seen the great pagoda tower of Tanjore on the horizon, and as we rumbled the thirty miles across the Kaveri plain in the early, showery afternoon it rose in height as we advanced, and the train stopped fairly in its shadow. Leaving David to watch the luggage at the station, Samuel Daniel hurried us to the temple gate and under the two gopuras to the striped inner court, where the thirteen-story vimana, or tower, of Shiva tapers away until its great trisul seems to touch the very sky.

"Ah! you see here the cleverosity of the Old World builders and the numerosity of their carvings," said Daniel, proudly.

After the French occupied the temple as a fortress in 1777, it was never purified or sanctified again, and the deserted court was a contrast to the other temples we had seen. Two barefooted priests slipped silently across an angle of the cloisters, the colossal stone bull crouched under its grease and garlands, and only the fluttering parrakeets gave any sign or sound of life to the vast inclosure. We gazed in wonderment at the court, the tower, and the exquisite little temple of Subrahmanya, the martial son of Shiva, on whose steps we met two glib, sightseeing babus, who began at once to upbraid us for the proselytizing work of the missionaries. The one with the largest Vishnu mark on his brow had graduated as a civil engineer at Calcutta University, but the exact sciences had not taught him to disbelieve in greasy images, or opened his eyes to any absurdities in his creed, and his torrent of words came like the flow of a phonograph. "Why do you come here to destroy our religion?" he pattered. I denied the charge. "Why do you wish us to give up our gods for your gods?" I denied the plural, and after the twittering parrakeet had followed us awhile, we left him shouting the rest of his set speech to the empty court.

It was a rest to find one heathen temple deserted, to be spared the oily Brahman guide, and to trace in peace the details of this most beautiful of Dravidian temples, the purest example of that style. The great vimana, or pagoda, thirteen stories in height, mounts like the gopuras of Madura, course upon course, carved over with figures and ornaments, two hundred feet to the ball at the peak—a granite mass weighing more than twelve tons, and which could have been placed there only by rolling it up an inclined plane more than a mile in length. In repairing the tower a few centuries ago, the sculptors introduced a face in one floral medallion that was not of any Hindu type. The local prophets said that it wore the features of the people who would conquer India, and it is easily recognized now as an admirable portrait of John Bright. We found Flaxman's beautiful tablet to the memory of Schwartz in the church where the great missionary preached. The church faces a tank where picturesque files of women with brass jars on their heads went up and down four separate flights of terrace steps, each for a special caste.

The elephants, which are kept "for the honor and glory of the palace," now that rajas ride in landaus and automobiles, were swaying uneasily at their posts in the palace courtyard, trumpeting and tossing trunk-loads of leaves and straw on their backs. We were shown the black and white marble durbar hall of the palace, and the library full of illuminated Persian books, and of precious Tamil manuscripts written on strips of palm leaves. When we had wandered through all the inner courts, such a train of guides, lackeys, ushers, keepers, sweepers, porters, and gardeners fawned with extended palms that even Samuel Daniel was dismayed, laid the coins on the flagstones, and walked away from the ensuing scene of combat. We were just in time to see the mahouts scramble to the elephants' necks as a fanfare of trumpets and two scarlet lancers heralded a landau holding two pale yellow, heavily jeweled grandchildren of the raja returning from a drive. A bearer with a red umbrella ran after them, the elephants saluted with trunk and foot, and the sad-faced princelings disappeared in the palace.

The railway station was as deserted as the temple court in the late afternoon, and we had the table brought out to the platform and enjoyed tea in the open air. A white tramp, a pure specimen of the genus hobo, the only one of his kind encountered in India, appeared silently with: "You are a European like myself, lady. Please give me a few rupees to get to Tuticorin." David and Daniel came running in alarm, and hastily swept table, books, chairs, and ourselves inside the refreshment-room and banged the doors, and the beery beggar slunk away to the native bazaar. The butler was decorating his white dinner-cloth with interlacing arabesques of black seeds dropped from a funnel, after which he arranged finger-bowls filled with black-eyed marigolds among his traceries and stood off to admire the effect. Again and again we marveled that the Hindu, with his gross stupidities and incompetencies, had yet been able so thoroughly to master the intricacies of an English dinner, the decoration of the table, the procession of the courses, the ceremony and decorum of it all, with little of the incongruity and inequalities, the mixed splendor and shabbiness, that mark everything of the Hindu's own.

CHAPTER III

WITH CHIDAMBRAM'S BRAHMANS

IT was our fine old Tamil Turveydrop, Samuel Daniel, who induced us to visit Chidambram after we had abandoned it in favor of Conjeveram, where the temple was said to be richer, the jewels more splendid. This artful one pictured "the cleverosity and numerosity of the sculptures," also "the numberlesses of the goddesses and the beauteousness of the temple's dancers, which makes it so popular for visitors," and our interest revived.

As necessary precedent to every move one makes in India, enough telegrams were sent to negotiate a treaty. We wired the Chidambram station-master to have conveyances ready the next midnight to take us the three miles to the dak bangla. We wired the bangla-keeper that we were coming, two beds strong. We informed the local magistrate and the high priest that we wished to make an offering to the temple and to celebrate in honor of the goddess with a great dance in the Hall of a Thousand Columns and to see the famous temple jewels. Last, we besought the section superintendent of the railway to reserve a compartment in the next midnight train that would bear us away from Chidambram.

With the remoteness and seeming isolation among the black faces one has no fear or concern in these Hindu communities, trusting implicitly to that safety and order guaranteed one wherever the British flag floats and Kaiser-i-Hind's initial letters grace official property. Else, when we stepped out on the lonely platform at Chidambram that rainy midnight, we would have thought twice before picking our way through sleeping pilgrims in the open waiting-room, and stowing ourselves away with every joint bent in a tiny box of a native cart, or "lie-down-bandy," for the ride into unknown blackness beyond. Daniel compressed himself with David and the larger luggage bundles into another small box on wheels, and the ponies spattered down a muddy road in the black shadows of overarching trees. Our driver had no turban, his hair was long and snaky, and the jerky motion of the bandy, and the driver's frequent flights out over the shafts to lead the pony by the bridle over bridges and around corners, sent those locks rippling down his back—and my back, too, as I sat hatless, crouched flat on the bandy floor behind him. After what seemed a long race through the reek and blackness, past sodden fields and through dreary mud hamlets, we came in under the shadows of the great trees surrounding the dak bangla.

With the abrupt reining up we slid out, or fell out, of the bandbox of a bandy, and our cramped members slowly jointed out straight again. Knocks, thumps, and calls brought no response from two front doors, and there was an uncanny quarter-hour of waiting before the swaying lantern of Daniel and

David's bandy turned in at the gates—and yet another eerie quarter of an hour while the bandy drivers muttered in the near darkness, and our two protectors pounded and shouted at a far-away door. The moon struggled out in rare glimpses and gave us suggestion now and then of a great lawn and trees, a long, low, white building whose eaves extended over a continuous flagged porch—the regulation rest-house built by government for the use of traveling officials and other Europeans.

A babel of angry voices came from the back of the compound, the loud talk and back talk, the incessant wrangle and jangle of untuned bells and Hindu servants, the most quarrelsome lower class in the world, after the Chinese. Their bickerings are an annoyance that frets the spirit and wears the nerves of the most adamantine traveler, and it is no wonder that the Buddha, and all saints and reformers, first fled to the jungle for years of silent meditation. The keeper of the bangla appeared with his keys and a lantern. "Oh, yes, certingly, mem-sahib," he had received the telegram in due time and had tightly locked up the bangla and his own quarters and gone soundly to sleep—Hindu irresponsibility, ungraciousness, and indifference to the usual degree.

The door clanged open and showed us the regulation lofty, cheerless, cement-floored room, as fit for prison as superior occupancy. One remembered those creepy "other stories" of Rudyard Kipling where lunatics and delirium tremens subjects habited, and suicides took themselves off in, just such cheerless rooms, and that other more grisly story of the dead man concealed on rafters overhead in just such a forlorn place. The candles burning sullenly in tall glass bells showed us a great dining-table, ponderous arm-chairs and lounging-chair, and a broad cane-seated settee for a bed. Another such hygienic couch of the country was brought in from a black, echoing room beyond, and the servants spread out our red *razais,* or wadded calico quilts, which every traveler in India must carry with him as bedding and covering, just as the Klondike miner carries his blankets when he "hits the trail." The rubber pillows were inflated, and the apartment was completely furnished and in order for occupancy. Before the alcohol lamp had boiled the water for the beef-tea of our midnight feast, the servants were snoring on the flags of the portico, lying on the door-mats with only a thin bit of dhurrie covering them, despite all one hears of the deadly effect of night air and the chill before the dawn. The most awful stillness succeeded, a silence that made one's ears ring, hushed our voices, and made us unconsciously put down spoons and cups noiselessly. No one had raised my terrors then with tales of the still occasionally existent thugs of southern India, of thieves who throttle by night and stealthily kill or maim an unbeliever as an act acceptable to Kali and the other destroying divinities. The situation was all novel and amusing, and the poverty-stricken interior, the forlorn banquet-hall of this Waldorf of the neighborhood, furnished all the real color one could want. The stealthy dripping of the trees told of another gentle shower, and the steady snoring on the porch was as comforting and hypnotic as the purring of a home cat by the hearth —sufficient assurance that all was well at one o'clock and that the British government in India still lived and protected us.

At seven o'clock repeated calls brought no answer from the portico; the silence of broad daylight was more complete than that of midnight. The flagstones were deserted, and not a sign of life appeared on either side of the bangla. David and Daniel had most literally taken up their beds and walked—far away beyond hearing. A little girl with a nose-ring crept out and looked at us, another one joined her, and the two stared and smiled, nodded their nose-rings with friendly flops, and looked their fill—a steady, continuous, fascinated scrutiny—for a whole half-hour before David and Daniel appeared bearing tea and toast. Then David's irate voice rose in volume, well-sweeps creaked and tubs were filled, chickens ran cackling, smoke rose and sounds of life and cheer came from the keeper's house and kitchen. David wrathfully told how he had had to go to the village bazaar, a mile away, to get even the firewood to cook the first breakfast.

While David ruled in the primitive mud kitchen the keeper of the bangla laid the table on the front portico, overlooking the broad, glistening green lawn, where squirrels frisked and little green parrots squawked and flew about. The china, glass, and cutlery provided at these dak banglas are always good, and there is usually some attempt at splendor in electroplated toast-racks and marmalade-stands. Our esthetic keeper of Chidambram put a great bouquet of yellow crysanthemums on the table, but the tablecloth was a thick honeycomb stuff, either a bed-spread or a bath-towel that some guest had left behind; and it was frescoed with hospitable records of a useful past in egg, coffee, and claret stains on a ground toned by the roadside's red dust of a season.

The local magistrate appeared for a morning call, entering the gates in a large bullock-bandy, or covered cart, drawn by two magnificent white bullocks with humps on their shoulders, the bells on their necks announcing the pace of their leisurely trot. The turbaned and white-draperied grandee had hardly descended from this seeming vehicle of state or chariot of religious ceremony when the driver loosened the yoke, tilted the bandy over, and turned the splendid creatures loose to graze on the lawn. This custom of southern India, of releasing bullocks and ponies of their harness at once, gives hotel and bangla grounds in the Madras Presidency always a homely look, suggestive alike of pasture, race-course, and stable-yard.

The magistrate was one of the finer types of high-caste Hindu, who added to his own Brahmanic culture and inherited refinement an English university education and acquaintance with other ways of living and thinking. He had all the Oriental suavity and graceful address, and talked with us two of the despised sex quite on a social equality. He sat long at his ease, commenting upon the customs of his people and the peculiarities of life and architecture in southern India. He deplored the low estate and want of education among women; praised the new era and the blessings of British rule, the good roads, schools, hospitals, and things not dreamed of before, that had come with the Western education, which had only begun to reach the mass of the people. His Western education had not, however, steeled him to shaking hands with a casteless unbeliever, and he kept tables and chairs between us as he rose to go.

"I must go and hurry up the priests," said the suave judicial. "Since they know you cannot leave until midnight, they will not try to be ready before late afternoon. At one o'clock I will send my bandy and peon for you. You will find my bullocks faster than those you would get from the bazaar." And with more beautiful speeches about the honor of our visit to Chidambram and our appreciation of Dravidian art, he backed and bowed himself away to his bandy, with furtive glances lest we yet lay defiling hand on him, and send him through all the details of his morning toilet again, as the least of ills.

It was past one o'clock when the stately bullocks again tinkled down the road to the bangla; a peon with a broad sash and metal plate on his breast forming an escort of honor. There was no telling how much our occupancy defiled the magistrate's bandy while we progressed magnificently along a shaded road, between garnered fields and the lines of mud houses constituting villages—mud houses with mud floors, and mud porticos or shelves where the occupants loll by day and sleep at night. Men and women gave friendly looks, the women draped gracefully in the single long sari, or winding-cloth, that, either red or white, is a foil to the dark skin and lends majesty and picturesqueness to the frowziest. Nearly every woman wore silver bracelets and anklets, armlets, finger-rings, ear-rings, nose-rings, and necklaces past counting, and one never knows what silver jewelry can effect, nor its artistic value, until he sees it against these sooty Tamil skins.

The village of Chidambram clusters low before the soaring gopura of this oldest Shivaite temple of the south, and its seventy rest-houses shelter thousands of pilgrims at every December mela. Four of these great pagoda-like structures, each 160 feet in height, carved, painted, and gilded over, with a massive trisul, or trident ornament of Shiva, for capstone, admit to the quadrangular space of thirty-two acres occupied by the labyrinth of shrines and courts and halls around the great tank. The temple was built a thousand years ago by a pious raja, who had seen Shiva and Parvati dancing on the near-by sea-shore; and the holy of holies is a golden shrine dedicated to the god of dancing. Another tradition says that a Kashmir prince of the fifth century brought three thousand Brahmans with him from the north and founded the temple. The greatest popularity was given the temple when "the golden-colored emperor," a leper prince who had come south on a pilgrimage, was cured by bathing in the temple tank, and thousands emulate him every year.

Repairs were being executed in many places, at the instance of a pious Hindu of Madras, and we picked our way through damp and dripping courts littered with freshly carved stones, crawled under scaffoldings and inclined planks, until we were well confused with the multiplicity of shrines, the garlanded and greased images of Shiva, Parvati, Ganesha, and the Bull, and always the figure of the dancing god with one knee acutely bent and the other foot flung with abandon. The courts were empty, the shrines deserted, no worshipers, no workmen, no priests, no crowd of idlers, as in the busy Madura and Srirangam temples. No signs of preparation for our visit were evident, and we sent the peon and Daniel and lay brethren in hot haste to give the alarm, lest the function be delayed past sunset. A few languid villagers stole in and stared, the longitudinal sect-mark of Vishnu on the forehead and the loosely drawn dhotee drapery around their shoulders giving them a strong resemblance to our red Indians of the prairies in war-paint and reservation blankets. Then more waiting succeeded, more messengers were despatched with more vehement advices, and Daniel, with the air of great cares pressing on him, paced the arcades meditating, speaking now and then with magnificent gestures, like a real raja. "My birthly is Christian," he had informed us in the first sanctuary of heathendom, that we might feel free to comment and question at will.

A band of Brahmans in fresh war-paint finally arrived, and their fierce hawk-like gaze, their eager, excited, hurried air, might have given one qualms of alarm at our isolation in this labyrinthine fortress of a temple, remote from any European settlement,

GOPURA AND TANK, CHIDAMBRAM TEMPLE.

and miles from a white official or any pale-face. But Daniel reassured one by his calm magnificence, his grandiloquent phrases and evident pride in the amazing spectacle which he, as grand impresario, was about to present. Three hundred of these highest-caste Dikshatar Brahmans, or priestly ones, descended from a first Cholukyan king, they say, live with their families within the temple inclosure. All are rich, enjoying inherited wealth and the great income which this popular temple derives from its votaries and pilgrims. There were fine, intelligent faces among them, and, barring the disfigurement of the painted sect-mark on the forehead, one could easily appreciate how much finer is the type and the cast of countenance of these long-descended aristocrats than the common Hindu face seen in bazaars and street crowds. All had fine, straight noses, level brows, and well-formed heads, the hair shaved all around the edges as though for a Chinese queue, and then drawn and knotted at the side behind the left ear, precisely as small children in north China twist their locks. All wore the white dhotee, twisted as a skirt around the body, left nude to the waist, save as one and another chose to fling the end of the long cloth over the head and shoulders as protection from the alternating sun and rain. The sacred white cord over one shoulder and the carved Brahman bead on a thread around the neck were the only other bits of apparel worn, although each one carried, in a twist of the girdle, a silver or brass box filled with the ashes of sandalwood or the dung of the sacred cow, with which to paint the caste- and sect-marks on their brows. Generations of superior folk, carefully nurtured, highly educated and cultivated in Brahman lore, have produced these splendid specimens of their race, these fine intellectual faces and athletic bodies overlaid with dark-brown skin of a grain and patina finer than any inanimate bronze—aristocrats of thirty centuries' direct descent.

They looked at us, their prey, with eager interest, and with shouts appropriate to those about to offer living sacrifice to the gods; with whoops and hurrahs this band of Brahmans conducted us to the main shrine and struck the gong to announce our presence to the god—an ugly, greasy, black little image, hidden somewhere out of sight in an innermost sanctuary. We saw only an open-fronted chapel, whose floor was three or four feet above the level of the court-yard; and as we advanced to it the priests brought gold plates heaped with garlands of strung flowers, which they flung around our necks. The gold plate was extended for our offerings, and at sight of the rupees of propitiation the Brahmans pushed, pointed, gesticulated, and shouted to one another. Only the Arabs of the Nile, or the boatwomen of Canton, could raise such din and hullabaloo, produce such waves and volumes of harsh, ear-splitting sounds. It seemed as if they were about to tear us to pieces and were quarreling about the lead, but it was only intense interest, pleased excitement, and glee at the prospect of another gala day for Chidambram, with a fine lot of rupees to be divided afterward among the charter members of the close corporation. They shouted, screamed, pushed, and all but defiled themselves by touching us, in order to point out things to us and attract attention. A half-dozen tried to be leaders of the expedition, to establish a special protectorate over us, each leading a separate way, the magistrate's peon making appealing dumb show for us to follow him in another direction, while Daniel, disentangling himself from the Brahman mob, made deprecatory gestures to them, bowed low to us, swept his hand obsequiously to guide us in a still different quarter, and said in mild, honeyed tones: "This way, your ladyships, this way." His suavity won, and all garlanded, as if ready for slaughter, and preceded by the band of temple musicians, we were led on and on, from shrine to shrine, the hawk-eyed Brahmans shouting wild acclaims, just as in a triumphant progress on the stage. It was all well-mounted grand opera, a deafening Wagnerian representation; and when we stood with the great chorus grouped before one gilded shrine with a golden roof and a golden flag-staff—a mainmast plated with hammered gold—it was a fine scene for the curtain to have fallen on. They led us to a store-room full of silver palanquins, chariots and platforms, silver bulls, elephants, goats, and peacocks, and explained how these and the sacred images are drawn in procession through Chidambram streets and courts on the great days of the heathen year. There the temple musicians fought and won chance for fullest action; and drum, trumpets, and castanets raised such echoing din in the holy inclosure that we were literally distracted when, having "visited the architectures,"we were conducted to the treasury and given chairs around a long, low table covered with a greasy red-silk cover. Deafened by the thump and blast of instruments and the vent of sacerdotal lungs, and overpowered by the weight and suffocating odors of the garlands of jasmine, tuberoses, marigolds, and chrysanthemums around our necks, we let those twenty-pound weights of vegetable adornments slip on to the backs of the chairs, and had Daniel hint to the Brahmans that our presents to the temple would be greater if the noise were less. He explained delicately that we were from another country than that of the usual visitors to Chidambram; that people in America were accustomed to speak in soft, low voices, and to keep very silent in their temples. What a Talleyrand was spoiled when that soul in its present incarnation habited the body of Trichinopoli's great guide! Daniel spoke, and the hush of midnight succeeded for about ten seconds. Then the Brahmans whispered; their buzz rose to audible speech, and our ear-drums were again violently beaten until the mercenary company was hushed by significant gestures from Daniel. The musicians fingered their instruments sadly, but Daniel was supreme, and when one strapping head Brahman fully caught the cue, he outdid Daniel in silencing the sacerdotal screamers for the rest of the afternoon.

When the magistrate came, followed by temple peons bearing great boxes tied up in red silk, he brought with him his six-year-old daughter, Thungama, the "little golden lady," as her pet name was translated, a disdainful, arrogant mite, who snubbed us soundly, but gave such cool, supercilious glances of high-caste scorn from such deep, dark, liquid, mysterious eyes that we forgave her. She wore a little cotton skirt and jacket, and silver anklets; and her hair, divided at the brow in two plaits that framed the face, held a semicircular rayed ornament of pearls. This star-eyed beauty did not want to be looked at nor addressed by us, and had a dread of being touched by pale strangers with uncovered faces and no caste-marks, stamps, or guarantees of position on their brows. This imperious mite ruled her father royally, received the respectful homage of the sleek old Brahmans, and was petted and passed from papa to priest and peon as suited her whims. There was the finest ethnological exhibit around that treasury table,—the magistrate, his daughter, and ourselves in front, and the Brahmans ranged in triple circle of fine, spirited faces above splendid shoulders, a prosperous-looking, sleek, and well-groomed board of temple aldermen, directors of that close corporation of Chidambram, living for so many generations on the fat of the land and the offerings of pilgrims, and inheriting the intellectual monopoly of ages. Each one had been invested in his youth with the sacred white cord, had served his time of probation, had married and raised a family, and now was enjoying his magnificent prime before disappearing from Chidambram and following the strict Brahman routine of the end of life. It seemed amazing that there should be a community where the physical average was so high; and commenting on the many fine, noble, and dignified countenances and the statuesque shoulders, Daniel explained it all: "Yes, the Brahmans are always splendid of appearance like these. It is the *hereditary heirness* of their high descent."

CHAPTER IV

FOR THE HONOR AND GLORY OF SHIVA

THE temple jewels are kept in iron-bound chests in a room fastened by many locks. The magistrate, the high priest, and a half-dozen other Brahmans of different castes each holds a key, and all must be present to unlock the room. Count and record are kept of each article; many of the jewels are historic and famous, and all are so well known to the community that the loss of even one stone would be as quickly noted on display days as the disappearance of an idol itself. When the jewels are thus shown, it is customary for visitors to leave from ten to twenty rupees for cleansing them pure from outcast touch. The rupee is a great leveler, and has purifying effect unaided; for nothing could be dingier, greasier, more in need of alcohol, jeweler's sawdust, and a touch of chamois than these jewels of Chidambram, unless it were the jewels at Srirangam or the famously dirty sapphires at Madura.

There was earnest effort and long parley over a first iron-bound chest that would not open. All the head Brahmans shouted and struggled with the obdurate padlock until the key broke. An agile brother whipped out a knife and tried to pick the lock, with an assurance that bespoke familiarity with such processes, but the rusty clamp would not yield. A longer and a louder clamor, and then a lusty Brahman seized one of the big keys on the table, a bar of iron as solid as the key of the Bastille, and began hammering the clasp, laying on blacksmith's blows with a will. The padlock flew off, the heavy lid creaked back, and with deafening yells the riches of Chidambram came in view.

They drew out all the jeweled ornaments, the crowns, caps, hand- and arm-coverings, necklaces, ear-rings, nose-rings, bracelets, anklets, and staffs given to the temple's precious idols for centuries back, laid them on the table, and passed them to us to handle and defile at will. The Brahmans shouted, talked, oh'd and ah'd, stretched hands over our shoulders to call attention to some special beauty or marvel, and even snatched them from our hands. Their eyes shone and their faces glowed with pride and joy in these treasures, their delight at seeing them childlike in its expression. They all told at once how the ruby bracelets were given the goddess by the rani, wife of the Raja of Tanjore, in fulfilment of a vow; and how, when the pious rani learned that the goddess had no ear-bosses, she despoiled her own jewel-boxes of her most magnificent ones. Then they told of Patcheapper Mudalier, the rich man of Madras, who had given the goddess pairs of gold serpents scaled over with great jewels; and, at the sale of the effects of the late Raja of Tanjore in 1891, had bought and presented the temple with a huge Phrygian cap, or war-bonnet, covered with hundreds of cabochon rubies and table-cut diamonds, along with a great breastplate over six inches square, set solidly with large flat rubies—rubies of the most perfect tint, and set double, ruby on top of ruby, as was the old Hindu custom, until the depth and richness of color surpass anything to be otherwise obtained. Patcheapper had not only given modern jewels, but he had had the old gems reset, adding lost stones to historic settings, and putting the accumulation of loose stones into telling form.

Two enormous water-bottles of solid gold were lifted out—"for bringing the sacred water to wash the goddess," said Daniel. "Six thousand rupees! Six thousand rupees!" yelled the Brahmans, anxious to impress us with the exceeding value of these toilet articles. A two-foot-long pendant of linked medallions set with rubies and diamonds, worn hanging from the back of the goddess's crown, was vouched for as valued at twenty-five thousand rupees, and a huge crested headpiece glowing with gems was quoted at thirty thousand rupees; and then, through Daniel, the Brahmans were besought kindly to omit price-marks and quarreling over and outbidding one another in values, since we had not come to buy nor to appraise the temple jewels, and had no interest in their money value.

That shabby table was spread over with more precious things than one can remember—gold crowns, crests, tiaras, plumes, bosses for the ears, ornaments for the hair and the forehead, nose-rings, necklaces, armlets, bracelets, zones, girdles, anklets, and every possible article of Hindu jewelry worn for these two thousand years—forms and designs but little changed in two thousand years; the same ancient, archaic Swami or Dravidian style of ornaments having been worn centuries before Chidambram's building, according to the sculptured records of the Buddhist monuments. Every piece was crusted over, inlaid with rubies and diamonds, sapphires, emeralds, and pearls; with emeralds as big as bullets—great drops of green dew; with sapphires the size of filberts and walnuts, sunk in pure, dull yellow gold as soft as wax. There were rubies, rubies, rubies—rubies everywhere—thick as pebbles on a beach,—and all of them smoothly rounded drops, blobs, or uneven lumps of warm and splendid color that went to the heart. A Western lapidary or jeweler would scoff at and perhaps scorn these masses of roughly cut cabochon gems, whose flaws and feathers and cloudings make them of little commercial but of such great artistic value. Crystalline perfection was not the first test which the old Hindu jewelers applied to their gems. With an eye first to color effects and rich combinations of color, all the flawed stones, the splinters and scales and pinpoints of color, had their value to them, and with them they achieved results of such richness, such gorgeousness and splendor, that our mechanically perfect, geometrically exact, many-faceted, flashing gems of Western jewelry seem cold, characterless, expressionless beside these living gems of the East. We were fairly dizzy with the glow and glitter and gorgeousness of the display, the feast of gems and flow of jewels, the barbaric splendors literally heaped upon Oriental magnificence within touch before us. One hardly knows the ruby, its glorious tones, its true uses and possibilities, until he has had some such feast of rubies in an Indian temple, and the taste there acquired is little satisfied afterward with the glassy, regular polyhedrons of the West. That deep, clear, warm red ruby, the concentration of all heat and gorgeous light, the glowing, burning stone of the tropics, is India's own, its most typical, tropical gem. It became hard to believe, though, that rubies were rare and precious when, after all seen elsewhere, Chidambram's Brahmans laid plates and sheets of rubies—dozens, hundreds, thousands of them—before us. One could almost think they came like buttons on a haberdasher's card, and that one bought them by the gross or great gross as required, or by dry measure perhaps—by heaped-up pints and overflowing quarts.

For nearly two hours we handled the collars and crowns and ornaments passed out to us, until we were well surfeited with splendors, until pear-shaped pearls in rains and fringes could excite no more surprise, until big tallow-drop emeralds were the common thing, and star sapphires had to be of thumb's-end size to command any praise. Ropes of necklaces made of overlapping gold pieces clanged in dead weight on the table; the famous parrot cut from a single emerald was produced with cheers, and broad manacle-bracelets, set with ancient stones recut in European facetings, closed the list. The lid of the last chest was slammed down, the Brahmans voiced their pent-up joy, and we sank back in our chairs, well exhausted with the strain of long-continued attention to such dazzling surprises. More flower garlands were dropped on our shoulders and enormous bouquets were presented us. Trays of fruit and cake and sugar things were offered, which we formally praised, accepted, and touched according to custom; and, by the same sign and custom, we never saw the defiled stuff again.

The musicians struck up a deafening pæan, the crowd in the courtyard made way, and we were borne triumphantly on for the great Nautch dance in the choltry, or Hall of a Thousand Columns. That noblest Brahman of them all, who had maintained a particular protectorate over us in the jewel-room and so summarily checked the other Brahmans when they extolled the jewels too full-lunged, all but gave his arm as he escorted us across the court, waving the others aside or pushing them with force when necessary. This arch-heathen, Pattu Thacheadar, the Superb, highest-caste Dikshatar Brahman of the white cord and the carved bead, was altogether the finest specimen Chidambram afforded, and sculptor or painter would equally delight in him as model. This big Brahman beau-ed us gallantly across the courts, up into the lofty pillared hall, and seated us in the waiting arm-chairs with a grace and address that would have become a leader of cotillions —barefooted, with only a red-bordered sheet for his full-dress uniform of social ceremony!

The magistrate, in his scholarly, gold-bowed spectacles, and the disdainful little goddess, Thun-

PATTU THACHEADAR.

gama, throned upon the peons' shoulders, were with us; and the august company of Brahmans seated themselves in a half-circle upon the stone floor, Pattu, the Superb, towering head and shoulders in the front row of the highest-caste marks. There was a May-pole in the middle of the vaulted hall, hung over with long streamers.

Six barefooted, neat-looking colored girls in starched muslin dress skirts and velvet jackets of antiquated cut and no fit whatever, stepped forward and, in methodical march and countermarch to a nasal chorus, braided the May-pole's ribbons down to their hands; in reverse order unbraided them, and stepped demurely back in line. We were breathless with surprise.

Was that the famous sacred temple dance? Could six octoroons, matter-of-fact young "yaller gals," shuffling slowly around a May-pole, ever give rise to such visions of beauty and grace as only the name of the Nautch dance conjures up? Oh, no! It was surely coming next. There would be something graceful and bewitching, something in gorgeous native costume, after this purposely tame and tedious cake-walk by colored church members in velveteen basques trimmed with cotton lace.

The same wooden young persons marched out again in line. We cheered ourselves, noting then that they were almost Oriental from the collar upward—what with necklaces and ear-studs and earrings looped back to the decorated waterfall, the "bath bun" of hair at the back of their heads, and nose-rings whose lowest pearl trembled on their lips, the literal pearls of speech. We questioned Daniel closely to know if these really were the picked dancers, the flower of Chidambram's beauties; if he had never seen them dance in voluminous, diaphanous, graceful native dress?

"No, your ladyship. These are their richest clothings. You see the magnificent velvets of their costumes. They never wear the common sari now that they have *these.* It is always this splendid dress they wear for the dancing when I bring European visitors."

The dance went on, a tame and tedious cake-walk, purely callisthenic school-girl exercise to the end, save in one or two less shuffling measures where they made undeniable eyes at us, posed one finger against the cheek, and looked unutterable archness. "Notice the postures, see the sentiments of the countenance," said Daniel, who was a connoisseur in such dances, and gifted with the second sight needed to make anything at all fascinating out of the languid measures. "It is praise of the goddess," said the old gentleman, rapturously, delighted with the spectacle. But such a dreary ballet! Such a monotonous walk-around to minor airs thumped and blown by the earnest temple musicians, and plaintive choruses wailed by the dancers themselves, would never fill a theater nor a side-show in the West, and the Midway Plaisance would have closed for lack of patronage had its Oriental dances been like this.

The sun struggled through the clouds and sent shafts and ladders of gold down from the high windows, that, touching the white draperies of the seated

Brahmans, illuminated them as if with lime-light. Pattu Thacheadar was radiant and smiling, nodding his approval and delight, and enjoying the great day and his prominent part in it with all of a boy's vain glee. He hung upon and watched closely the evolutions of the dancers, and all the Brahmans buzzed approval when the six advanced and retreated, rapping little sticks together in the measure of some very old dance to Shiva. That was the liveliest measure trod—very literally trod, with the flat of the bare foot—by these star-eyed serpents and enchanters of the Coromandel coast.

"It is the most difficult to do this dance, you see. They are trained to it from little girls. Their limbs are very movable," said Daniel, aglow with delight.

When the placid program came to an end, Daniel put on his spectacles, took his place by the May-pole, and, more like a head schoolmaster giving diplomas than like the grand almoner of royalty, presented a rupee to each girl. Each one advanced and received it with a bow, and each one then stepped on to us, stood rigid, and made the regulation military salute with one hand—a figure only a little more formal and automatic than the whole gay revel of the sacred dance had been, something very plainly learned from a British drill-sergeant's code. The musicians received their gratuities in the same formal manner, and the Brahmans, dancers, and orchestra trooped with us down the hall to the court surrounding the temple tank, where the afternoon sun lighted a scene of splendor and picturesqueness. Despite the late and yellow light, I snapped the camera to right and left, on gilded gopuras, the mirror tank, and the staircase of the great hall where the dancers and Brahmans were grouped unconscious. Little Thungama and her adoring peon stood for me; and then Pattu Thacheadar, special protector and personal conductor, impresario, and grand manager of the Brahman troupe, was asked to take the steps, to pose magnificent, all flower-garlanded as he was. He assented with excited delight, the other Brahmans shouted their satisfaction, and with much chaff and back-talk to his Brahman brethren, this splendid creature spread out his flower necklaces and stood, facing the sun, breathing slowly and not winking for seconds after the button was pressed.

The bullock-bandy carried us and our load of floral gifts home to the bangla, and after a quick dinner and long nap carried us on to the station, where Pattu, the Superb, was parading the platform in waiting. He had walked the eight miles to take leave of us, to present more flower garlands and a rare lemon brought from a grove some miles away on the Coromandel coast. He wore classic sandals, or shoes bound by rawhide thongs, and the end of his long white drapery was thrown up over his head and shoulders like an Arab burnoose. He swung a quaint, archaic lantern, and in the flashes of light from the station-rooms he was more paintable and operatic than at the temple. And this son of the Sun, descendant of ten thousand Brahmans, masher of most magnificent order, was posing for effect as unmistakably as others of his kind pose in Western drawing-rooms—the handsome man and his little arts—the same transparency the world over.

The station-master interpreted for him while we waited a whole midnight hour for the train. Pattu wanted to know when we would come to Chidambram again; how far away was America; how many days would it take us to get back there; how much would it cost; had we railways there; or any temples as splendid as Chidambram.

"Then," said the station-master, "he has been telling me of the great festival at the temple to-day. He says there was a crowd there to see the dance, more than two hundred Brahmans, and he was the best-looking man there, and you took his picture to carry to America to show."

Oh! Pattu! Pattu Thacheadar!

CHAPTER V

MADRAS AND THE SEVEN PAGODAS

WE had expected to have another feast of jewels at Conjeveram, the Benares of southern India, but at Chingleput Junction the constable from that sacred city was waiting to tell us that we could not see the temple jewels, owing to a recent theft of three thousand rupees' worth of treasure and the arrest of the head high priest, who held one of the five keys. "I have just brought forty Brahmans up with me as witnesses. There has been a big quarrel on among the high-caste families, one trying to run the other out; but as all the temple offices, even the keepers of the oil, are hereditary, only civil suits and criminal imprisonment ever oust them. Each steals a little from the god himself, but does not want any one else to do so."

When we arrived at the great railway station of Madras, the largest and oldest city in southern India, with a population of half a million, there were no European vehicles to be had—only bullock-carts and the bandbox jutkas, or native pony-cabs. "There is a convention of Theosophists on now," said the station-master in explanation, but he could not tell what people with astral bodies wanted with material cabs.

The jutka was such torture and indignity that we walked the last block to the hotel in a great garden, where a hen-brained lot of "don't-know" servants held the summer-house, which served as hotel office.

There were no manager, no rooms, no memorandum of our telegrams, no anything at this only hotel. There was no other place to go; no steamer leaving for five days. The butler led us to a neglected row of rooms that we might prepare for tiffin and await the return of the manager. Ants ran riot over the beds and the torn matting on the dirty cement floor; the ragged, brown mosquito-netting suggested horrors in the darkness; and the bath-water of days ago stood iridescent in the tubs. We retreated to the stone porch and then to the dining-room, where there was painted as a decorative frieze: "Recommend us. Recommend us. The best hotel in India." There was a veteran table cloth, but a charming floral decoration, and we were served a pallid and tasteless soup, potato croquettes, grilled bones, and "cornflower cream," *i. e.*, a watery blanc-mange. Meanwhile, our robust British table neighbors—all resident Anglo-Indians, with a proper scorn for tourists—ate broiled birds, dressed the most inviting tomato-salads, and closed their feast with red bananas and cheese. "Oh! that belongs gentlemans. Gentlemans self buy bazaar," hissed the butler, when we had sternly pointed to and ordered birds and salad and bananas.

Then the manager came and bowed us into a carriage and off to a branch house, "a residential hotel," where he said he had most spacious rooms reserved. Remembering the bath-tubs, the grilled bones, and the legend on the dining-room walls of the parent establishment, we had small expectation of anything sybaritic at the offshoot hostelry. Yet we were rewarded with a great mansion, in a garden that was almost a park; the house was clean and admirably kept by a black, black butler, twin to the end-man of the old minstrel shows.

We drove miles and miles through tree-lined streets to the water-front of the city to find the post, telegraph, and steamship offices and the bank. All Madras and all southern India, planters from Bangalur and the Nilgiri Hills, and officials from everywhere, were doing their Christmas shopping those days, the races were on, and the streets and bazaars were full of life and animation. We drove into beautiful grounds and around under a great portico of a mansion to find the chemist's shop; into another splendid place to find, not the lord chief justice, but the grocer; and this extravagance of space makes Madras a city of frightfully magnificent distances.

The burnt-cork butler welcomed us home to our residential hotel, himself brought the dainty tea-tray to the marble-floored portico, and stood by with ear-to-ear smiles, watching us enjoy his crisp toast and fresh seed-cakes. We began to have a Christmas feeling of peace and good will to all Madras. The loggia was so attractive that we ordered dinner to be served there, rather than dress and dine with any more self-supplying guests, as at that "best hotel in India." The butler assented joyfully, a whole minstrel troupe ran in with bouquets, fruit pyramids,

MONOLITHIC TEMPLES AT MAHABALIPUR

candle-bells, and a British profusion of electroplated furnishings. The butler, three assistants, David and Daniel, a pankha boy, and whispering coolies uncounted beyond the latticed door, combined to serve a good dinner to perfection. We wondered how the residential guests were faring with so much of the headquarters staff on duty in our apartment, and the next day learned that we were the only guests in the new hotel; that the invisible manager was a myth, and the black butler the greatest Pooh Bah off the stage.

Madras residents had, long in advance, engaged all the "budgery-boats" on the Buckingham Canal for Christmas week; and instead of one of those comfortable house-boats, where civilized existence continues its regular routine, we had to content ourselves with a coal-barge—a "spacious and commodious fourteen-passenger-boat," Samuel Daniel called it—for the visit to the Seven Pagodas, the ruins of Mahabalipur. Our Turveydrop assured us that all tourists went in such craft; that Bishop Phillips Brooks had traveled that way to see this one of the seven great wonders of the Indian world; and as he talked on, we almost forgot the ignominious cargo-lighter.

The guide-book said to pay seven rupees for such a boat to go to the Seven Pagodas; the butler said fifty rupees; Daniel and David stoutly maintained fifteen rupees; and we finally gave ten rupees. Coal-barge No. 1350 was some twenty feet long, with a mat roof, side awnings, and a single mast; and when swept, scrubbed, and drenched under our eyes, we embarked with mattresses, chairs, a few pots and pans and provisions from the hotel, and a great supply of our own stores to augment the tiffin-basket. Instead of driving to Marmalong or Guindy Bridge, and trusting to meet the dilatory boatmen there, we embarked at Governor's Basin, and for reward found the Buckingham Canal drag a stagnant, sewery way past Madras commons and dead walls, past hedges and kitchen-gardens, for six miles to Guindy Bridge, where the open country began. We posted a letter in the mail-box at the bridge, ordering a carriage to be waiting there at five o'clock the second morning, and then were towed and poled at a comfortable gait southward through the long, lazy afternoon, curtained from the western sun, with a fresh little breeze from the sea pleasantly stirring the air.

It was a flat, level country, lying close to the Coromandel coast. Once the canal debouched into a great lagoon, and the trackers plashed like a file of storks across a few miles of shallow water, and often we heard the long boom of the breakers. Villages nestled under palm and banian groves; villagers trod the high embankment paths like so many white storks or red flamingos; and market, cargo, and fire-wood boats slipped silently by. We walked past a series of locks in the late afternoon, and when the great triangular sail dropped we took our chairs to the roof and glided down such a sunset stretch as met one's ideal of the tropics. Two Tamil coolies, tandem, towed us; a tall boatman poled; and Daniel's brilliant red turban at the fore gave the high keynote to the sunset color scheme, while his voice rose in sonorous passages descriptive of his country and his people. Even the untutored blacks of the crew crept close to hear the foreign language roll from his tongue in such unctuous streams. He told of the temple jewels we had not seen; of the stores of the finest old Indian jewels which the Nautch girls everywhere own, since the women of the great families are continually robbed by degenerate sons, who have learned only more forms of vice and extravagance with Western education. Then of the Brahmans and their "hereditary heirness" he said with a sneer: "Those Brahman priests say they are the gods visible in the world. Once they may have taught truths, but now they only humbug the poor people." Buddhism as it flourishes in Ceylon? "More humbug," he averred.

The palm-trees grew darker than violet against the rosy west, until they were black skeletons against a steely blue, star-spangled firmament, where Jupiter shone like a small moon and Orion's three great belt-jewels streamed golden tracks across the lagoon. We could hear the boom of the Coromandel surf; dark palm groves stopped the gentle sea breeze; the sail, spread to catch any breath, dragged and flapped against the mast, then filled with the soft sea air when the star-dotted horizon was visible again, and drew canal-boat No. 1350 along through the enchanted night.

In the middle of the darkness came the clatter of the falling sail and an angry colloquy by the bank-side, David and Daniel together venting their strongest language at invisible retorters.

"It is the twenty-mile lock," said David, shaking with wrath. "The manager has gone to bed and will not open the lock again until morning, and we shall not get to Seven Pagodas before ten o'clock. They will always do it for the gentries, but they do not believe when poor native says he has gentries waiting in a boat." With one lantern and an escort of innumerable shadows in ghostly clothes, we went and pounded on the lock-keeper's door, and besought him as the most courteous of a whole race of kindly disposed people to consider a tourist's precious time and consuming zeal for rock-sculpture, and open his locks and let us wing and track our way to Mahabalipur. "Certingly, certingly. Right away, mem-sahib," and the lock-keeper came out with his keys, our crew worked the gates and levers, and while we walked and talked with our benefactor of the tropic night, the waters swirled in and lifted the boat to the next level.

They drove a stake in the soft sand and made fast at three in the morning, and in the gray-blue dawn we woke to find ourselves and three budgery-boats lying at the edge of a great sandy flat, beyond which a white house and some palm-trees promised government cheer. We went over to the dak bangla and demanded baths, breakfasts, and chair-bearers at once. The first two demands were complied with; but at six o'clock it was "wait a little," as it had been at five-thirty, and, realizing that the sooner we began the five-mile walk in the sun and sand the better were our chances of surviving and accomplishing it all before noon, we set forth in the cool of the

December morning. Slowly, quite slowly, we strolled out past great lily-ponds, through sandy commons and underbrush, for a mile and a half to the sculptured raths of Mahabalipur, the boulder-temples of the once great city of Bali.

When the pious ones of that place, whether in the sixth century or still earlier, wished to build a temple they took a boulder of the desired size, carved it outwardly until it looked as if built by masons' hands, block by block and course by course, and then hollowed the interior into chambers, even one and two stories of pillared and vaulted chambers. Five such monolithic raths, or temples, remain in this lonely strand, with guardian lions, elephants, and bulls hewn from lesser boulders before them. Two of the raths are mere sentry-box shrines, or image-cells, eleven feet square and twenty feet high, carved with a wealth of exterior and interior ornament. The largest rath is the Split Temple, forty-two feet in length, with an impressive interior hall. All the raths stand empty and deserted, as if touched by the enchanter's wand, miraculously turned to stone. There was no moving thing, no sound but the distant moan of the surf and the rustling clash of palm-branches. The seven-o'clock sun already burned the sands and was reflected scorchingly from the rock masses, whose burned, yellow-brown tones seemed the very expression of heat.

Very slowly we walked for a mile through a plantation of young fir-trees, proof that the government of India considers the welfare of this region, whose long-denuded sands are being reforested for both economic and climatic reasons. We came out on the hard sand beach where the ocean lapped in soft, creamy wavelets, and the terrible Coromandel surges we had heard and read of only splashed gently on the steps of a quaint little pyramidal temple carved, course upon course, to its final bell-cap. Posts and columns stand far out in the water, and a line of breakers, a mile still further out, mark where legend says other pagodas stand intact beneath the waves. Southey has imaged it in "The Curse of Kehama," but prosaic surveyors say that there is only a reef of needle-rocks below the surface. That lonely little temple at the edge of the loud-sounding sea, although a common thing of masons' construction, is most impressive of all the seven temples. Its stone façade is rounded with sand-blast, spray, and surge, its walls are broken, its portico and platform half wrecked by the fury of past storms, and its cool, wet chambers hold Vishnu's images in his different incarnations,—Buddha, Vishnu's ninth avatar, occupying a last cool grotto.

The sun was burning with full strength then, and we sought the mud and thatch Tamil village under a cluster of palm-trees. The villagers swarmed out, and an inky, sooty flock of cherubs ran beside us to another boulder-temple, where we sat in the shade and regarded a huge stone hollowed like a churn or bowl, where "the gopis made butter for Krishna in the forest"—"But the cat ran away with the butter," said Daniel, regretfully. Krishna, the dancing god of Hindu mythology, very nearly corresponds to the Greek Apollo or Hercules, and the gopis parallel the naiads and muses.

The palm-tree was our Christmas-tree that day, and the villagers, having already stripped it of gifts, pierced the green cocoanuts and gave us reviving drinks. The Tamil cupids folded palm-leaves into drinking-cups and drank such portions as their elders gave them. It was a pretty, primitive scene, purely and ideally Indian, when around the rock came a British tourist in a pith helmet, a lady in a helmet, too, with streaming green veil ends. They looked at the churn, they looked at the temple on which we sat, but they saw us no more than they would see canal-boat No. 1350 at anchor beside their splendid budgery-boat. We opened more cocoanuts and drank to the merry day, to the Superior Person, to the Pharisee wherever he may find himself. "Peace on earth—good will to men." Blessed is the Christmas spirit and the Briton's sense of decorum. Alas, that we had no letters of introduction with us!

Slowly we walked up over a great scarped rock—and it was like walking across a hot stove—and descended steps in its front to see the carving known as Arjuna's Penance—a rock-front, thirty-seven feet high and ninety feet long, carved all over with life-sized figures and animals in high relief, a whole picture-book of earliest mythology. The wicked cat who stole the gopi's lump of butter was triumphantly pointed out, standing on its hind legs in penance, while mice ran about its feet. "Really," said Daniel, "he is waiting for the sea to dry that he may eat all the fish in it." This gigantic bas-relief sculpture, beside which Thorvaldsen's lion at Lucerne is a toy, is from an earlier time than the monolithic raths by the sea, and marks the dateless era of serpent-worship. But the sunny rock-front radiated heat like a bonfire, and there was no wish to stand and study it.

It was then past nine o'clock, the sun was scorching high overhead, and nothing Daniel could say about the "numberlesses of gods and goddesses," or lesser cave-temples, could stir us. Not "Krishna and the gopis, his sweethearts in paradise," not Ganesha, all black, greasy, and garlanded in his own rock-cut temple, could attract us longer—all interest in art, archæology, and architecture scorched and scotched for the day. For a half-mile we had made Daniel give guarantees of importance before we would look within a cave or take one extra step in that terrible scorch and sun-glare of a midwinter morning.

The sands were blinding and our boats quivered in heat-waves as we went toward them at noon; but while the coolies splashed along over tow-paths submerged by the tide, we were cooled by a gentle head-wind all the afternoon. The water was a-splash with bits of silver, and one of the trackers stopped, wrestled with something under his foot, and threw a large fish into the boat. At sunset we could see a faint line of surf beyond the sand wastes, and the beat of the sea was heard through hours of darkness succeeding the most beautiful, moist pink sunset.

When the candles were lighted a great, two-inch brown cockroach ran up the side of the boat, stood upside down on the mat ceiling, and waved his feelers.

THE VILLAGE STREET.

Others followed the beckoning leader until the place was swarming, and we retreated to the chairs at the stern, where, with breakneck naps, we spent the night, shuddering to think of the preceding night, when, preferring starlight to candles, we had gone to bed in the dark.

The sky was full of big, yellow, pulsing stars, but the Southern Cross was not visible. Orion gradually changed its angle and tilted itself almost in reverse; and Orion was a great offense to me in those low latitudes. As if one went to latitude 0° and to 6° N. and 13° N. to see one's most familiar northern constellation!

"Meh lady! Meh lady! The Holy Cross is here in the sky now," said faithful David at four o'clock, and he crossed himself as became a good Romanist. There, straightaway in our wake to southward, were two lopsided crosses, or diamonds, each outlined by four great, glowing yellow stars where the narrow cut of the Buckingham Canal exactly underlay and reflected the great southern constellation, the filmy trails of Magellan's clouds floating near.

CHAPTER VI

MADRAS AND CALCUTTA

THERE is a splendid show of old armor and weapons in the Madras Museum, but those trophies of metal-work are not unique like the relics and fragments from the great Buddhist shrines of the south. Room after room is filled with bas-reliefs and images dating from the noblest period of Greco-Buddhist art, the great tope of Amraoti having been, like the temple of Boro Boedor in Java, a picture-Bible of Buddhism. The exquisite marble bas-reliefs, portraying events in the life of Buddha and scenes of religious ceremony, and the bands of ornament give but a starting-point for the imagination to reconstruct the shrines of twelve and fifteen centuries ago. There are treasured relics dating centuries before the Christian era, and one bit of bone in a beryl cylinder, found in the excavations at the Bhattiprolu mound, is an undoubted fragment of the body of Gautama Buddha. Our guides were not eloquent over these Buddhist relics, knowing more about the jeweled and damascened swords, goads, spears, and daggers of the late Raja of Tanjore, whose treasures had lately come to the "wonder-house," as the natives term a museum. A wonder-guide had attached himself to us as we made the rounds, greatly to the annoyance of Samuel Daniel, whose severest manner could not rout him. At the door each handed us an umbrella, and as we went down the steps Daniel thrust away the self-appointed guide and began: "Your ladyships"; but the rival slipped past, opened the carriage door, and, bowing, said: "Your highnesses." The constant "ladyships" that we everywhere received declared how the wily Hindu sees and plays upon the weaknesses of the alien race he knows best, and the "highnesses" was climax of the play upon snobbery.

One never could have greater need for an astral body than in Madras, where we drove and drove to get to any place—through miles of banian tunnels and green-vaulted avenues, along the Marina road by the sea, and through the Adyar suburb, where Theosophists still congregate, despite the cruel exposure of the whole Blavatsky-Mahatma-Yogi frauds in that very quarter years ago.

Life is lived on narrow margins in India. One cannot get "something for nothing" in Madras; and every purchase sent to the hotel came with a footnote to the bill: "Coolie not paid." When Samuel Daniel had left for his home, the next post brought us a card: "Your ladyships: I forgetfully leave my carpet and blanket with David's bed at Guindy Bridge. Please David have send to, as railway parcel, to station-master at Trichinopoli." We ordered the room butler to send a responsible person to the station and—but before I could finish my remarks and tell how to prepay the parcel, his grins changed and he began to storm angrily: "Who pays that coolie? Who pays that railway? I am poor man. Suppose I never see Daniel again? Suppose I die, and Daniel does n't come? What becomes of my family then? You pay the coolie. You pay the coolie. God will bless you. God will bless the good lady who helps the poor. Think of my family! Oh, think of my family! You pay the coolie! You pay the coolie! God will bless you!" he implored, working himself into a very frenzy. There was a rush and rustle of starched clothing and the frenzy suddenly ended as David cuffed him out of the room with word that the memsahib had expected to pay the coolie anyhow.

The butler presented a bill that was many rupees too much. "I must see the manager about this," I said, rising to leave the room. "Oh, your ladyship! Your ladyship! Write a chit! Write only a little chit—a little chit to the manager, and he will understand and make it right," implored the end-man. "But I must see him," I said. A torrent of agitated pleas poured from the minstrel. "The manager is away. He is at the fort."

"Then I will wait and speak to him when he returns."

"But, your ladyship, suppose your ship comes! Oh, your ladyship, write just a little chit," and the butler wrung his hands in real despair.

That act of the farce having lasted long enough, I wrote "too much" on the back of the bill. The butler carried it out on the silver salver, went to a table at the end of the hall, and wrote something on the face of the bill. Pooh Bah had literally gone over to the other side of the stage and become manager himself. He returned in less than three minutes with the corrected bill, with apologies from the manager three miles away at the fort, and with his autograph "*Thanks*" written at the end. Then the combination butler-manager-bookkeeper took the money, went back to the hall table, and receipted the bill, which was all in the one handwriting.

All the doors of my room, the windows, the hall, staircase, and portico were full of salaaming servants when leave-taking came. The neighborhood must have been emptied for our farewell, as well as the village of servants in the back yard. From the triple-part chief to the humblest coolie, gardener, water-carrier, sweeper, and the despised woman slavey, all stood expectant, rubbing their noses upward with their palms and extending their hands as they wailed: "Prissint! Prissint! Oh, memsahib, prissint!"

"Will you kindly telephone to the hotel when the ship is sighted Sunday morning. There are eight passengers there," I had said to the clerk on Saturday. "Oh, madam," said the pink Englishman in a shocked tone, "the telephone cannot be used on Sundays. The telephone office is closed."

At sunrise and at sunset we drove to the empty harbor, and a black babu at the door of the steamship office said: "The *Khedive, she* will not come until morning now. *She* cannot get in the entrance of the breakwater without daylight."

"When will the launch go off to the ship?"

"Oh, we don't get the passengers out. You just put yourself in a massoula-boat when you see the ship and go out to it yourself."

We engaged a massoula-boat from him with the agreement that one of the crew should rouse the hotel when the *Khedive* was sighted. And he did, with such fervor and fury that we all drove at a Gilpin-speed for the harbor lest we miss the ship. Black boatmen ran the last mile beside us, screeching their numbers, holding out their tin license-tags, and dodging the blows of our own courier boatman, who resented any approaches toward his legal fares. We and our trunks and traps were but atoms in the bottom of the cavernous massoula-boat that the black babu had engaged for us—a primitive native boat whose timbers, fitted and tied together, only can withstand the famous Madras surf. Six black man-apes plied arrow-headed poles that passed for oars, and with a wild, resounding chant shot away from the iron pier. We clung to the high gunwales as we stood on the loose lattice of poles and mats and wondered when the first great roller would lift us. But we rowed only a few hundred yards to a ship within the still pool of the artificial harbor, sheltered by a breakwater whose opposing arms, bearing twin lighthouses, were far enough apart for fleets to have manœuvered there after dark. Madras people went past us in dingies and dories and any sort of row-boats, and we in our arks of massoula-boats were as ridiculous as tourists generally are in strange lands. Enough tourists had been duped into engaging these huge surf-boats to make a very imposing appearance when the fleet approached the gangway in line. There was a smooth, smiling sunlit sea flickering beyond the breakwater that serene December day, and the fabled surf of the Coromandel coast and the "life-in-your-hand" embarkations at Madras were other outlived illusions.

There had been a bedlam of coolies at the pier, but there was ten times more bedlam at the one gangway of the *Khedive;* one stream of passengers, servants, and baggage-coolies ascending the narrow, swaying gangway, and another stream trying to descend, every lung and muscle in the lot working overtime. We hesitated long, but David, scenting a fray, was as intractable as a war-horse, and, leaping ahead, screamed, pushed, kicked, and slapped a way for us through the struggling bearers, the toppling trunks and bags. The others did the same, and one would rather have jumped over than have attempted to return. As one woman was jerked up by both arms from the rocking massoula-boat, a lurch sent her against the gangway chains and knocked her chatelaine-bag off and into the water. With it went watch, purse, keys, tickets, and letter of credit. And the ship was to sail in an hour! The purser sent a boatman in haste, a lighter came alongside, and the diver was dressed, his headpiece screwed on before our eyes, and his leaden knapsack arranged as his weighted feet were lowered from rung to rung of the ladder until beneath the water. A line of bubbles showed where he walked about at the bottom of the sea, and in five minutes he came up with the bag on his wrist, the whole proceeding as orderly and matter-of-fact as if it were the usual thing to drop and recover articles in Madras harbor.

The completed railway now gives one choice of a land route to Calcutta in half the time a ship requires; but with the dust, heat, and discomfort considered, it is not always preferred.

"The *Khedive*, she" made the seven hundred and eighty miles from Madras to Calcutta in four days and a half, counting in the whole night that we anchored among a brilliant constellation of ships' lights at the Hugli mouth of the Ganges. When the ship started up the sacred, muddy stream of such ill omen, with a famous Hugli pilot in an enormous mushroom solar hat shading him like an umbrella, ports were closed, ropes laid out, and every officer, lascar, and stoker was at his post. The ship sailed smoothly over the shoals and quicksands of such dire record and nothing happened.

We hastened to the Great Eastern Hotel, to which we had written in November, again in December, and twice telegraphed of our coming from Madras.

"We never reserve rooms unless money is inclosed with the order," said the haughty brown clerk. "This hotel is full."

"Have you any mail for us?"

"Oh, yes. Many letters. They have been coming for some time. The bank messenger brought many to-day. You will find them in that desk over there," pointing to a box where every one rummaged and chose at will.

We drove in the fast-falling dusk to five hotels

and four boarding-houses. Not a room nor a tent could be had, and we were deciding whether to lay ourselves on an orphan asylum's door-step, seek the consul as really distressed Americans, or go back to the ship and insist upon their keeping us until morning, when the peon of one of the hotels screamed and ran after us as we drove past. We hurried in and sat on the upper backstairs until we could make an instantaneous exchange of luggage with an officer called back to his hill station. The small back room had such shabby furnishings as would cause an American cook to give notice, and we commanded a view of tin roofs, chimney-pots, and clothes-lines. A half-clad, hairy man came in with a bloated goatskin of water over his shoulder. He pulled the goatskin neck around and filled the bath-tub from the leather reservoir—this primitive method surviving in the "city of palaces" after a century of British rule and long official example of luxury and splendor.

In the dining-room each guest had his own servant standing behind his chair. One hundred guests sat at meat, and more than that many turbaned bearers stepped silently over the marble floor. Each retainer looked grim determination, and had a row of knives, forks, and spoons thrust dagger-wise in his belt. Then we discovered that the table d'hôte was the battle-ground of the bearers, that food and forks were for the forehanded, for the swiftest and strongest only. Our Tamil was quivering for the fray and soon in the midst of it, wresting soup and fish, entrée, roast, and game, trophy by trophy, and emerging from each hand-to-hand struggle with turban awry and eyes flashing. Although this football rush was going on in the pantry and dining-room, the swiftly moving, barefooted contestants made no sound on the marble floor, and only a suppressed hissing indicated the death-scuffle behind the screen. Each bearer put down the hard-won plate before his master, pulled a fresh knife and fork from his belt, gave them a rub on his voluminous garments, and fell into statuesque pose again behind the chair.

CHAPTER VII

CALCUTTA IN CHRISTMAS WEEK

ANOTHER winter I took heed and reached Calcutta betimes, making sure of hotel accommodations for Christmas week, the gala season of the Anglo-Indian year, when all the fifteen hundred civilians who rule India, and all the officers who can be spared from cantonments, seek the capital.

Going from and returning to Singapore there was opportunity to stop in Burma, politically a province of India, but a country quite unique, where the life and the people are so distinct from those of India that one cannot class it with Hindustan any more than Siam. A different religion has made the Burmese a different people, and the absence of caste, the freedom, the equality, in fact, the acknowledged superiority of the attractive, capable, Burmese women have evolved a wholly different social order. There is light, and laughter and gaiety among its people, and the Burman is Malay enough to enjoy a life of leisure. The Chinese come and do the trading, and the Madrasi come to do the work, and the Burmese woman keeps the shop, rules the family, smokes her "whacking white cheroot" with grace, and exerts rare charm.

In all sight-seeing nothing is such surprise, so Oriental, so dazzling and fascinating as the great Shoëdagong pagoda at Rangoon. It repays one for all the entomological revels of the " B. I." boats to see that colossal, gilded, and jeweled monument surrounded by picturesque worshipers; to watch "the elephants a-pilin' teak"; to see the colossal Sleeping Buddha at Pegu; and to travel past one hundred miles of sacked rice awaiting the overtaxed railway transportation, as one rumbles by rail to Mandalay, where the fantastic gilt and mirror-covered temples, monasteries, and palaces equal one's dreams of "the gorgeous East." Only seeing can convince one what Buddhism can do for a people in contrast with Hinduism or Mohammedanism, and that the pagoda is always in sight in Burma—the swelling, white bodies tapering to needle spires often gilded and tipped with jewels—the sites of deserted cities like Amarapura and Pagan on the lower Irawadi dotted as thickly with temples and pagodas as ever they could have been with houses. Too many chapters would be required for anything like an adequate exploitation of this picturesque country and attractive people; but until the great European mail-steamers touch at Rangoon the pleasure traveler is warned against the slow coasting steamers on which one lives with the heat and the smells and the motion at the very stern, and where huge brown tropical roaches swarm, past any figures of speech to give idea.

THE RUINS AND PAGODAS OF PAGAN.

THE FORT AT MANDALAY.

There were brilliant panoramas on Calcutta streets, those glittering noondays and golden afternoons, but the hotels had only increased in numbers, and advanced in price in the few years. Hotels in India are all conducted on the *pension* or American plan of a fixed rate per day, with everything save wine included, and the charges had risen from the average five and seven rupees to ten and fifteen rupees, to the indignation of Anglo-Indians, who, in no gentle terms, blame increasing tourist travel for the increased cost of living.

I was conducted across a back yard and up a flight of outer steps to a room whose reed matting had not been disturbed in many seasons. "But the Bishop of New York occupied that room last year and made no complaint," said the landlady, dramatically.

"Think how much more Christian fortitude and saving grace a bishop has to have"—and she countermanded the order for a new matting to be laid on top of the old one in shiftless Indian fashion, and decreed a cleaning instead. Two inches of dust, that had to be shoveled off, underlay the matting, then the cement floor was washed with disinfectants, and there was one clean room in one Calcutta hotel that night. When the washstand, grimed with the wear of many seasons, had received a coat of white paint, —without a bowl or article being removed,—it was a splendid apartment—for an Indian hotel. I almost hesitated to exchange it for "one of the best rooms in the house"—a lofty, whitewashed cell with worn cocoa matting on the floor, where twilight reigned all day and no pernicious ray of sunlight fell. "This is Room 66 in the —— Hotel in Calcutta, one of the best in the house," said an American lecturer once, and at sight of the lantern picture the audience roared with laughter.

" Go and see the Black Hole of Calcutta," said the Viceroy, who had finally determined and marked the exact spot. " I have no need to, Your Excellency. I live there now. Room 18, —— Hotel," said another winter visitor.

There is little of stock sight-seeing for the tourist —only the Zoölogical and Botanical Gardens and the Temple of Kali; there are no specialties or local opportunities in souvenir shopping in Calcutta, and the European life is not what one comes half-way around the world to see; so that the traveler's stay in this city is usually brief. The fact of its being the capital for so short a season gives Calcutta much of a watering-place atmosphere.

Except for innumerable turbaned and bare-footed servants, the pankha, and the use of many Hindustani words, the life is the life of London—a London with the chill taken off and the sun shining gloriously. Every one waits for the London *Times* to know the real news of the world; and although the Calcutta newspapers hold diverting advertisements of cinder-picking and ash-sifting rights for sale, and "20 Rhinoceroses Wanted, Rupees 2000 each," local opinion waits on the daily arrival of the *Allahabad Pioneer*, a nursery of genius wherein Sinnett and Kipling and Marion Crawford first won public applause.

Even in December there is summer heat at noon, and one wears the white gowns of the tropics at that high social hour in Calcutta; for one writes his name in the visitors' book at Government House, all formal calls are made, and letters of introduction are presented between twelve and two o'clock; and on Sundays, after church, every drawing-room hums with visitors' chat. The solid two-o'clock tiffin, following the heavy ten-o'clock breakfast, is so soon succeeded by the four-o'clock tea and the eight-o'clock dinner, that it is a surprise that any one survives the constant feasting which fills Anglo-Indian life. Little can be urged against a climate that permits such Gargantuan feats. The London menu goes with the British drum-beat round the world, and the beef and beer and cheese, the boiled potato, the cauliflower, and orange marmalade are fixed and omnipresent. More continuous than the imperial drum-beat is the sound of the soda-water bottle, on which, with the quinine sulphate, British rule rests. A chill and piercing dampness succeeds sunset, and often at night dense fogs shroud lamp-posts and landmarks until street travel is at a standstill. The modern Calcutta houses have fireplaces where a few lumps of coal diffuse a cheerful dryness, but in the older mansions one is bidden quite seriously to sit nearer the lamp and enjoy its benign radiation.

The Viceroy comes down from Simla in November, and goes on a provincial tour, reaching Calcutta before Christmas, when tents for extra guests decorate the lawns of Government House, of the clubs and great residences; and the empire revolves within the white viceregal palace. The standard flies above the main entrance, red lancers of the body-guard pose statuesque before the portico, and at times a red carpet rolls down the steps and the Viceroy goes in state to return princely visits, or to stand on a pearl and bullion embroidered carpet before his silver arm-chair and lay a corner-stone, unveil a statue, or open some new public building. The great event of the racing week is the Viceroy's Cup, when all sporting India has its eye on the Maidan, remotest cantonments as heavily interested as the cheering crowds on the oval. The Viceroy comes in state, and his loge and lawn are the center of interest and the social heaven of the ambitious, who, between events, parade in the hats and gowns brought out from London and Paris for the races. Rajas and nabobs of degree make a brave show too, with their jeweled turbans, and necklaces worn outside frock coats of flowered satins; the tight-fitting trousers to match as often trimmed with tinsel braid and French passementerie. Thousands of natives, in the universal white garments and turbans of every hue, make such patches of shifting rainbow color in the field, such a living tulip-bed, as fascinates the eye more than any scramble of running horses.

Then all the world drives in the Maidan, making a grand defile down the Red Road and the avenue of statues, along the Strand and the Esplanade by the Eden Gardens, where the band plays at sunset. Eastern and Western fashions are strangely contrasted. The bhisti, with swollen goatskins on their backs, sprinkle the dust, as in the times of Alexander the Great and Cyrus, while automobiles fly by, electric lights prick the blue mists of distance, and night falls with tropic swiftness.

The Viceroy and his wife together hold a drawing-room a few days after Christmas, when a procession of women winds slowly up the white staircase of Government House lined with red-coated red-turbaned servants, and past the many barriers to the throne-room, where the knee is bent to viceroyalty, and one train and bouquet give way to the long procession of trains and bouquets. One does not soon forget the scenes of Lord Curzon's rule in India. The Viceroy, in his white satin smallclothes, girt with his orders and stars and the insignia of the Garter, and Lady Curzon, that supremely beautiful woman of her day, on the dais beside him in glittering tiara and ropes of pearls, her long train rippling away over the edge of the steps, remind one of certain of David's historical pictures. Lady Curzon has held all native and Anglo-India under the spell of her charm during her stay. There could be no rivalry in beauty, and her unfailing tact and sweet gentleness carry all before her. The Indian people exhausted the imagery of their several hundred languages to describe her beauty, the sun, moon, stars, jewels, and all the goddesses and gopis of their pantheon being drawn into comparison to describe the lovely "Lady Sahib."

A still larger company of men are presented to the Viceroy, receiving alone, at the levee, and then the state balls and state dinners, small dinners and dances rapidly succeed one another, while the Viceroy's private hospitalities are continuous. At the end of each week the viceregal family go to their country house at Barrackpur, fourteen miles up the Hugli, the large house-party reinforced by a company of guests brought up on the yacht to lunch under the great banian-tree. Like Lord Auckland, Lord Curzon, with the Dowager Empress of China, rules half the human race and still finds time to breakfast under that banian-tree. Possessed of that same tireless energy as those two other strenuous rulers of his day, President Roosevelt and the Emperor William, Lord Curzon has given Anglo-India daily shock and sensation since his arrival, and sleepy bureaus and slow officials were galvanized to a life that has known no resting since. There has been no monotony during Lord Curzon's time, and those who have waited for him to weary of hustling the East, to sit back in conventional viceregal fashion and sign the papers brought him, have had to resign themselves to his omnipresence and terrible activity, his thirst for information, and his frenzy for work. He has impressed his vigorous personality upon every branch of the imperial service, and already has visited more native states and distant provinces than any predecessor; ordering, with equal attention to minutiæ, the least details of the increased state and ceremony now attending the viceregal court, the methods of famine relief and plague control, and of the organization of the new district created on the northwest frontier. He has brought India to the world's attention and given it an impetus in the path of progress and prosperity.

The "L. G." or Lieutenant-Governor of Bengal, ruler of sixty millions of people, carries on an elaborate program of hospitalities at Belvidere, his beautiful villa beyond the race-course, and the commander-in-chief and the local military officers at the fort do their part to crowd the January weeks with social events for the keenly pleasure-loving English in exile. It is only at investment ceremonies and at durbars on the arrival of a new viceroy that the native princes assemble at the Calcutta court in great numbers. A few Parsi women in graceful head draperies of pale silks, and loaded with jewels, attend the functions at Government House, and a few elderly and widowed Hindu ladies of rank receive visitors of their own sex; but otherwise the native women of the higher classes remain in as great seclusion as ever, veiled even when they drive in closed carriages. On one afternoon of the week, the India Museum is closed to men visitors, and native women and children come by the gharry-load to the "wonder-house." Foreign women can enter the museum then, mingle with their purdah sisters, and watch the jeweled persons as they stroll about as curious and as ignorant as the smaller children.

The India Museum is rich beyond rivalry in treasures of ancient art. The magnificent carved gateway and rail from the Buddhist tope at Sanchi, original of the casts in London and in Paris, bas-reliefs and images from Gandhara and Amraoti, with treasures and relics from the great temple at Buddha-Gaya, have long made the fame of the museum. When the Piprawah mound at Padaria on the Nepal frontier was excavated, and the stone coffer containing the relics and fragments of the body of Gautama Buddha were found, no archæologist or representative of the government was present, and the " L. G." of the Northwest Provinces, when communicated with, divided the treasures between the India Museum and the King of Siam, the only Buddhist sovereign of this day. The sandstone coffer, a soapstone vase, a crystal vase, some bits of bone and crumbling particles of wood, many pearls, tiny gold beads and flowers, and cut amethyst, topaz, carnelian, coral, garnet, beryl, and jade stars, together with larger beaten gold ornaments in the shape of the swastika, came to this museum—more authentic relics of the founder of a great religion than any European cathedral contains. It possesses also the inscription recording the deposit of these relics of the body of the Buddha in that mound by the members of the Sakya clan—a treasure of archæology which makes real the personality of the Buddha, the founder of that religion no longer a solar myth. This museum has an average of sixty thousand visitors a month, equaling nearly the throngs at the Louvre; but the company of barefooted, sheeted Bengalis are so aimless and vacant-looking that one questions whether the carefully planned exhibits reach beyond the retina, whether they have any comprehension of the objects.

One does not expect to find a great leisure class in India, where the struggle for existence is so close and bitter, but watching the idle drift of natives past this stretch of Chowringee Road, and the Maidan before the museum, even more than through the labyrinthine bazaars, one is appalled and oppressed with the realization of India's population—294,360,356. All day the lean, wistful, apathetic men stream up and down, up and down, going nowhere, doing nothing—hundreds passing at any moment, thousands in an hour, with no women and rarely a child in sight. Each Hindu, in his dirty head-sheet, represents a family crowded back somewhere in the city slums or in mud villages beyond. One easily believes the census figures, and sees how the frightful problem of over-population besets the empire; how necessary, almost, are plague and famine, in lieu of wars, to reduce the swarms and herds of these lank, inert, torpid, half-fed, half-clothed, half-alive Bengalis. When the sixty million Bengalis are crowded seven hundred and even nine hundred to the square mile of this fertile province, and are the most prolific of Indian races, they must reap three harvests a year even to half live, as they do. Long-continued peace and the sanitary blessings of English rule have so preserved and increased human life that disease and starvation seem too slow agents to accomplish the necessary reduction. Only tidal waves and earthquakes, annual disasters like those of Pompeii and Martinique, could keep the population within bounds.

The Hindus are not a laughing, light-hearted, joyous people, and the Bengali is the most melancholy of them. He has little, almost no sense of humor, his voice is always in a sad minor key when not quarreling, and the corners of his mouth are permanently drawn down. A sad sobriety is his sense of dignity and good form. The hotel porter calls a "fitton" (phaëton), not with the tyrant voice of command, but with the sad, piercing wail of a banshee. The sais, wrapped in melancholy and a quilted bed-spread, responds with a mournful loon cry, and urges his lean, despondent horses forward, the running sais in tattered sheet hanging on behind, like an old dust-cloth, with bags of green fodder. He jeers but never laughs, and one wonders if he can, with so little room for a normal pair of lungs in that thin, flat body and narrow chest. With no oxygen to speak of for generations, they can hardly be cheerful or energetic. Athletic sports are not in the line of the young Bengalis of the Brahman castes who crowd the schools, take all the prizes, and fill the government offices,—Young Bengal being usually a superficially educated poll-parrot quite as offensive and hopeless as Young China. The Bengalis are slow to reward the Christian missionaries who have worked among them for a century, but they are converted to Mohammedanism in droves, whole villages adopting that casteless creed.

The laboring Hindu seems generally incompetent, and sadly lacks inventiveness, originality, ingenuity, and the all-embracing but indescribable faculty known as "gumption." His appliances, tools, and instruments are unchanged since the day of Alexander, and the mechanical sense seems wholly denied him. Everything has come to him with his conquerors. With spindle legs, flat chest, and shrunken arms, one wonders how one of them can do the heavy work of dock-yards, harbors, railway yards, and iron foundries. Everything is hoisted on the head and shoulder, and so little is carried in the hand that handles are superfluous ornaments on luggage. One meets grand pianos and packing-cases of equal size carried on the heads of eight and twelve men, who step together with locked arms. I watched one coolie's seven attempts to carry ten pasteboard boxes from one shop counter to another. Each time he heaped the load on one arm his draped head-sheet fell away. Each time he reflung the sheet the boxes dropped from the limp arm, and the alternating play went on, until one would have expected an employer to deal blows—or for any rational creature to throw away the sheet and get to work. Centuries have not evolved a way of tying or pinning the woman's veil fast, and weary housekeepers describe the ayah's efforts to make a bed and keep her veil in place as an alternating affair like that of my coolie and the ten boxes.

The curse of caste and all the difficulties its observance implies further complicate dealings with these people, and a century of enlightened rule has not freed them from its tyranny. The railway has done something toward leveling castes, but for the journey only. Instead of reviling and recoiling from the railway as an invention of the defiling European for the express purpose of destroying caste, the Brahman artfully calls steam one of the thousand and eight uncatalogued manifestations of Vishnu. He conceals his sacred thread, washes off his caste-mark, and rides in the jam of a third-class car, touching sweepers and water-carriers and corpse-burners, and trusts to after-purification. Instead of the Chinese hostility to railways, they have so much adopted them for their own that there is already a hereditary railway caste, and railway workers of the third generation are following their fathers' occupation as naturally as if it were an occupation of centuries' inheritance. One never arrives at an end of the puzzling caste distinctions. With the four great castes of Brahmans subdivided into eighteen hundred and eighty-six castes, it is beyond any European mind to master its intricacies. Because of caste, no one jostles you in the street, and insistent touts keep a safe distance.

CHAPTER VIII

THE GREATEST THING IN THE WORLD

IN traveling north from Calcutta toward Darjiling, we had the same springless, cheerless, dusty railway cars as in southern India; the same bare floors, hard, leather-covered sofas, and rattling windows of violet glass that gave a wintry, melancholy look to the flat Bengal plain that we jolted over all the afternoon. After sunset it grew really cold in the bare, dimly lighted box, that finally halted amid clamoring torch-bearers on a siding by a river bank. It might as well have been the crumbling mud banks of the upper Missouri as those of the sacred Ganges that we descended to reach a flat-bottomed, stern-wheel river steamer of American model; but no band of Sioux or Crees on the war-path ever raised such din as the coolies at Damookdea when the "up-mail" arrived. The very stars seemed to reel from the noise, and we breathed deep sighs of thanksgiving when the boat wheezed away from the movable station and on across "sacred Mother Ganges" to Sara Ghat, where another horde of coolies lay in wait, shrieking and gesticulating in the torchlight as the boat advanced. "I catch coolies," said David, and he did so, dragging them on board by leg, arm, or turban end, as chanced. Although we had telegraphed to have lower sofas reserved, the Anglo-Indian railway brain has not been equal to devising or borrowing a system of numbering and definitely securing such a reservation. Possession was to the swiftest, and the foot-race up a soft bank and over ends of railway ties by torchlight warmed one at least. The air grew colder, and bitterly colder, as we rumbled along through the night, and the loose-fitting doors and windows sent frosty currents across us. From dreams of Pullman curtains, blankets, soft mattresses and springs, of double windows and thick carpets, of sixteen-wheeled trucks with cylindrical springs under long cars hung far above the dusty road-bed, we woke to the cold reality of our freight- and cattle-car comforts. Before daylight tea-trays flashed in the lamplight of way stations, and cups of freshly made tea thawed one and cheered the gray hour of dawn, while the thick frost haze of the plain half obscured the sky.

By six o'clock it was light enough to see that the people had changed overnight with the temperature. We had left the sleek, supple, barefooted Bengali in his sheeted drapery, with his thin nose and deep eyes, and come to a race with high cheek bones and flat Mongol faces, first cousins to the Chinese, even to the cut of their loose-sleeved coats with overlapping fronts, and their high cloth boots. The queue and the turban were worn together; and that was not more incongruous than the Hindu caste-mark on the brow of a flat, Mongol face. There were ruddy-faced mountaineers in Tatar caps on the platforms, and unveiled women with elaborate head-dresses and necklaces of silver, coral, and turquoises. Beyond the trees and houses of Haldibari station there loomed a great rose-pink line of peaks and snowy battlements, stretching across the upper sky and resting above ridges of tremendous blue and hazily purple mountains. As the sun rose, the peaks paled, turned to gold and silvery white, and the greatest mountain wall in the world stood sharply revealed, twenty-eight thousand feet in air, a parapet of high heaven, the first sight of which leaves one breathless. Beyond all other mountain views is that first sight of the Himalayas, as the great line of snow-peaks towers from the Siliguri-plain.

After such mundane things as coffee and eggs, the most absurd little narrow-gage cars, with only canvas curtains as protection from the changes of mountain weather, trundled us across a few level miles, and more slowly began climbing through shady jungles and along cleared hillsides, with now a view out to the level, yellow plain where a shining river stretched to hazy distance, and now a view toward silvery peaks that rose continually higher. The tiny engine gained a thousand feet in altitude each hour, creeping along hillsides planted with monotonous lines of tea-bushes, through dry and dusty jungles where trees and tree-ferns, creepers and underbrush, were parched and frost-nipped, dull with the dust of the dry season. The toy train crawled over curves and loops, and one wished that the Gladstone family, owning the line, had provided, instead of the string of cabs linked together, one well-built and windowed trolley-car, that one might sit in comfort and enjoy the views that continually opened. Flat-faced Lepcha and Bhutia women stared with uncovered faces and Chinese stolidity as the train slowly passed them, each woman a family savings-bank with the hoarded rupees strung in overlapping rows on her head and neck. Tibetans, too, were seen, and at Kurseong, five thousand feet above the sea, in the midst of tea-gardens, we were only nineteen miles from the Tibetan frontier. After tiffin in the chill, whitewashed dining-room of the Kurseong hotel, we thawed ourselves in the sunny garden, where a Catholic priest from the adjoining mission-house pointed the way to the pass at the edge of Tibet, where he had been spending some months. Although the Tibetans come freely across the boundary to trade and to work in the tea plantations, all English and Europeans are rigorously excluded, and none of the Indian tea openly reaches Tibet; the Chinese monopoly of the tea trade being the chief reason for the severe exclusion laws the lamas maintain.

Kunchinjinga seemed no nearer, only higher, still higher, and looming larger against the sky. The air was decidedly a nipping one, and with all our rugs and razais and hot-water cans at our feet, we found the foolish little open tram-car anything but a rational conveyance for high mountain travel, still less appropriate when we ran into a dense, woolly white cloud that hid everything for half an hour. The toy engine screeched, wheezed, panted, and slowly drew us up to cloudland by many loops and switchbacks; going backward and forward, but always upward, until we came to Ghoom, a double row of huts lining the track. There were picturesque folk in that bazaar, and foremost was the "witch of Ghoom," a wrinkled squaw who claimed to be one hundred years old, and begged for an anna on that account. A stumpy little Gurkha officer boarded the train there, his breast covered with war medals, and his wife covered with rows and rows of gold and silver coin necklaces and strings of coral, turquoise, and amber beads; her head as thickly plated with family assets, and her costume only richer in material than the bright purple, red, green, orange, and yellow garments of the hill folk that made Ghoom's one street a lane of color and light. Children rode pickaback instead of astride the Hindu hip; all loads were carried on the back by a strap over the brow, and after the inert and melancholy Hindus, these hill folk seemed a light-hearted, laughing people.

We were eight hours in accomplishing the fifty miles, reaching an elevation of 7470 feet at Ghoom, and descending to 6000 feet at Darjiling, a whole daylight of child's play with a toy train to any one who has traveled on Colorado's narrow-gage mountain railways.

We were carried from the station to the hotel in dandy-wallahs, carrying-chairs like the swan and shell chariots of stage pantomimes, the bearers turning them backward to climb steps or steep places. From the hotel windows and the terraced roads of the town, which occupies the crest of a knife-edged ridge, one has a full view of the front of Kunchinjinga and the long running line of snows across the deep chasm of the Ranjit. All too soon sunset reversed the pageant of the morning, and as the white peaks changed to gold, flame color, and rose-pink, blue and purple mists filled each ravine and valley. The rosy phantom lingered long before fading to cold gray and silver, the western sky glowing for a full hour, and a young white moon showing through the leafless trees.

The bazaar or market-place was empty then, for its gala time is on Sunday morning, when the tea-pickers come from remotest plantations to show and buy their finery; but there was a curio-shop whose owner was chiefest curio of the lot—one of the many who announce that they will surely reach Lhasa. He was then studying Tibetan, and produced an alleged lama who was disloyally teaching him the language and the religious exercises and formula that would help him to enter Lhasa in disguise. The lama fitted well into the room full of prayer-wheels, skull drums, skull bowls, tobacco-pouches, relic-boxes, bells, and images, and his presence surely helped business. With serious face the would-be explorer told how he should be welcomed to Lhasa as an envoy of the Theosophical Societies of Paris and London; how he should gather religious objects for Prince Ferdinand d'Este, and butterflies for Baron Rothschild, the latter guaranteeing all the expenses of the trip for the sake of the resulting collections. He had butterflies by the hundreds, great jewel-winged creatures of every color, with iridescent shadings and velvet bloom that were a delight to the eye. Tibet may still be worth penetrating for unknown butterflies, but from the early visits of French priests and English travelers down to the recent visit of Pundit Chandra Das, of native members of the Geological Survey of India, and of the Japanese Buddhist priests, about all that the world in general wants to know about Lhasa is known. Photographs of its streets and monasteries prove the correctness of the old engravings; Dr. Waddell has translated and edited the very complete local guide for Lhasa; and three women have gone as near to Lhasa as any explorer since Abbé Huc. All the blue-eyed travelers naturally failed to disguise themselves, and the Japanese had least difficulty in the enterprise.

Long before daylight the next morning we started in chairs in frosty darkness, a sky full of glittering stars lighting dimly the gigantic white shadows so strangely high in the sky. We passed through the military station and sanatorium of Jelapahar, along the side of the knife-ridge to Ghoom, and up to the isolated summit of Tiger Hill, fifteen hundred feet higher than Darjiling, where nothing interrupts the view of the whole range of snow-peaks from Kunchinjinga to Mount Everest. We sat in the lee of a boulder, wrapped in rugs and razais, our veins freezing in that thin, icy, mountain-top air, while the mixed lot of coolies and horse-boys accompanying the tourist contingent were unconscious of the cold; coolie No. 108 improving the time by tying large turquoises to holes in the lobes of his ears. They all wore these rough Tibetan turquoise ornaments, and turned many rupees by their sale while we waited for the sun, the lobe of the ear being the regulation showcase for these regular agents of a regular jewel merchant. The smart tourist always suspects the professional dealer, and much more confidingly trusts the simple hillman, and pays him a better price for bits of chalk dyed blue or ground glass of cerulean hue. The tip of Kunchinjinga, 28,150 feet in air, first turned rose-red and then caught the sun's rays, that flashed electrically down the long white line—a spectacle unequaled. Even the tourist's perpetual-motion tongue was silenced as the color pageant proceeded, and Kunchinjinga, with half of its height snow-covered, so transcended all one's imaginings that it did not seem the vision could be reality. Mount Everest, to our bitter disappointment, sulked in a tent of clouds to westward; but Kunchinjinga was visible all day long from our windows, and at sunset ran through its color changes once more.

It was degrees and degrees colder the next morning, but the sky was clearer, and the dazzling stars lighted the white phantom across the Ranjit more clearly. The frost lay like snow on Tiger Hill; the water by the wayside was frozen; and the wind blew with glacial edge that benumbed the little company of sun-worshipers gathered there at dawn. Again the world was suffused with a rose flush, a flash of sunlight touched Kunchinjinga and ran along the line of peaks clear to the three white pinnacles that rise above the depression of Chola Pass. I had not expected Mount Everest to be merely one small finger-tip of snow one hundred and twenty miles away. It was hardly worth while to hold up field-glasses in that arctic wind to look at that trifling nodule on the far horizon. It did not look like the greatest mountain in the world, "the highest measured elevation on earth." Imagination could not invest it with any superiority—not while splendid Kunchinjinga was there before us, with snow streamers and pennants and rosy cloud-banners floating away from those storehouse peaks of gold, silver, gems, and grains, as the Tibetans describe the five summits.

"Why are the globe-trotters so bent on seeing Mount Everest?" asked a Geological Survey officer. "It is not the finest peak, if it is the highest. It is only megalomania that takes the tourists off to Tiger Hill to see the highest peak in the world. Everest is not to be compared for looks with Peak XIII and Peak D^2. Those are the finest arrangements in rock and snow in the Himalayas. And then, Mount Everest is not in British territory, you know, and until we annex Nepal, I object to its being made so much of."

When we had come down from the Himalayan heights to the commonplace level of the plains again, and recrossed the Ganges, we had to share the two-sofa compartment with a severely silent and resentful Anglo-Indian matron, who stared at us heartlessly, contemptuously, and evidently denied us the right to occupy any part of her compartment and hemisphere. For the trip to Calcutta, she had brought with her into the compartment a tin steamer-trunk, a canvas hold-all, two dressing-bags, a Gladstone bag, a tiffin-basket, a basket tea-pot, a tin bonnet-box, a roll of razais and fur rugs, a shawl-strap bundle of cloaks and jackets, and one large bouquet. Her "boxes" were in the luggage-van.

But this lady of luggage was only forerunner to the memsahib we met when we left Calcutta the next night. We had sent the bearer ahead with our luggage two hours before train time. When we reached the Howrah station, we found that while our man was called off to pay a charge for extra luggage the paper of reservation had been unpinned from one lower berth and fastened to the upper one by an Anglo-Indian lady, who then unrolled her bedding, seated herself on it, and became deaf to any remarks or remonstrance. She had brought with her into the compartment the usual British impedimenta—tin steamer-trunk, canvas hold-all, Gladstone bag, laundry-bag, dressing-bag, tiffin-basket, a roll of umbrellas, a tennis racket, a bag with her pith hat, also a wicker chair, a collection of garments which hung from every available hook, *and* a large round-topped Saratoga trunk. When we protested to the station-master about the changing of his reservations, he could or dared do nothing. Possession was nine points, and the tenth was a gleam in her eye that might have warned away a lion-tamer. We produced our receipts and insisted that the station-master should send our large trunks into the compartment, too, and give us back the sixteen rupees we had paid for extra luggage, or else the memsahib's trunks should go. They went; and she paid six rupees through the window with wrath and threats. Only the thinnest veneer of civilization prevented her from laying violent hands upon us then, or strangling us in the night. Nothing so shocks and offends the Anglo-Indian traveler on American transcontinental trains as the publicity of the Pullman cars, where each berth has its curtain and number, and is as securely reserved as a theater chair. May they always occupy four-berthed, uncurtained carriages with infuriated strangers who have stolen their lower berths and owe them a grudge besides!

CHAPTER IX

MAHABODHI, THE PLACE OF GREAT INTELLIGENCE

NOT Jerusalem nor even Mecca is held in greater reverence by the millions of Christians and Mohammedans than is Buddha-Gaya by many more millions of Buddhists, who, inhabiting every part of Asia save India, look upon the temple at Mahabodhi as their greatest shrine, to the Sacred Bo-tree beside it as their most holy relic and living symbol, the most venerated, if not strictly the most venerable, tree on earth—Bodhi-druma, the Tree of Knowledge, beneath which Gautama became the Buddha, the Awakened, the Enlightened.

The so-called Buddhist Holy Land, the ancient Magadha, lies east of Benares and south of the Ganges River, within a radius of one hundred and fifty miles from Buddha-Gaya. The birthplace of the Nepalese prince Siddhartha, and the original burial-place of Gautama Buddha, so recently identified and excavated, are two hundred miles north of Buddha-Gaya, near the Nepal frontier. Every place associated with the life of the Great Teacher was marked by an inscribed column or a votive stupa by the emperor Asoka 250 B.C.; and from the abundant Pali, Sanskrit, and Chinese accounts, every place has been exactly determined, the recent finding of the very bones of the body of Buddha in the inscribed casket which his family had deposited beneath the great mound at Piprawah adding the last historic link in the chain, and leaving the life of Gautama Buddha an open book.

Very evidently no other place in India has such historical importance, and yet no place is so seldom visited by the legion of winter tourists, as this Buddha-Gaya of modern Behar, the Uruwela of ancient Magadha, the birthplace of one of the world's greatest religions. Until Lord Elgin's visit in 1895, no viceroy had sought this most ancient and historic spot in the empire. Outward India and the life of the people have changed so little that one easily pictures the scenes occurring twenty-five centuries ago in the same setting—when the Great Knight, Siddhartha, the Rajput, having made the Great Renunciation, left family and home and high estate on the full-moon night of July, and, with his five disciples, journeyed southward from his capital at Kapilavastu to Rajagriha, and finally along the river bank to the jungles of Uruwela, where, for six years, he practised the most rigorous penance, self-torture, and mortification. When he had reduced himself to living on one grain of rice a day, he fell as in death; and then, convinced of the uselessness of such a life of extreme bodily penance, he partook of food. His disciples forsook this starved ascetic for so basely yielding to the body, and the monk Gautama wandered to the river bank, where Sujata, a villager's daughter, gave him a bowl of milk and honey which he consumed in the shade of a bo-tree. Still sitting there, facing eastward, he attained full and perfect wisdom, the supreme knowledge, in four meditations. For seven times seven days and nights he continued his vigils, assailed by all temptations and evils, say the legends. For one space he paced to and fro beyond the Bo-tree—a path immortalized and literally made the Jeweled Cloister. For another space he regarded the tree day and night, without removing his eyes, the great Nagas, or cobra kings, protecting him with their outspread hoods from the chilling rain, and the snails covering his head with their cool, moist bodies from the scorching sun. He could then have entered into Nirvana, but upon further meditation he determined to share his treasure of wisdom with his fellow-men. Resuming his staff and begging-bowl, he walked on to Benares and there converted his lost disciples and ultimately the world, Gautama Buddha being first to preach universal equality and the brotherhood of man; enjoining pity, love, and charity for all; protesting against caste distinctions, against propitiation by sacrifices, penances, and offerings; and teaching that man must attain divine favor and perfect wisdom by his moral qualities and pure life alone, and thus reach the peace of Nirvana, the calm that follows upon self-victory, the extinction of anger, lust, and ignorance.

At the end of six months he sent his sixty disciples forth to preach the new wisdom, and himself returned to the foot of this Bo-tree at Uruwela, and, there converting the three fire-worshiping Brahman hermits who lived in that solitude, he gained Kasyapa, best-beloved disciple after his cousin Ananda. As a mendicant, begging from door to door, he revisited Kapilavastu and saw again his aged father and his widowed wife, Yasodhara, who adopted the religious life and became the first Buddhist nun. His son, Rahula, demanding his inheritance, was endowed with some of the wisdom acquired by the Buddha beneath the Bo-tree and admitted to the order, and Gautama's half-brother also assumed the mendicant's robe and bowl. For forty-four years after the great struggle beneath the Bo-tree, Buddha taught in the Deer Park at Benares, beneath this sacred Bo-tree at Uruwela, or in the Bamboo Grove at Rajagriha during the rainy season; and for the rest of the year wandered through Magadha, preaching the religion that has held sway over a great part of Asia for twenty-five centuries, and in corrupt form now holds more adherents than any other faith. Preaching the equality of men, he yet attracted disciples of high birth and station; and with no praises or reverence for women, voicing only the bitterest accusations and charges against the whole sex, women flocked to his teachings, and he established unwillingly, after much hesitation, the crowded orders of female mendicants.

After these forty-four years of active proselytism and conversion, he announced that he was about to die. He was then in his eightieth year; and while begging his way toward Kapilavastu, he ate of some rice and young pork given him in his begging-bowl, and died that night beneath a bo-tree in a grove near Kusinagara—543 B.C., if we accept the older Pali or Cingalese records of the southern Buddhists, 400 B.C., or 478 B.C., according to the Sanskrit records. Then all nature mourned, and the Bo-tree, for the only time, shed its leaves. His remains were cremated on the spot where he died, and a great stupa raised by the Sakya clan over the one-eighth portion of the ashes and relics allotted them. The rest of the relics were distributed to seven centers of his doctrinal teachings, where similar monuments were raised. Excavations at Buddha-Gaya, Bhattiprolu, and Piprawah have yielded relic-caskets containing these undoubted fragments of the body of Buddha, accompanied in every instance by stores of pearls and precious stones, gold-leaf ornaments in the form of swastikas, seals, and inscribed tablets. The soapstone, crystal, and beryl vases and cylinders containing these relics are admirable pieces of workmanship, but the only inscriptions dating from Gautama's lifetime now visible are those from the Piprawah mound, housed in the India Museum at Calcutta.

The doctrines were preserved in oral versions, which were correctly chanted for months at a time by the priests participating in the First and Second Councils, held one hundred and two hundred years after his death. At the Third Council, called by the emperor Asoka in 244 B.C., a first record of the Orthodox Canon was written on palm leaves in Pali, the language of Magadha. A fourth council of Buddhists was held by the Scythian king Ka-

VASES FROM THE SAKYA STUPA AT PIPRAWAH.

THE SARCOPHAGUS IN THE CAVE.

nishka in 1, or 40 A.D., and elaborate commentaries were written in Sanskrit and, it is said, engraved on copper plates and buried beneath a great stupa—a prize for archæologists to search for, and for sensation-seekers to manufacture fraudulently. The separation between the Northern or Sanskrit school and the Pali or Southern school of Buddhists was definite then, and in 634 A.D. Hiouen Thsang, the Chinese priest, attended the great Sanskrit Council of Siladitya, when the Cingalese versions, the "Little Vehicle" of the Pali teachers, were formally condemned by the adherents of the Sanskrit "Great Vehicle." Hiouen Thsang acquired both languages, and studied both vehicles in monasteries in Kashmir and Magadha, translated innumerable works into Chinese, and by his description of the surroundings, the monuments, the images, treasures, and relics of the sacred places, made the work of archæologists and historians comparatively easy—his descriptions as precise as those of a modern Baedeker, his services comparable to those of Pausanias in classic Greece. A modern council of Buddhists was held in Ceylon in 1875, looking to the translation, revision, and publication of the Cingalese and Pali texts, and a Pali Text Society has forwarded the effort to present these oldest Buddhist books to modern readers, Dr. Rhys Davids having done most to introduce Buddhist literature to English-speaking people. Dr. Max Müller and many Continental scholars have given translations of the Sacred Sanskrit books.

It was a raw January morning, with the yellow

dust whirling in clouds, when I reached Gaya station on my pilgrimage to the Tree of Knowledge, and it was a cold, dull, prosaic drive of a mile in a rattling gharry to Gaya town and the dak bangla, where the government provides chill cheer for the few European travelers who ever rest there. One

THE EKKA.

elephant passed by on the station road,—a touch of the ancient East, the Hindu India, that did not accord with the background of barbed-wire fences, telegraph poles, and railway tracks, nor with the well-metaled highway of British India that the creature trod upon. A string of dusty brown camels filed across the neutral, dusty distance, and turbaned folk sped by in bullock-carts or gay *ekkas,* the native cabs, mere curtained canopies hung with balls and bells, and the ponies caparisoned to match, with high, peaked collars and blue bead necklaces.

Modern Gaya, the Sahibs' market, is an orderly new town with broad thoroughfares and busy bazaars, the whitewashed houses, the tidy streets and drains betraying the infallible signs of model British rule, prosperity, and eternal sanitation. It is distinct from the more ancient Brahm-Gaya, where huddled houses cut by narrow streets crowd around the great Brahman temple of the Vishnupad by the river bank, to which more than one hundred thousand Hindu pilgrims come to bathe and pray each year—a temple crowded with Buddhist sculptures and wreck from older temples.

The dak bangla at Gaya stands in a great shady compound, which looks upon a busy part of a main street, a continuous panorama of half-clad and sheeted figures, of absurd ekkas and bullock-carts going by beyond the bangla lawn, as if drawn across a stage for one's delight. There is a well at one side of the compound, to which we watched all the neighbor folk come to fill their brass lotas or heavy, red earthen jars—half-veiled women, who needed help to lift the great weights and poise them on their heads, their slender, feeble figures bending under the weight. Others, balancing these great amphoræ with ease, passed out with the graceful, noble tread of goddesses, the living figures of a Greek frieze. On the bangla's covered portico we were sheltered from the wind and dust, the sun shone warmly, and little parrakeets twittered and shrieked, flying about the lawn. We were so well entertained with this spectacle and play of Hindu life, that we sat for an hour—balanced ourselves, rather, for that space

—on decrepit chairs which, rocking on uncertain legs, threatened momently to fall beneath us, if the torn and sagging rush seats did not sooner engulf us. "If the dak bangla's chairs were then as they are now, no wonder Buddha sat for six years under the Bo-tree," wrote the one American visitor of six seasons in the visitors' book. In time we ate an early and hurried tiffin—our daily goat-chop, garnished with green peas that rattled upon the plate like so much bird-shot, and the usual cold and sodden Indian rice poured over with a blackish curry mixture diversified by pools of clear grease—the worst-made curry in the world, always served one at Indian hotels, dak banglas, and railway refreshment-rooms. "Chutney? Chutney? No!" came the regular Indian response of surprise when we asked for some palliative, some condiment to make the dish of the country go down protesting throats; but the khansamah boasted that he would be able to produce "a vary splendid dinner, with cauliflower, mem," in the evening.

The road southward for seven miles to Buddha-Gaya was broad, smooth, and well made, shaded with tamarisk- and bo-trees, strung along with little hamlets and mud huts, and following the banks of the Phalgu River. Each group of dwellings had its common well, and, under some wide-spreading tree, a plastered-up terrace or altar supported a tiny shrine, or the greasy image of a Hindu god,—this the same pagan, heathen India, the life little changed since the all-perfect Gautama Buddha used to pass this way in his yellow robes, with his golden

THE GREAT TEMPLE AT BUDDHA-GAYA AND THE SACRED BO-TREE.

begging-bowl and a glory of six cubits height extending around his head. Brown fields stretched on either hand; brown hills bounded the view; and narrow streams loitered here and there among the stones of the broad, sandy river-bed. A few barefooted people moved by in silence, and the brown monotony, the comforting warmth of the hot midday sun, and the quivering heat-rays in the air, soon gave an eerie, unreal look to things, a strange, hazy, hypnotic effect, a sense of dreamy spell.

We turned from the Gaya road to a massive white gateway, where sheeted Brahmans and turbaned folk lay in leisured wait for us, and noble white bullocks rested beside tilted carts that had brought priestly visitors to this Sannyasi or Shivaite college of Buddha-Gaya. A much-marked Brahman, with the sacred white thread across his shoulder, led us off by a sandy path toward the pinnacle of a temple roof just showing beyond some tree-tops, when suddenly all Mahabodhi, the Place of Great Intelligence, was revealed to us. The sunken courtyard of the Sacred Bo-tree lay at our feet, and a great nine-storied, pyramidal temple soared one hundred and sixty feet in air, seemingly perfect in every line, from foundation-stone to the gilded pineapple pinnacle,—precisely the temple built in the second or in the sixth century, as may some time be agreed upon, but certainly the great temple that Hiouen Thsang saw. There was, at the first glance, nothing ruinous or hoary or venerable about the apparently well-preserved monument. The good repair was too disenchantingly obtrusive and conspicuous, and for sentiment's sake one would almost rather have seen the temple crumbling and vine-grown in a rubbish-choked court, as it was in 1860. There was a chilling neatness and a forbidding order, too, about the crowded monuments, remains of monuments, and foundations of monuments in that flagged area thirty feet below us, which told of the archæologist with his tape-measure, his numbers and labels, the restorer with his healing plaster and illusive cement. The view came so suddenly, there was such silence, with no moving object anywhere in sight, that it was as unreal as if a vast drop-curtain had blocked the path. The silence, too, was befitting the sacred place, the actual scene of the great penance and struggle, the illumining of the Light of Asia, the birthplace of India's noblest religious system, a place hallowed by the traditions and associations of twenty-five centuries of religious life. No other visitors, not a pilgrim nor a worshiper, came to that court for hours. Our melancholy Moslem servant, the big, sheeted Brahman, who knew as little as the Moslem of this treasure-spot, and the languid, lesser Brahman, more brainless still, were the only moving creatures in all that sunny space. The shrieks of little parakeets, as they flew with flashes of emerald light in and out of the niches of the temple and the branches of the Sacred Bo-tree, were the only sounds in the mellow, slumbering air, that same perfect midday atmosphere that belongs to the ideal days of the East Indian winter, as to the sun-ripe days of the American Indian summer. All the world drowsed in that golden calm—it was the ideal Mahabodhi.

In Hiouen Thsang's time buildings and monuments were crowded together, almost touching for a mile and a half, all round the Sacred Tree. There remain only what one sees in the single glance at the sunken area; save as archæologists, digging here and there, have found the remnants of palace and temple and monastery walls, of cloisters and tanks and towers. Where we stood had been the great entrance of the monastery, where three thousand priests once lived, and treasures incalculable accumulated around an inner arcanum, whose solid gold statue was covered from foot to crown with jewel offerings. Instead of the great tower-capped walls stretching a thousand feet either way, and the throngs of yellow-robed priests, there is a very modern little galvanized iron pavilion sheltering a collection of broken images, sculptured and inscribed stones, salved from the pits and rubbish-heaps around, wreckage gathered after centuries of abandonment and final Mohammedan vandalism. The most valuable and interesting stones have been sent to the Calcutta Museum, and some few to London. The guides, of course, knew next to nothing about these relics. "General Cunningham put them there"—"General Cunningham vary high essteemed them," etc. The Brahman knew nothing of the history of the temple, the tree, or the place, and was perhaps the most aggravatingly disappointing of all his vampire tribe that fasten upon one in the show-places of India. Our gloomy and monosyllabic Mohammedan—may all travelers in India beware of that professional traveling servant, Foglou Rahman!—knew far, far less. I had to cross-question, call for and demand to be shown this and that; to poke and pry, push and insist and rack my memory for the very little it held of Fahien's or Hiouen Thsang's travels. "He duss-sunt know-ah. People never ask—just memsahib want to know," sighed the melancholy Moslem.

"Where are the caves in the hills where the Buddha lived? Up there?" I asked, pointing. "Is there a cave there with carvings all over the walls?"

The Brahman could not have looked blanker if I had asked for the Eiffel Tower. It took long consultation and visible guesswork by both Brahman and Foglou Rahman for them to answer: "Maybe there are some holes in the hills over there—but—he duss-sunt know, memsahib." One might hope for better things in the next incarnation of the twice-born Brahman blockhead, the long-descended Aryan decadent and degenerate—but for the Moslem there ought to be all that the wrath of the Prophet has promised to the unworthy. The exasperation of being there, of having eyes, yet almost seeing not, went far toward quelling any deep emotions and dissipating the spell of the place, the somnolent calm, the soothing peace, the atmosphere almost as of Nirvana which brooded there, as we sat on the ancient stones and looked down upon the Place of Great Intelligence, the Veranda of and the veritable Tree of Knowledge.

CHAPTER X

THE SACRED BO-TREE

THE broad stone staircase which leads down to the court from the north commands the view of the temple and tree which uncounted thousands have drunk in with ecstasy, a place which has resounded for centuries with prayers and chants; for Gautama Buddha said in his lifetime: "If any one look with a pleasant mind at a dagoba, or at the Court of the Bo-tree, he will undoubtedly be born in a dewa loka,"[1] a pilgrimage to Buddha-Gaya being therefore a certain advance toward Nirvana. Aside from the historic and religious associations of this particular bo- or pipul-tree, the *Ficus religiosa* has a character and interest quite its own, the effect of its symmetrical growth and well-balanced foliage masses, heightened by the continual agitation of its brilliant, dark-green leaves. Even on that still afternoon each individual, heart-shaped leaf, with its long-drawn, tapering tendril tip, was trembling and spinning on its slender foot-stalk, until the whole tree mass was in agitation—every one of the myriad

[1] *Dewa loka* is one of the six celestial worlds between earth and heaven.

glossy, green leaves flashing with a separate light as these thousands of perpetually moving mirrors caught the sun. The restlessness and activity of these bo-leaves, vibrating and striking together with a tinkling noise like the patter of soft raindrops on still nights, make the pipul the most grateful shade-tree, and the reflections of its glossy leaves suggest always the first stir of a rising breeze. This flashing, sparkling, flickering play of light all over the tree gives the pipul its unique and individual character—something like the dazzling, glittering trees that one sees in pictures by imperfect vitascope. The pipul trembles to this day in reverence for the one who became Buddha beneath its branches, and as symbol of the continual change and motion, the impermanency of the world. The pipul whispers to Rishaba, the Hindus say, every word it hears, for which reason it is never planted in the bazaar where trade must employ the lie. Brahmans claim that Brahma planted the pipul-tree, and that Vishnu, who in his ninth avatar became Buddha, was born beneath a pipul-tree. The Hindu pilgrims, who come in such thousands every year to offer unleavened cakes and repeat mantras to this tree at Buddha-Gaya, before worshiping the print of Vishnu's footsteps at Brahm-Gaya, believe that a service beneath its branches will relieve their ancestors for one hundred generations back.

The Bo-tree was always worshiped, swept around, sprinkled with milk and perfumes, and hung with offerings in the Buddha's lifetime, and he taught, from his seat beneath it, that he was but one of a series of Buddhas who appear on earth as faith wanes and the world needs purification; that his religious system would continue for five thousand years and then suffer extinction, when all relics, having lost honor and worshipers, would return to the foot of this same Bo-tree, and there, assuming the form of the Buddha's body, be consumed in their own refulgence, as in a flame. Then a new Buddha shall come, Maitreya Buddha, the Buddha of Kindness, who shall redeem the world by love and again show the way to Nirvana.

To devout Buddhists the Sacred Bo-tree is the most sacred symbol and object in all the world, the living representative of Buddha himself, who distinctly enjoined its worship. When the pilgrims, bringing flowers and perfumes and offerings to Sewet, failed to find him, Ananda suggested that some object be designated for them to worship in his absence, and Buddha said: "The objects that are proper to receive worship are of three kinds. . . . In the last division is the tree at the foot of which I became Buddha. Therefore send to obtain a branch of that tree and set it in the court of this vihara. He who worships it will receive the same reward as if he worshiped me in person." When requested to honor this tree by sitting at the foot of it, Buddha said that when he sat under the tree at Gaya he became Buddha, and that "it was not meet he should sit in the same manner near any other tree."

Buddhists regard the Bo-tree as too sacred to be touched or robbed of a leaf, and devout Burmese pilgrims kneel, fix their eyes upon it, and in a trance of prayer wait until a miraculous leaf detaches itself and flutters down. It seemed sacrilege when the Brahman snapped off a leaf and offered it to me with the universal Indian gesture of the begging palm, and, at a request for more, snatched off a whole handful of trembling green hearts, as ruthlessly and brainlessly as the troop of monkeys in the bo-tree at Anuradhpura had done a few weeks before.

Despite the reverently worded mantra with which his own people address the tree, this Brahman butcher, responsive to a single rupee, continued to snatch off and break away twig after twig until I had a great green bouquet of nearly one hundred living, quivering leaves of Buddhist prayer. With no seeming appreciation of the sacrilege, he said: " Some people are satisfied with just one leaf. They bow to it, pray to it, and carry it away in a gold box." Then he set himself down on the Vajrasana, the Diamond Throne, the Bodhi Manda, or Veranda of Knowledge, to yawn and scratch his lean arms as he adjusted his drapery.

Three centuries after the death of the Buddha the emperor Asoka, grandson of that Asoka who drove the Greeks from India and who ruled from Kabul to the sea, began a relentless persecution of Buddhists. He ordered the Sacred Bo-tree cut down and burned; but when two trees sprang uninjured from the flames and a priest emerged unharmed, the "raging Asoka" was humbled, converted. He built a wall around the tree, and marked the Great Teacher's seat by a carved stone altar or table—the Vajrasana, or Diamond Throne, the reputed center of the universe, the jewel that came up from the center of the earth to mark where Buddha sat when he attained perfect wisdom—Bodhi Manda, the Veranda of Knowledge. Asoka erected a small brick temple, made pilgrimages to every spot connected with the life of Buddha, and marked them by stupas, or inscribed columns. He summoned the Great Council, when the doctrines were first put in writing in the square Pali characters of his day; he sent missionaries to all parts of the world, even despatching his own son as evangelist to Ceylon, and making his daughter bearer of the cutting of the Sacred Bo-tree sent to Anuradhpura.

Asoka's wife became jealous of the sacred tree, and tried vainly to destroy it; persecuting rajas cut it down and filled the roots with fire; but it sprang always to the same stature again. The Chinese pilgrims saw and described it; the first English travelers found it green and vigorous, and it was perpetuated, of course, like its congener at Anuradhpura, by the dropping of a seed in the fork or hollow of the dying trunk. The archæologists found in 1861 that the tree was growing forty-five feet above the original level of the court, traces of sixteen successive cement platforms showing where that many trees had mounted upon the roots of preceding trees. That venerable pipul, with many dead branches and stumps, was blown over in 1876, and the stripling Bo-tree flourishing in its mold was carefully replanted at the level of the earliest tree, and the

Diamond Throne, a slab of polished sandstone, replaced in its afternoon shade. There were unusual numbers of pilgrims for a few years, and the pious Burmese covered the stem and branches with so much gold leaf, poured so much milk, perfumery, cologne, oil, incense, tins of sardines, European food and confections around its roots, that it began to droop and die. General Cunningham put in a new tree in 1885, and surrounded it by a brick wall inlaid with old carved stones around the window openings on each side. A marble table or altar was erected by a pious Cingalese to receive the Burmese and Hindu offerings, and that sturdy tree glitters and grows magnificently.

There was no building of any kind at Mahabodhi in the Buddha's lifetime, nor can any stone or inscription be traced to his day. The First Council met in the great sculptured cave on the hillside, and it was not until the Third Council, 244 B.C., that Asoka erected a temple. Buddhism, having found its Constantine in the "sorrowless Asoka," remained the state religion throughout the great empire.

The temple became a treasury of relics and riches. The window-frames and door-frames of gold and silver were set with gems, the Diamond Throne was heaped with all the jewels of the East, and, like the Jeweled Cloister, was literally what its name indicates. Archæologists are not all agreed whether the present temple was built by the Scythian conquerors in the second century, or by a Brahman in the sixth century. Between the second and fourth centuries the priests had left Mahabodhi, and Buddhism was at such an ebb that Brahmans seized the temple, cast out the golden image, and installed their emblems in its place. "All was desolate and abandoned" when Fahien arrived from China, 400 A.D.; but, later, Hiouen Thsang saw and minutely described the great temple which stands to-day where stood "the chief of the eighty-four thousand shrines erected by Dharma Asoka, ruler of the earth at the close of the two hundred and eighteenth year of Buddha's Nirvana, upon the holy spot where our Lord tasted the milk and honey," as the inscribed stone declares.

In all the romance of religion, nothing equals the vicissitudes and alternating fortunes of this sacred place; for, soon after Hiouen Thsang's visit, Buddhism degenerated, the Brahmans again took over the sanctuary, and the monastery became a fort. In the sixteenth century of Buddhism, about 1000 A.D., there was a revival and a reformation of the faith; the temple was restored, and priests gathered in numbers. Again it fell away, and at the time of the Mohammedan conquest the Buddhists were persecuted like other infidels, and the ruins of their temples and monasteries tell how hundreds of priests met death by fire and sword in such asylums. In the fourteenth century the King of Burma sent an embassy to restore the temple, when a few Buddhist priests were found in the lonely place.

Floods came and left their sand deposits in the court, brick and plaster crumbled, the jungle crept upon the open space, trees flourished in every piece of masonry, and Mahabodhi was without a history until a Shivaite mendicant wandered there in the first years of the eighteenth century, as the mendicant Gautama had come in his yellow robe so long before. He lived a hermit among the ruins, attracting other wanderers until he had a sufficient following to build a monastery by the river bank. Little heed was paid these pious squatters, but as their numbers increased the chief mahant obtained a firman from the emperor Shah Alum, confirming them in their ownership of the ground they had built upon. The sacred courtyard was the quarry for these builders, and they chose the most accessible stones—frequently those that were carved and inscribed.

The King of Burma sent missions to rebuild and restore the temple in 1805 and in 1831, and one of the Shivaite priests, who later guided Buchanan Hamilton around the ruins, claimed to have been converted by the Burmese visitors, and from their books to have been taught the history of each monument within the sacred court. The Archæological Survey made examinations and excavations at Buddha-Gaya in 1861 and 1863, found the true level of the old court, and brought to light the Diamond Throne and the greater part of Asoka's rail.

In 1877 another mission from the King of Burma obtained the consent of the Bengal government and of the mahant at Buddha-Gaya to restore the temple. Word reached Calcutta of the zeal with which these Burmese were razing and obliterating old structures and monuments, and Dr. Mitra was sent to investigate; but the wreck and transformation of the temple court had gone too far for any interference to avail. The Burmese had demolished gateways, pavilions, and monuments, leveled ruin-heaps, swept away terraces and votive stupas, used carved stones for foundations or minor constructions; or, casting them recklessly on different rubbish-heaps, made it impossible to identify what Hiouen Thsang had so carefully described.

In 1879 General Cunningham, chief of the Archæological Survey, cleared out the entire temple court of the sand and rubbish of ages, completely restored the temple within and without, and rebuilt the portico over the east entrance door and the four corner pavilions. A miniature stone temple found in excavating, and repeated in bas-reliefs and Buddhist sculptures everywhere from Amraoti to Gandhara, and at many places in Burma, gave the model for the restorations. Every measurement now corresponds precisely to the Chinese priest's account, and the temple lacks only the hundreds of gilded images in the tiers of niches that mount to the gilded amalika at the summit. The temple stands exactly over the site of Asoka's temple, and the original floor and altar are uncovered. A ball of clay in an altar niche contained a rich treasure—bits of gold leaf and beaten gold in the form of flowers and stars, pearls, rough sapphires and rubies, bits of beryl, jade, agate, and crystal. Even the plaster of this altar was composed of pounded coral, pearl, ivory, and precious stones mixed with lime. A similar treasure was found in a vase beneath the image niched in the outer temple wall; and all these relics are now to be seen in the India Museum at Calcutta, together with tablets bearing Chinese inscriptions and scores of terra-cotta lamps, seals, and votive tablets molded within the outlines of a bo-leaf.

Of the Jeweled Cloister—that long pavilion covering the path where Buddha paced to and fro and flowers sprang up as he trod, whose carved columns were hung with garlands of flowers and strings of jewels and half incased in silver and gold—only fragments remain to mark the position and extent. Asoka's carved sandstone rail, "the oldest sculptured monument in India," has been carefully replaced, as far as possible, and in long stretches shows us that curious carpenter's arrangement of mortised posts and rails and carved rosette ornaments over each joint and cross-piece. The great pillars and cross-beams of the toran gateway, precursor of the Chinese pailow and the Japanese torii, have been raised before the entrance, but too much of it is missing to tell whether it was as splendid and monumental as the toran of Sanchi which Asoka later began erecting. Twenty posts and many rosettes of the carved rail had been built into the walls and courts of the mahants' college, and no amount of persuasion could induce the heathens to restore them to the temple court.

All about the Bo-tree, the Diamond Throne, the Cloister, and the temple doorway, the stones were daubed with gold-leaf and ocher. The Brahman guide was just able to tell that these yellow smears were the offerings of pious Burmese, but to any

ASOKA'S RAIL, BUDDHA-GAYA.

further questions concerning the Burmese and their intermittent gilding the Brahman returned a dumb stare. He led us up into the temple, through an archway in a wall twenty feet thick, to a square whitewashed cell, and up to a second chilly, white vault where the light fell through a triangular east window full upon the image on the carved basalt altar. It was a tawdry, gilded image, more asleep than serenely meditating, with a Hindu caste-mark on its brow—"Buddha's mother!" said the Brahman. For further shock and disillusionment, it was only necessary to note that the image was attired in a red merino petticoat and a tinsel-bordered cape —"to keep the image warm," said the Brahman, winding his grimy sheet more closely around him in that chill sanctuary. There was a litter of food and flower, incense and candle offerings on the altar in true Burmese fashion, scores of Tibetan flags and streamers in the corners of the room, while old Buddhist bas-reliefs built into the wall were buttered and garlanded in the Hindu manner—a medley of religions in the one shrine. It was hard to believe that this untidy vault, this religious lumber-room, was the supreme shrine, the ark, the tabernacle, the holy of holies. It was harder to realize that the stone image, the shabby old "Buddha's mother," all daubed with gold-leaf, successor to innumerable images of gold, perfumed paste, basalt, sandstone, and stucco—this clumsy image, with its stolid, vacant face, was intended for the same beautiful, passionless Teacher who meditates, steeped in the peace of eternal Nirvana, in the gilded temples of Japan or beneath Kamakura's pine-trees.

The Brahman had little interest in the big Burmese bells by the temple door, in the venerable statues, or in the sacred sites. Whether this place was the cloistered flower-tank or the lotus-pond, or only where Buddha washed his robe or his bowl, he cared not; but he showed us insistently the cylindrical monument to the first mahant of the Shivaite monastery, who there performed the great penance, or rather feat, of "the five fires." To attain great spiritual reward, this sacred salamander sat between four fires, with the midsummer sun overhead, and survived to enjoy the expected sanctity. Another monument marked where one of the fraternity had been devoured by a tiger while at prayer, and the Brahman could not understand our affected depression when he had assured us and reassured us that the tigers did not come to the courtyard now—"not eat the priests any more, surely, truly, memsahib. Be not uneasy."

The Brahman boasted of the number of pilgrims who came to Buddha-Gaya—"from everywhere!—from Colombo, Rangoon, Tibet-ty, China, Japan!—oh, from everywhere! Now is there a Japanese over there at the palace," pointing toward the monastery by the river bank. He led us to the mahants' college, and through a labyrinth of stone courts, where scores of Shivaite priests lounged and loafed over their bowls and messes of food, and across a garden full of little Burmese pagodas, to the rest-house built for resting Burmese by King Mindon Min. The Brahman routed out a languid creature in loose garments with yards of a pale pink sarong wobbling between his knees, a short white jacket fastened closely at the neck, and a topknot of hair under a cap. A queer-looking Japanese, surely.

"Where are you from?" we asked.

"Rangoon!" drawled the ghostly Maung Somebody, and when we protested to the Brahman that he had deceived us with a mere every-day, near-by Burmese, he said: "Oh! Burmese, Japanese, just the same. Their country is a long way off, but they all come to Buddha-Gaya."

The shadows were lengthening and palms and pipuls were rustling in the afternoon wind, but even after hours spent in Mahabodhi there was something wanting, something inharmonious in one's general impression. The temple was too well preserved, and proclaimed too loudly the plumb-line and the trowel's work. Sentiment and day-dreams could not play upon those precise angles and sharp edges. And the Tree of Knowledge! as trim, compact and shapely as a California orange-tree, with squawking parrots flashing in and out of its flickering foliage, as if it were but a common tree for birds to perch upon! There was too much of shock and disillusionment at Mahabodhi; too much of the garish every day; a lack of romance and mystery, and of any real sense of antiquity and of chance for imagination.

We drove back with our treasure of sacred leaves, and saw the busy bazaars of Gaya before a salmon and saffron sunset of blinding glory held us at the dak bangla's gate, while the blind beggar wailed by the roadside, the women went to and fro with their water-jars, the parrakeets flew shrieking among the tamarind-trees before they settled for the night, and our lank Moslem knelt and bent to the ground in repeated prayers to the Mecca beyond the sunset.

When we went to the midnight train that was to take us away, a raja and his suite were just arriving from Bankipur. There was hurry and excitement, a rushing to and fro of richly dressed attendants, and much glitter and splendor and flash of color, as the torch-bearers led the raja in his jeweled turban to the low dhoolie suspended from a curved silver yoke, and, lifting it, bore him out into the night. The voices of his followers died away as the flicker of the torches was finally lost down the road, but the last impression of Gaya was of that raja sitting cross-legged, like a god, in his silver and velvet car, departing by torch-light to some palace, whence he would issue before sunrise to bathe in the Phalgu, to worship the Bo-tree and the Vishnupad—all living traces of the great religion obliterated, like Gautama's own footprints in that dusty road; the Light of Asia forever extinguished on the spot where it first rose upon the world; the great temple and the Sacred Bo-tree drowsing, neglected, in the sunshine of an empty, lifeless court; the temple of a sleeping Buddha, of a dead religion, everything turned to stone, when there have passed but half of those five thousand years that the Master declared his religion would endure, an annihilation greater and more complete than Nirvana already come to the faith in its birthplace.

CHAPTER XI

THE GREATEST SIGHT IN THE WORLD

AT Mogul Sarai junction, three Englishmen stood over as many hillocks of leather- and tin-covered luggage, directing its removal to the Benares train. The servants bore it off and flung it through doors and windows, covering the floor, heaping the seats, filling all the racks and hooks, until the owners themselves, looking in, said: "Oh, I say, now. There is no room left for us. We had best sit in this next carriage, where we can watch them." When I spoke of this dilemma of the men and their luggage to others of their nationality, they said bewilderedly: "For the life of me, I do not see why you Americans should laugh at that. I thought you always traveled with so much luggage. Those enormous trunks—Saratogas, you call them." It argued nothing to them, no matter how much we explained it, that we sent the Saratogas to the baggage-car and never sat with malodorous sole-leather heaped around us in our richly finished and furnished cars.

We crossed a muddy river by a high bridge with fortress turrets at either end—the very bridge of "Voices in the Night"—and were then in the usual glaring, sun-baked European suburb, where broad roads and waste spaces, new houses in large grounds, and dusty lines of banian-trees certainly did not go to make up the Benares of one's dreams. The hotel was more like the hotels of Java, the dining-room in a central building by itself, and long rows of bedrooms in adjacent buildings. Peddlers, guides, jugglers, and snake-charmers haunted the long, flagged porches all the afternoon. Cobras were drawn out from small, round baskets like so many yards of sausage, and made to dance on their tails to plaintive pipings, and then crowded back into their baskets with as little ceremony; and a weary little mongoose was shaken and cuffed and made to battle with the hooded horror.

Chaturgam Lal, in a flowered and cotton-wadded chintz overcoat, a worsted comforter around his neck, large spectacles under a fat turban, the caste-mark freshly painted on his brow, and an unctuous smile set for the day, rapped on our door long before dawn. We looked out to see a long line of sleeping bearers on the brick-floored portico, each before his master's door, every turban-topped bundle rolled in a stripped dhurrie with a pair of bare brown legs protruding. The air was keen and frosty, and I wondered if any estate on earth, any future reincarnation, could be more replete with bodily misery and discomfort than the regular life of an Indian bearer or traveling servant—sleeping on cold stone porches, snatching bits of food at irregular hours, traveling all day and all night, and as often standing for hours in the crowded compartments.

THE WOMEN'S GHAT, BENARES.

The greatest human spectacle in India, the chief incident and motive of Benares life, and the most extraordinary manifestation of religious zeal and superstition in all the world, begins at sunrise by the Ganges bank and lasts for several hours. We started in the first gray light of the dawn, drove two miles across the city, and, descending the ghats, or broad staircases, to the water's edge, were rowed slowly up and down the three-mile crescent of river-front, watching Brahmans and humbler believers bathe and pray to the rising sun, repeating the oldest Vedic hymns. That picturesque sweep of the city front —a high cliff with palaces, temples, and gardens clinging to its terraced embankments and long flights of steps descending to the water—is spectacle enough when lighted by the first yellow flash of sunlight, without the thousands of white-clad worshipers at the Ganges brink and far out in its turbid flood. After three sunrise visits to the river bank, the spectacle was as amazing and incomprehensible as at first, as incredible, as dreamlike, as the afternoon memory of it. I saw it with equal surprise each time, the key-note, the soul of India revealed in Benares as nowhere else,—since all India flocks to Benares in sickness and health, in trouble and rejoicing, to pray and to commit crimes, the sacred city being the meeting-place and hiding-place of all criminals, the hatching-place of all conspiracies.

We sped through empty cantonment streets, but in the native city every thoroughfare was crowded. All were streaming one way, and a hum of voices filled the air as we reached the ghats and came upon sight of the multitude standing waist-deep in the sacred stream or crouching on platforms built out over the water. From twenty-five to fifty thousand people regularly—on special occasions one hundred thousand bathers and worshipers, Brahmans and believers of every caste—perform their daily rites in the Ganges. They are so rapt, ecstatic, bent on and absorbed in the mechanical formula, the endless minutiæ of their worship, that they are unconscious of the few curious strangers who may drift up and down the river-front in the brief tourist season. A Brahman cannot let eye or mind wander for one moment lest, omitting something, or changing the order of invocation, prayers, and movements, he should have to begin the long ritual afresh. The daily religious observances should occupy nearly twelve hours, so that a repetition is something of a penance.

The lowlands across the river were veiled in haze as, seated in our comfortable arm-chairs on the boat's deck, we floated off into the stream. Just as the sun's disk rose above the hazy, blue plain, a louder murmur arose, a general chant, the measured responses of a great congregation. Each one standing in the stream lifted up an offering of water, tossed a handful three times in the air, dipped the body beneath the surface, repeating the while the sacred mantras, the ancient Vedic hymns, the names of the gods, and the sacred syllable "Om." They sipped handfuls of the holy water, rinsed their mouths, lifted the water and let it stream through their fingers or pour back down the arm, facing always to the east, and moving their lips in prayer. They filled their water-jars and poured it over their heads, and they drank it "to purify themselves," our mentor said, although one group of purity-seekers stood two feet from the mouth of a rapidly discharging sewer, every sort of city filth floating to their hands and water-jars, the bodies of men and animals and decaying flowers floating by. They drank the pestilent fluid, they carried it home for household use, and bottles were being filled to be sent and carried to the remotest parts of India. Western education and sanitary science avail nothing against the Ganges superstition. The British have provided a pure water supply for Benares, but the people prefer the sacred dilution of sewerage and cremation-ground refuse, thus inviting and encouraging every disease.

Whole platforms of Brahmans went through their morning ceremonies before us as if on a theater stage. Some sat with fixed or upraised eyes, some with eyes closed—all absorbed, as if in hypnotic trance, slowly whispering and muttering their prayers, lost in contemplation of their fingers, symbols of different gods, dipping each one in the river many times and praying to it fervently as the water trickled off. They dipped wisps of grass in the river and contemplated them prayerfully, meditating on the one hundred and eight manifestations of Shiva, the ten hundred and eight manifestations of Vishnu. They emptied their jars by rule; they prayed, touching their arms, breasts, knees in slow callisthenics as they vowed themselves to one and an-

9

other of the pantheon; they produced boxes of ashes of sacred cow-dung and painted their foreheads and smeared their arms and breasts for the day. Others, standing in the stream, drew in deep breaths, closed first one nostril, then the other, and then held both nostrils with the fingers for uncounted seconds. "They hold the nose so. It is a prayer. It is a ceremony," said Chaturgam Lal, beaming with proud omniscience. "Sometimes they pray with the right nose, sometimes with the left nose."

There were some serious and thorough ablutions going on also, vigorous scrubbings and tubbings that were good imitations of the Anglo-Indian form of godlincss. Men waded out to their shoulders, removed their garments, and washed them in the holy water, assuming dry garments as they dropped the wet ones at the steps. Others energetically shampooed their heads with river mud, for soap is impure to their notion. Women came down to the river's edge, scoured their brass jars, rinsed, filled them, and walked away in never-ending processions upon the broad steps. Even babus in gold spectacles and worsted comforters carried off jars of water to pour over some chosen image. The high-caste women had bathed and gone before sunrise, the wives of rajas and potentates rowed off in curtained boats to bathe and pray far from the common horde. The women specially congregate at one ghat, barely uncovering their faces to the rising sun, and gracefully and ingeniously draping the fresh sari over the wet one as they reach the steps again. "These are nearly all widows," said our guide, condescendingly; and certainly no people in the world have more need to implore divine aid than these Indian widows, accursed things who, as they themselves and all others believe, have brought the calamity of death upon their husbands.

And then there were the fakirs; the real things of one's Sunday-school books, ragged, unkempt, ash-smeared objects that seemed hardly human, sitting rigid in their insane, consequential sanctity. Some were so utterly absurd and ridiculous with their fantastic ash powderings, that the young American boy on our boat vented peal after peal of laughter that continued to tears as one ash-heap, crouched like Humpty Dumpty on a sunny wall, mouthed and gibbered back at him spitefully. There were lean old fakirs, mere wrinkles of skin laid loosely over some bones, and strapping young fakirs, whom the police should move on or put to road-making. One able-bodied specimen of lazy holiness sat with clenched hand and uplifted arm, wearing the most consciously self-righteous air; another posed like a dirty salt image on a broken stone pedestal at a corner of the ghat; and a row of toothless old relics sat in their dirt and ashes waiting for certain Brahman princes to come along, as in a stage tableau, and distribute daily alms of rice—"to acquire merit." Each whining, mumbling old fakir held out his hands, his begging-bowl, or a dirty end of rag drapery, the almoner doled out a few spoonfuls of cheap rice, and the rich man moved on to a chorus of blessings, conspicuously well pleased with himself and the increased assets of acquired merit—precisely the

Pharisee of Judea. There are more than two million fakirs in India, all leading lives of leisure and comparative plenty; but the prize fakir of them all on the Ganges bank was surely the well-fed and plumped out one who had all his bones painted in white outline on his brown skin, and sat comfortably in the sun, waiting for his breakfast to come to him—a living skeleton of the impressionist school. There was finally a dead fakir, propped up against a wall, covered with flower garlands, and soon to be richly spiced and committed to the Ganges, since fire is not needed to purify such holy men.

At sunrise the ghouls of the cremation-ground or burning-ghat began heaping funeral piles for the day's work, and others of this lowest caste were carrying yesterday's ashes to the water's edge, washing them in sieves and pans like any placer-miner to recover the gold, silver, and jewels burned with the bodies. The domri, who conduct cremations, surpass the Occidental undertakers in their extortionate charges—for firewood, oil, and the flaming brand for starting the blaze. Shrouded and flower-decked bodies, lashed to litters of poles, were borne down the steps and laid at the water's edge, the feet resting in the sacred river while the pyre was made ready and the relatives paid the domri and paid for prayers by the "Sons of the Ganges"—a legion of fat priests shouting under great umbrellas—brigand Brahmans of the river bank, no less mercenary and rapacious than the outcast domri. A dead woman shrouded in white and roped over with marigold chains was laid where the foul waters

THE BURNING-GHAT, BENARES

could lave the feet, a sewer arch discharging but a yard away, and the evil domri panning out their treasure close by. When the pyre was ready, the body was completely immersed for a moment, carried up and laid on the fagots, and a sobbing, frightened little boy, his tunic wet in Ganges water, laid sandalwood and spices on his mother's body, ran five times around the pile as priests and relatives pushed and pulled him through his part, and, touching the torch to the oil-drenched fagots, ran shrieking to a servant's arms. The flames leaped and crackled, jets of thick smoke curled around, the fire lapped over the edges of the grave-clothes, and smoke mercifully concealed the rest. The domri stood by with long irons arranging the fire, adding wood and oil, while the family group waited there until all should be consumed. A prisoner's body from the jail was laid by the sewer's mouth, and instead of being burned in the later, cheaper hours of the afternoon, was to be cremated at once at the expense of a rich Brahman, who waited to commit the ashes to the river and thereby "acquire merit."

At the near-by ghat a boy's body had been laid on the lowest step, and without cover or shroud, clothed as in life, his relatives wailed and dashed Ganges water over him. He had probably died within the hour. He might even have been gasping as they hurried him through the streets to be burned and committed to the Ganges before noon. The body was not yet rigid as the relatives poured and sprinkled water over the graceful young statue, wrapped it in a Ganges-soaked sheet, fastened it to a litter of boughs, and bore it off to the burning-ghat. The group of women remained behind, and standing in a circle facing inward, wailed and tossed their arms. Some were dry-eyed and watched us while they wailed and beat their breasts, but the mother was unmistakable in the group—her cries and gestures in pathetic contrast to those of the others.

When we had twice gone the length of the ghats, drifting down to the railroad bridge and rowing back to the upper ghats, reviewing seven miles of bathing, praying, misguided people, we landed where the crowds were thickest, the din loudest. The well filled with Vishnu's perspiration, and in which Devi dropped her ear-jewel, and the stone footprint of Vishnu make this spot the center of busiest religious life on the river bank. There priests and people swarmed thickest, all bellowing the history of the pool in one's ears; and the sick and the well, the diseased and the robust, crowded the inclosing steps of this tank of filth, an abominable ooze of Ganges slime, decaying flowers, spices, sweetmeats, butter, and milk. They sipped and drank this liquid death, and we hastened from the noisy crowd of priests, pilgrims, fakirs, beggars, Brahmans, jugglers, snake-charmers, money-changers, and idlers with sacred cows wearing bead and flower necklaces, pushing their way when it was not obsequiously cleared for them.

Processions of people carrying water to their homes and the temples, and spilling it as they went, made walking dangerously slippery, and we barely looked into the court of the Golden Temple, where worshipers crowded to jangle the bells, sprinkle grease, and garland the images. The courtyard of the Well of Knowledge, in which Shiva resides, was so offensive that we had no wish to approach the curb and see the pit of decaying food, flowers, incense, milk, and butter. We took a peep at the Temple of the Stick, where sugar dogs are the acceptable offering, and a greedy Brahman whips repentent sinners and then grants them absolution and indulgence—whips them with peacock feathers—even gives the unbeliever a swish of the feathers for two annas and laughs with him at the deluded divinity he serves!

It was then ten o'clock, and after four hours in the headquarters of heathendom we were glad to return to the quiet, empty spaces of the cantonment, realizing more than before what an appalling task confronts the missionaries, and what generations of such blindly bigoted Ganges worshipers must pass away before any change can be hoped for. A century of British law, order, cleanliness, and sanitary improvement avails nothing against the superstitions and practices of twenty-five centuries. Yet in this same center of bigotry and superstition Gautama Buddha won the people from their idolatry, their superstitions and caste creed, and for eight hundred years his doctrines prevailed. With this precedent, the ultimate conversion of the Hindus need not be despaired of. We drove out that afternoon by a dusty, tamarind-shaded road to Sarnath, the Deer Park of Benares, where the Buddha preached, defied the Brahmans, and built up his great following.

Only a few ruins remain of the great group of buildings, the crumbling tope in a deserted common the only object above ground described by Fahien and Hiouen Thsang. "Did Sarnath pay?" asked my table d'hôte neighbor that night, and I stammered for an answer. "Because," she said, "they told us there was nothing to see, that it would n't pay us to drive out there just to see some rubbishy old stones and brick heaps."

CHAPTER XII

BENARES

IT did not seem possible that the Ganges banks could ever show such another sight; yet a second and a third morning we rose by starlight, drove through streets all blue and lilac with frost haze, to the ghats where the rising sun again glorified the whole fantastic, picturesque line; turning adobe, sandstone and grimy whitewashed buildings into the richest temples and palaces of dreams, and lighting the faces of the thousands of believers standing in the swirling mud stream, as thousands have stood at sunrise for centuries. Even then, one can figure it out that many thousands shirk their religious duties—a cheering sign in a way—for, if the two thousand temples of Benares with their five hundred thousand idols are tended by eighty thousand priests, the sacerdotal company alone would exceed the crowds we saw on any one morning. The priests are supposed to be driven all day, to have time for nothing but sacred observances, the bathing, buttering, garlanding, tiring, fanning, and tending of the idols, and always to begin the day with the dip in the Ganges. Many of them surely omit it on these frosty mornings. While the mummery goes on in the temples, the babus and pundits, even those who have taken degrees in Western universities, insist that this worship is not idolatry, that these images of Vishnu, Shiva, Parvati, Krishna, Ganesha, and the rest, the stone bulls, the sacred cows, sacred wells, and sacred monkeys, are but symbols—symbols of the purest and simplest creed, of the noblest faith, the highest philosophy—a symbolism that the masses of course recognize. One has all of a Mohammedan's impatience and contempt for the puerilities, the grossness, the unreasonable imbecility of it all.

One remembers the Scala Santa in Rome, the scenes at Assisi and Lourdes, when he sees fakirs and fanatics making the rounds of all the shrines of Benares on their knees, and measuring with their bodies the fifty miles of sacred road that sweeps in a semicircle around the suburbs of the holy city of the Brahman's soul, known to the pious Hindu as Kasi the Magnificent—a city which rests, not on the earth, but on the point of Shiva's trident.

The bazaars of Benares, particularly the noisy brass bazaar, are picturesque in a general way, but the wares exposed are the coarsest and crudest that the debased taste and careless hand of the day can produce. Heavy, ill-shapen, vulgar brass pieces scratched over with thin and poor designs replace the deeply cut and finely chased brass-work that used to distinguish Benares. But the glint and glow and color of the base metal in its myriad forms make of the narrow street of brass-beaters' dens a long genre picture. The fruit and flower bazaar carries on the dominant, decorative yellow note, and the orange of marigolds blends well with the rich reds of earthenware in the pottery bazaar, where the lotas and chatties have preserved the same lines from earliest times recorded in sculptures. The kincobs, or gold brocades, of Benares are tawdry and tinselly past belief, commonplace in design and color.

If anything could further disenchant one with Hindu forms of worship, it is provided at the temple of Durga, the Monkey Temple. One steps into a red sandstone and pink stucco court, where priests wait for gifts and gray apes with red faces sit in rows on the parapets, cornice, and roof, swarm up and down columns, drop noiselessly beside one and stretch long, lean, gray arms over his shoulder and clutch at his garments. The big apes chatter and mouth and make faces, and the little ones run screaming to safety, for when gift cakes are impending, the big apes are violent. The priests seem little more intelligent than the other sacred servitors, and as more and more apes drop noiselessly to the crowded pavement the tourist turns and flees.

I had unceasingly demanded the great mahatma, a certain holy man and miracle-worker who was reported as living in some palace garden of Benares, and but a little way beyond the Monkey Temple. We left the carriage, disputed passage with a sacred cow in a narrow lane, and found the green paradise of the Annanbag Garden, where dwelt Swamji, the living god. This aged seer and sage, a Brahman of so high a caste and sphere that no touch or deed can defile him, to whom no sin is possible, sits in his garden, "air clad," summer and winter alike, indifferent to heat and cold, hunger and thirst, feeling neither joy nor sorrow, a soul uplifted beyond all further test or trial. He sits there imparting wisdom to his disciples and followers, as Gautama Buddha taught once in the Deer Park, presenting the same old unchanging picture of religious life in the East. Like the Prince Siddhartha, Swamji left home and wife upon the birth of a son. His duty to the world was then done, and all the years since have been given to study, meditation, and the welfare of his soul, learning the great yoga mysteries and passing continually to higher stages. Two disciples early attached themselves to him, begged for him, and devoutly served him, accompanying the holy man on his pilgrimages to sacred places, and finally to his home, where with tearless indifference he learned of the death of his son, and addressing words of wisdom to his parents and wife, passed on. Without money, with only a shred of clothing, and no care for the morrow, he traveled all India, and, preserved through heat and snow, flood, storm, cold, hunger, and sickness, he came finally to Benares when he felt that he had attained supreme wisdom and triumphed over the world. A pious raja put the beautiful Annanbag (Garden of Happiness) at his disposal, and, dropping the one bit of raiment, his last earthly possession, Paribrajakacharya Sri Bhaskarananda Saraswati Swamji lives, air clad, in the same state of nature as primeval man, sitting beneath the trees by day discoursing to the

FAKIRS AT BENARES.

circle of disciples, sleeping uncovered on the bare earth at night, and eating only the offerings of fruit and rice which his devotees bring him. A jeweled youth with a great caste-mark on his brow was sitting with the holy man when we were announced by Chaturgam Lal and the favor of an audience asked; and the worshiping youth threw his own silky white chudda around the saint as we advanced down the garden path. The holy man sat there with knees bent, soles turned upward, and hand lifted in precisely the attitude of the Buddha in art. Birds twittered and the rustling trees overhead cast checkered shadows on the lean and wrinkled old ascetic beneath. He had a kindly face, a gentle, benevolent manner; he was very gracious, courteous, and human, and the living god began at once to talk of the impermanence of the world, of the delusions and fleeting joys of which we mistakenly make so much. His richly turbaned native visitors soon forgot our interruption, listening with rapt attention, and each one bowed reverently whenever the saint's eyes were directly turned in his direction. At Swamji's request, a disciple led us to a little marble shrine in the garden to see a portrait statue of the holy man, for this living god is worshiped in the flesh and in the image, there and in other cities.

When we returned to the teacher, he had evidently had more information concerning us from the omniscient Chaturgam Lal. "You write books," said the living god. "So do I. My books are commentaries on the Vedas and encouragements to the true religious life. I like your spirit. I will give you my book. And you shall learn Sanskrit and read it. You will give me your book. I already know English."

"You are yogi, you are mahatma. You are all-knowing and can perform miracles. Can you see to America and tell me what happens there?" I asked, "you can read my mind."

The smile faded from the venerable face. He looked pityingly, kindly at me. "No, my daughter. No one in India can see to America. Put away care. Do not think sorrow. Do not think money." And the renowned seer of seers, sage of sages, the living god, the Brahman above caste laid his hand in blessing like any noble old bishop. We spent a charming half-hour under the Annanbag trees, eating the saint's oranges, talking with him and his visitors as at any garden tea. When we were leaving, the saint threw over our shoulders the jasmine garlands his worshipers had laid at his feet, wound the borrowed chudda around him, and, rising, stalked with the swaying gait of extreme age to the gateway. He shook hands with us fearlessly and conventionally, for he was beyond defilement, and urged us to come again and talk with him in his garden.

Then Chaturgam Lal's tongue was loosened and he told us more of the great mahatma and of the miracles he had performed. "Why, once they sent officials to invite him to come to America. They wished him to perform miracles at the World's Fair in Chicago." This was shock and anticlimax, surely.

ON THE GANGES.

We took a boat at the next ghat, and were towed up-stream by a rope made fast to the tip of the mast, in the crazy Yang-tse and Asiatic fashion, and then were rowed quickly across to the marble palace of the Maharaja of Benares. Instead of landing at the inviting marble steps, we climbed the mud bank and walked around to an untidy back gate, the land entrance, seeing there an ill-kept menagerie and the frowzy soldiers of the body-guard. We passed through several courts and marble halls to the state apartments, where splendid rugs, tawdry European ornaments, and mechanical toys made extreme contrasts, and came out on the marble terraces and latticed loggias overlooking the river and the city's long line of palaces and temples. The jeweled beauties of the zenana should have been lounging there to complete the picture, but they were shut up behind latticed windows looking on the inside court. This Ramnuggur palace would seem to be the most desirable place to live in, but there is a strong prejudice against dying there or anywhere on that opposite bank of the Ganges. Generations ago, the maharaja tormented a Brahman by asking ninety-nine times where his soul would go to from the palace, and the Brahman, at the hundredth query, assured the great man that his soul would enter a donkey if he died there. Now when an illness becomes at all serious in Ramnuggur precincts, the victim is hurried to a boat and frantically ferried across.

As we were leaving the palace a fanfare of trumpets and bugles announced the arrival of the maharaja, and we stopped to watch the passing of the handsome young Hindu in his white and gold turban, a becoming red chudda wound around his shoulders. He stopped in front of us, bowed inquiringly, and Chaturgam Lal, in his flowered dressing-gown, introduced us by name, as democratically as any constituent might stop and introduce one to his congressman on the court-house steps. After a short conversation on lines of democratic equality, the maharaja asked us to return and see more rooms of the palace and take a cup of tea; but it was then sunset, darkness soon to follow, and we had instead to hurry around to the mud-bank landing, and drift back to the ghats by twinkling lamplights, a last dull glow indicating where the domri were burning the bodies of the poorest believers.

CHAPTER XIII

LUCKNOW

THERE was a truly Oriental hotel at Lucknow—a great, long, low, white palace of a building, with an arcaded front upon which the rooms opened. There was a noble drawing-room, strewn with the myriad little tables, dwarf chairs, and knickknacks of British middle-class esthetic fashion, but glorified by a great display of marigolds. The dinner-table was such another feast of marigolds that one forgave, or forgot, what came on the plates. The bedchambers were vast, cavernous, sunless caves, with their ceilings lost in remote shadows; the beds high, hard catafalques in the center of each such town hall. We spread rugs, blankets, and razais on these state couches, and, although the bundles of bedding had grown until they covered the top of a gharry, not all of them could soften or level those beds.

A typical, listless, shiftless, incompetent poll-parrot of a guide undertook to show us Lucknow. The most meager idea of the Mutiny, only the set phrases of local incident, had ever entered his head, along with a sordid idea of profit. "Two rupees a day, your ladyship,'' whined the creature, ''and, if you like me, a little more for bakshish, your ladyship.'' And so his woolen comforter and embroidered cap rode on our carriage-box to the Kaiserbaugh, where in its walled garden the wicked Queen of Oudh and the three hundred women of the zenana lived in jewels and idleness, envied and hated by the ninety nautch dancers housed in the gate pavilion.

Lucknow's museum is indeed a ''wonder-house,'' and, fortunate in having most energetic archæologists and ethnologists as its curators, its collections in those lines are most complete. This palace in a park contains in its first hall life-sized figures and groups illustrating the many races, tribes, and types of men in the empire, from the blue-eyed men of the Northwest to the inkiest Tamil and Andaman Islander. There is a distracting show of textiles and embroideries, of beasts, birds, metal-work, wood and ivory carving, and such treasures of sculptured relics from Buddhist ruins that the India of fifteen and twenty centuries ago is as well portrayed. The guide knew nothing about any of these things, and to our questions answered moodily: ''If your ladyship wishes me to tell you of the Mutiny, I can. If you will come down-stairs, I will explain the model of the Residency.'' Arrived at the model, the parrot glibly read off the names printed on each tiny roof, wall, and gate. ''This is the Bailly Gate. This is the hospital,'' etc., etc. ''Yes, yes,'' we answered. ''We can read that. You go on and explain the model, and we will follow you.'' ''But, your ladyship,'' wailed the parrot, ''I am explaining it to you now. This is the Bailly Gate." "Gate to what?" we asked pitilessly. "Who was Bailly that they should name a gate for him?" The poor poll-parrot's only answer to such conundrums was a rigmarole about the size of the Residency. "The mutineers," "the rebels," "our forces," "the natives," and "the king's forces" rolled from his tongue without any mental effort. "Eighteen hundred people were besieged here for six months. Many died. More than two thousand of them were buried here." When asked to explain how two thousand could die if there were only eighteen hundred in the beginning, he whimpered: "But, your ladyship, let me tell you a little more about the Mutiny. Those poor people, *how* they suffered!"

One has rather too much of the Mutiny in India. It is decidedly overdone. It may be well to keep the great incident alive in native memory, along with the justly terrible reprisals; but the tourist gets sated with England's woes and foes of '57, and recalls other wars and sieges since, and trusts that the next generation is not to be harrowed with the sieges of Ladysmith and Mafeking, Tientsin and Peking. Yet that tale of English courage and endurance is so familiar to all of us, that none can fail to be deeply stirred by the sight of the battered Bailly Gate and the pathetic, roofless Residency—a vine-wreathed, eloquent monument, England's flag still flying night and day from the tower that never surrendered. It is the most eloquent, the most human and speaking ruin that I know; and in that beautiful garden not a voice is raised, nor an irreverent word heard, every sound unconsciously hushed by the associations. The climax is reached at the grave of Henry Lawrence, that great soldier who "tried to do his duty. May the Lord have mercy on his soul."

We turned away from the Residency door surfeited with sorrows. We could stand no more mute memorials of suffering. "What, memsahib! Will you not even see *that cellar?*" implored the guide, a chastened, tongue-tied soul since being informed that he would be dismissed with six annas only if he again addressed us as ladyships. "But the memsahibs all like it. We do it to please," he wailed. An old soldier, survivor of the scene, is guardian of the Residency, and he saw that we saw every bullet-hole and shell-mark, and visited every room down to the underground chambers intended as luxurious retreats in hot weather. The old veteran who had come in with Outram's relief in September, and fought through the second siege until Colin Campbell's final relief in November, made very real to us how a thousand people lived in that one building all the unusually hot summer of '57, with a plague of flies that covered the floors and walls and buzzed sickeningly over the people and their food.

We had then supped full of Mutiny horrors, and we broke with the program of sight-seeing and drove for hours,—first to the river bank where the dhobie-men were swinging, pounding, slapping wet garments with might and main, and spreading them out in acres of white mosaic on bank and common. We heeded not ruined Dilkusha, where Havelock died, nor the route of Campbell's advance. "Will the memsahib not even see the Secunderabad?" wailed the guide when we refused to look into that slaughter-pen, where sixteen hundred and forty sepoys, fleeing from the Highlanders, were bayoneted in a cul-de-sac. Even Lord Roberts has said that that surging heap of dead and dying, more than shoulder high against the wall, was an incident of war that sickened men bent on avenging the atrocities of Cawnpore.

We saw with interest the great Mohammedan Imambara, the arches of its court framing pictures of other domes and minarets, its mihrab pointing westward to Mecca, and its deep baoli, or well, with encircling marble galleries where it is always cool in summer. The clock-tower, the white mosque filled with mirrors like a Champs-Elysées café, and the old palace of the kings of Oudh hung with portraits of those flabby and ill-favored royalties, were tedious stock sights. We saw with far more interest the latest American magazines lying on the table of the United Service Club, which now occupies the old Umbrella House of the nawab, an important place during the siege.

Although it was a real city of palaces long before the Mutiny, and a larger place then than Calcutta or Bombay, the bazaars of this old native capital were not so very interesting; and, except in the silver bazaar, a plague of torpid flies tormented us. The perfume-shops were countless, and we sniffed gums, grasses, woods, and attars of all the flowers, until we could not tell the precious rose attar, that sells at four times its weight in silver, from the rose-water at twelve cents a quart that one carries for ablutions on railway trains.

Again we caught sight of the square gray tower, —the tower that Mrs. Steele has introduced so well in "Voices of the Night,"—and the dreadful depression of Mutiny memories fell upon us. The dark, vaulted bedchambers of the hotel were too suggestive of the Residency cellar, and rather than pass a night in the city of such associations, or stop the next day to feed on the greater horrors of Cawnpore, we took the afternoon train for Agra. Some tourists came on at Cawnpore, anxious to escape from the horror of it. They had seen it all, and suffered all the terrible deaths in imagination, from the ghats where the boat-loads of English were burned, drowned, or murdered in cold blood by the fiendish Nana Sahib, to the room where the women and children were bayoneted and clubbed against the wall, and the crowning agony of the memorial angel over the well of burial—all explained in detail by an old soldier survivor.

Regarding Agra as the most important tourist place in India, it is disconcerting to have to reach it by cross-roads, way-trains, and branch lines, arriving always between midnight and daylight. We changed at Tundla Junction in a deluge of rain, and rode in a crowded car, seven in a single compartment, without any lamps, for an hour to Agra.

A huge turban from the hotel claimed us, and when the file of baggage coolies had trailed after us to the entrance, I said, "Get me a gharry." "Very well, madam. Very well. Very well," said the turban, flourishing his cane. After five minutes I repeated the order to turban tramping madly up and down the flagstones, cuffing coolies and bawling at every one and no one. "Very well, very well, madam," said this madman of Agra. Another appeal only pulled the string for another shower of "very wells," and nothing happened. I bade the bearer bring a gharry at once, and after big turban had beaten the air, beaten the bearer, and the two had screeched a mad dialogue, two lean horses and a rattletrap night-liner drew up and took us inside, the luggage on the roof, the turban on the box, and the bearer on behind. The ill-matched horses made a dash out from the lamplighted station, across the great common before Akbar's red sandstone fort, and took a turn entirely round a tree-box. After a second and a third turn around the tree, I put my head out and said severely, "Take us to the Hotel ——." "Very well. Very well, madam," floated down from the box, and with a jerk and a leap the ponies made another tour of the tree. We continued to whirl and circle around that sapling by the light of a thin, wet moon, wrangling voices and whip-crackings from overhead drowning any further directions to drive to the hotel. Our friends, following in the next gharry, thought the first circlings a runaway; then, hearing the voices from the box, arrived at another idea, and cried: "Oh, come on to the hotel. It 's no use trying to see the Taj now. It is after one o'clock."

Our answer was lost as the ponies ran around the

tree again. In time the bearer was made to understand, and to lead the ponies by the bridle out of the enchanted square, and they splashed along soberly enough through wet and gloomy avenues to the far-away hotel. This was an incongruous, opera-bouffe sort of arrival in and introduction to the city of one's soul and dreams, where more of sentiment, beauty, and haunting charm abide than in all the peninsula; but sentiment with difficulty survives the disenchantment and jarring contacts of Indian travel. One must see India and spend his sentiment on it afterward.

CHAPTER XIV

AGRA

TO the traveler Agra means, stands for, the Taj alone, the most interesting object in India; and, arrived there, one almost fears to precipitate the supreme moment, to put it to the test, to take the first look. There was no inspiration in the gray, cloudy morning or the tedious drive from the hotel in the farthest suburb three miles to the walled garden by the river bank. A sandstone gateway in a long wall admitted us to the serai, or outer court, where cabs and bullock-carts stood and touts, peddlers, and guides squatted waiting for prey, scenting the first tourist rupee of the day. There fronted the Great Gateway, a magnificent sandstone tower in itself worth coming to see, its arch inlaid with white verses and flowers, and a row of airy little bell cupolas fringing the roof-line. We went in through the drafty rotunda of a hall, and straight before us was the vision of beauty, the Taj Mahal—the most supremely beautiful building in all the world—the most perfect creation of that kind that the mind and hand of man have ever achieved—one of the great objectives of travel that does not disappoint, but far exceeds all anticipations—a reward for all the distance one may travel to reach it—recompense for all one endures in Indian travel. Well as one knows it from photographs and engravings, the reality is as astonishing, as overwhelming, as if he had never heard of it. Even while he first looks through the arch to the white dome above the cypress-trees, it seems too rarely perfect to be real, too incredibly beautiful to be true. It would not have surprised me if the light had faded, a curtain had fallen; or, still less, if one had found he could not enter, that no foot could touch the garden-path or the white terrace, which is mere pedestal for this marvelous work of art. After watching the entrance of some others, we paused for a first steadfast look, and then, all excitement and exaltation, followed the marble path and mounted the half-way platform that affords the perfect view-point, the white wonder reflected in the long marble canal at their feet.

The Taj on its high platform, with the red sandstone mosque at the west, the complementary building or "Response" on the east, and the whole sky-space over and beyond the river as background, presents the most harmonious and perfectly balanced composition and is the most admirably placed building in India. The eye travels from feature to feature and detail to detail, and the wonder of its perfection continually grows. The bands of low-relief carving, the panels and borders of inlaid work, afford endless study, and one easily accepts the guide's set story that forty varieties of carnelian

THE TAJ MAHAL.

are inlaid in one small flower, and that the whole Koran is inlaid, verse by verse, on the walls. There is a whole new set of sensations when one enters the softly lighted, dim white interior, with the echo repeating each word like the response of a chanted service—a single note from flute or guitar a whole theme. A trellis of marble tracery, with inlaid borders, screens the two tombs, low sarcophagi of jeweled marble resting on inlaid platforms. Mumtaz-i-Mahal in the center, where the Great Mogul laid her, and with Shah Jahan at her side are laid away in real simple white tombs in a vault immediately below the sarcophagi; and to them the aged guardian conducts one with a lantern.

We went back at sunset, and saw only an uninteresting yellow ball sink against a hazy horizon, and the clear-cut shadows in the arches of the Taj fade to white and gray. In a little while the yellow ball of the full moon rose beyond the river, and flooded the eastern arch with a splendor unimagined. On the platform in mid-garden were other moonlight pilgrims, and what did they talk about in face of this glorious apparition, this wonder of the world? The German professor told how the mutton chops were served at his hotel—brought in and passed around sizzling on the hot grill! Could sacrilege go further?

There was a British artist at our hotel, "painting Tajes," as he naïvely explained, for the "London spring market"—"four rather nice ones" already finished, and more to do while the fine weather lasted; since early in March the hot winds begin, a scorching gale is blowing by noon, and the air is filled with dust. "Yes, it is a bit chilly sitting in the garden so long, these days," he said, "and the tourists do bother a bit, you know; looking over one's shoulder and asking one if it is hard to do." When we hurried from dinner the next night for a second moonlight view, the artist said: "Oh, I say! You Americans have such a notion for seeing the Taj by moonlight. There were some American ladies here last month at the full of the moon, and they went down there after dinner, too."

"Have n't you seen it by moonlight yet?"

"Oh, dear, no! I am there all day, you know."

"But are you not going to-night?" we asked in amazement.

"No, I think not. I will go sometime, though. It might be nice to paint a moonlight Taj," and he went on eating cheese!

With the round silver moon shining high in the vault of the intense, indigo-blue sky, the Taj Mahal was the frost-palace of one's dreams, and from the dark arch of the entrance gateway it seemed fairly to shine and flash in the strong light poured full on its eastern face. There was silence in the enchanted garden, and as we walked toward the luminous white palace only the far murmur of running water and the scent of violets and mignonette told upon the other senses. We had the place to ourselves for one hour of silence and charm, sitting in the shadows of the Response. Then the chatter, clatter of the tourist contingent was heard at the gateway and down the path. *"Ach, Wunderschön!*

Wunderschön!" the loudest voice proclaimed. Then clouds skimmed over the moon, dimming the Taj, which was suddenly transformed to silver and frosted ivory again as the moon rode out. The "*Wunderschön*" voices continued down the path until smothered in the staircase inside the platform, came out full-lunged on the terrace, and there proclaimed with greater volume the wonderful beauty of the white building. Echoes came from the domed hall, then the faint, glow-worm light of the custodian's lantern led the voluble gutturals around the octagon and down to the tombs. Next cockney voices came down the garden walk—some "Tommies" from the cantonment with their "'Arriets," who, skylarking down to the terrace, with an all-hands-round at the entrance of the platform stairway, chased, shrieking, up the inner stairway and came out on the platform with shouts of laughter, each slim, trim figure in red coat and box cap standing out distinct in color in the moonlight. Disenchanted, we fled through the darkest garden paths. It was sacrilege of the rankest kind for those sweethearting couples to be skylarking around the marble screen of the tombs, dropping their barbarous "h's" to summon the echo, the pure soul of the Taj Mahal.

For four days we haunted the garden of the Taj, for by noonday, sunset, and moonlight it took on as many rarer qualities and aspects; and six times a day, as we drove those long miles to and from the gateway, we berated the hotel-keepers for not putting the hotel where it should be. The guardians and keepers at the Taj came to know us, the touts and guides let us alone. We found, after many comparative tests, that the best full view of the Taj is to be had from the second story of the entrance gateway; the best sunset view from the west pavilion over the river angle of the terrace, reached by a staircase in the mosque; and the best moonlight effect is that obtained from the opposite east pavilion, reached by the corresponding stairway in the Response.

There were Philistines among some of the early English commanders at Agra, the most soulless of them all being that Lord William Bentinck who wanted to sell the Taj Mahal, and actually considered the offer of thirty thousand pounds from a rich Hindu. One gasps, too, to hear how the Maharaja of Sindhia entertained a viceroy in the enchanted garden, serving supper in the Response, ham and champagne, "swine's flesh and wine," in the architectural counterpart of the Mosque. Lord Auckland also was entertained in the Taj, when there were games in the garden, with roars of laughter, and ham and champagne again in the Response. In the same way, a ball was given for Lord Ellenborough after the siege of Kabul, lanterns were strung on the cypress-trees, there was dancing to military music on the marble platform, and supper in the Response, as usual. The native press denounced this desecration of a tomb and place of worship, but the Agra officials argued that the Response was not a mosque, and, if it were, it had long since lost sanctity by its desecration by Jats and Hindus. Moreover, they said that the literal translation of its name was "the feast-place"—it was before the tomb was built, Tatar and Mogul alike preparing a beautiful garden in life that it might become their burial-place, after which it was never used for pleasuring, but given over to the care of priests. The Taj Mahal was held in great reverence in Mohammedan days, and visitors were blindfolded at the entrance and not uncovered until they reached the place of prayer. When the Jats took Agra and looted its palaces, they carried off the entrance gates with their thousands of silver nails, each with a rupee as its head. They took away the inner doors of the Taj, each a single translucent slab of agate, the gold spire and crescent, and the precious carpets laid three and four deep on the floor. No vandalism of that kind has taken place in British days, and there has been great interest shown in keeping the gardens in their original condition. In 1876 the whole place was thoroughly repaired and restored in preparation for the Prince of Wales's visit, and the closest watch is kept to prevent natives, soldiers, and tourists from picking out the precious bits of inlaid stone. Severe punishment is visited upon natives who pick flowers or otherwise transgress within the inclosure, and the query was always in my mind whether or not the natives had any comprehension of the beauty and sentiment of the place. It was ever a growing wonder that these people, the Hindus, had ever accomplished it—how even twenty-two thousand of them, working for seventeen or for twenty-two years under Moslem directors, had ever reared it. Like Sir Charles Dilke, one finds it hard to believe that "a people who paint their cows pink with green spots, and their houses orange or bright red, should be the authors of the Pearl Mosque or the Taj. It would be too wonderful." It is easier to credit the plans to the Frenchman Austin de Bordeaux or to any of the master masons or carvers who came from Bagdad, Constantinople, Samarkand, and from every Moslem center of note, and worked here during the same years that the Pilgrim Fathers were building their first log-house on Plymouth Bay.

Driving through the great fortress gate, we saw first the red palace of Akbar, sandstone prelude to the jeweled marble halls of Shah Jahan, the greatest builder of all the Moguls. The first or private audience-hall, the Khas Mahal, lies across the Grape Garden, its windows set in the solid battlemented walls that rise sheer from the moats. It is a dream in white—arches and walls of pure white marble carved in scrolls, traceries, and flowers in low relief, the windows filled with marble lattices. The scheme of white on white is offset by a ceiling of gold and colors, and the Khas Mahal is a model for architects and decorators for all time. By an open terrace on the battlements, and a series of marble halls with walls inlaid with graceful Persian arabesques and flowers in colored stones, we came to the Jasmine Tower, Shah Jahan's finest construction. The rounded balcony of the tower projects beyond the walls and commands the moats below, the long curve of the Jumna, and the white bubbles of the Taj beyond a flat, green foreground of river bottom mosaiced over with the washermen's white patches. The lovely Mumtaz-i-Mahal lived in these rooms around the fountain court, all their surface a maze of precious inlay, the floor of the court a marble pachisi-board, the walls of the inner chambers fitted with long, sunken pockets for jewels that only a woman's slender hand and wrist could reach into. A staircase leads down to the Shish Mahal, or Hall of Mirrors, a cool grotto of a bath set with tiny mirrors in carved plaster, where a cascade once tinkled down a stepped arrangement over colored lights. Overhead is the tiny Gem Mosque, where the women prayed the Prophet to grant them souls; this exquisite marble cell being afterward the prison place of Shah Jahan. Shah Jahan, the accepted Great Mogul of Europeans, and contemporary of Cromwell, was deposed by his son, Jahangir, but cheered in his seven years' captivity by his faithful daughter, Jahanira. Another passage leads along above the battlements from the Jasmine Tower to the Diwan-i-Khas, another private audience-hall with an inner decoration of white on white in low relief, the outer pillars and arches inlaid with color. A considerable annual outlay is required to keep these inlaid walls in order, to replace the bits of carnelian, jade, jasper, amethyst, agate, and lapis lazuli dug out by vicious tourists and idling hooligans of soldiers. This audience-hall fronts upon a terrace flush with the battlements, and there at close of day the Great Mogul used to lounge on a black marble throne, watching the domes and minarets of the Taj grow beneath the hands of the thousands of workmen. When the marauding Jats captured the fort they sacked the palace, despoiled the Diwan-i-Khas of its silver ceiling, but when they attempted to sit on this seat of the Great Mogul it broke under the indignity. Half of the court space was once a sunken pond, with a carved niche or throne in the surrounding gallery, where the great one used to sit to fish at ease. It is now but a dry stone court, and no trace remains of the bath-room of precious green marble, whose interior was stripped by the Marquis of Hastings, who wished to send it to England to be reërected as a bath-room for George IV. The loose marbles lay around for years, uncared for, and were finally sold for a trifle. It is not necessary for any outsider to vent his indignation at this barbaric proceeding, as Sir James Fergusson has said it all, with a vehemence none can approach, and has sufficiently laid the lash of his terrible sarcasm on his Philistine countrymen.

From this Court of the Fish-pond a door admits one directly to the Diwan-i-Am, or great audience-hall, its marble lattices and inlaid throne splendid reminders of the past, the rows of British cannon and the red-coated sentries beyond sufficient evidences of the present. We crossed the court and ascended the staircase to the Moti Musjid, the Pearl Mosque, over which three generations of writers have raved as an architectural chef-d'œuvre second only to the Taj. After all the splendid creations of Shah Jahan, this in some way failed to produce an equal impression, and it gave us a distinct sense of disappointment. The simplicity of the white mosque, relieved only by the blue and gray veins

PRIVATE AUDIENCE HALL AND JASMINE TOWER IN AGRA PALACE. TAJ MAHAL IN DISTANCE.

of the marble and the one long inscription in black inlay, did not appeal. The white court with its mirror tank, the white cloisters, the vista of white arches and columns, and the pale shadows of the interior had beauty,—Vereshchagin's painting had told one that,—but the Moti Musjid gave the chill of the first disappointment in Agra.

The tomb of I'tamadu-daulah, father of Nur Jahan, the famous wife of Jahangir, and grandfather of Mumtaz-i-Mahal, is on the opposite side of the Jumna; far above the Taj and from the high railway bridge and from the garden terraces one has still different views of the Taj. All the roads leading there were crowded one Sunday afternoon with strings of ekkas and bullock-carts overflowing with women and children, and the garden-paths and the marble platform around the marquetry tomb of the Persian treasurer were crowded with family parties. The women and children were all in their most brilliant holiday attire, their jewels and tinsel, fantastic fineries and fripperies of every kind making the green garden around the white pavilion a dazzle of color, a dream of India. Complacent fathers sat stocking-footed on outspread blankets, their veiled women and children, huddled near, regarding the superior being with awe—a joyous Indian family holiday of the middle classes. A small boy flashed by in a petunia satin coat and gold-embroidered cap, bare-legged and tugging at a bow and arrow. Another boy in gorgeous red satin top-clothes munched a green apple, and the petunia archer flew at him with the fury of a tiger. Screams from the combatants and all their female followers rent the air, and when forcibly separated neither was to be appeased by proffered peanuts. Then a small sister of the petunia coat dashed forward and dealt the green-apple boy such a clap on the ear that the female parliament was paralyzed. When we presented the intrepid little woman with some annas of admiration our dumfounded bearer asked, "Why do such curious thing?" and afterward tried half-heartedly to explain to the crouching women that it was our testimonial to the first woman in India with any backbone. With laughter, the four wives, the two daughters, and the wrinkled old nurse in pewter jewelry, who were with the father of the little "new woman," promised to keep her in the habit of resenting tyrant man and redressing promptly all the wrongs that came to her notice.

The garden rang with jingling anklets, and the play of colors was kaleidoscopic. Two beautiful young women raised their white head-sheets to look at us as they passed, red shoes and full yellow skirts and much coin jewelry making them fantastic figures fit for a fancy-dress ball. Scores of women flounced by in red skirts, green skirts, changeable silk skirts with tinsel borders, and wearing purple, green, yellow, and white head-sheets. A nautch-girl came jingling by, her pale-blue skirts the only touch of that color in the whole garden. After we had seen the tombs in the mosaic pavilion, whose inlaid walls were the first to be decorated in pietra dura in India, we mounted to the terrace roof around the upper story of the marble reliquary, which is a mass of fine relief-carving and lattice-work, and looked down upon the brilliant scene in the garden. And this spectacular gathering of so many hundreds of women and children was all to celebrate the ceremonial hair-cutting of the year —the clippings of the children's hair being brought to the terrace and there thrown into the Jumna, with flower offerings.

CHAPTER XV

AKBAR, THE GREATEST MOGUL OF THEM ALL

AT Agra, Akbar, the greatest of all the Mogul sovereigns, descendant of Baber and Timur, and of tribal connection with Genghis Khan, becomes a very real personage. He lived in that age of great sovereigns when Henry IV, Philip II, and Queen Elizabeth ruled in Europe. He has been called the Marcus Aurelius and the Frederick the Great of India, and he was the greatest builder the country had then known. Forts, palaces, tombs, and whole cities sprang up by his command, and at his court literature, art, and all religions were honored. Brahmans, Mohammedans, Sikhs, Jains, and Catholic priests expounded and argued with him in a first parliament of religions, and, regarding them all impartially, he devised a universal theology, a compromise creed which his vizier and not a few courtiers adopted. He himself worshiped the sun every morning, as representative of the divinity which animates and rules the world. He was a strenuous sort of ruler too, walking twenty and thirty miles a day, to the dismay of his courtiers; and once he rode from Ajmir to Agra in two days, covering the two hundred and twenty miles by innumerable relays of fast horses. Akbar wrote his memoirs, in worthy emulation of Baber, whose autobiography in illuminated Persian text is treasured in the Agra College library.

In the usual reverse order of all Indian sight-seeing, we first saw Akbar's tomb, and then his City of Victory. The tomb is at Secundra, a suburb of Agra. A great red sandstone gateway admits one to the flagged court, and the impressive pillared pavilion, rising story upon story, after the oldest Buddhist constructions, covers the remains of the greatest of the Moguls. A pierced marble screen walls the upper terrace, where the white sarcophagus, covered with carving, lies open to the sun and sky, the intended white dome never having been completed by Akbar's successors. The real tomb is reached by a sloping passageway, and the monarch lies in a grave scooped in the earth like the graves of his desert-chief ancestors.

Never on any sleigh-ride, nor in winter travel in the North, have I known such suffering from cold as during the twenty-two-mile ride from Agra to Fatehpur Sikri, Akbar's City of Victory. The heaviest winter clothing and all the wraps, rugs, razais, and hot-water bottles could not defy the insidious air. The sun shone, the trees were green, the road was smooth and well kept, but the keen, raw, icy wind of a Canadian March so benumbed us on our way to Akbar's Versailles that several times we ran beside the victoria in our efforts to restore circulation. We paused not for sights when once arrived there. What were Akbar's outer walls, his treasury, mint, or any lot of ruined stonework to us until we could reach the cold splendors of the dak bangla, once the Record Office and Akbar's House of Dreams, and thaw our fingers over the cook-house charcoals? We shut the mullioned windows in the cliff-like outer walls commanding the vast prospect of the plain, and supplemented the slight and shadowy, the sketchy, impressionist imitation of a breakfast of the Agra hotel with scalding chocolate and really hot toast, and embarked the sympathetic old khansamah on a more solid tiffin than he had contemplated. We proposed to stoke up with all the bodily fuel possible for the return drive in the teeth of the wind.

A troop of guides lay in wait for us, and luck let us have another of those stupid parrots who, in embroidered caps and winding chuddas, mislead one over all the show-places of India. This one stuttered—may all others know and avoid him by that sign!—and, like all of his gild, reversed the guide-book order of sight-seeing. We had already suffered enough in that way, and we ordered him to right about face and march to the Turkish queen's house, first on the Murray list and first object before the Hall of Records. "But, ladyship, I wish f-f-first to sh-sh-show you the mosque and my ancestor's grave." But we wanted none of his ancestors, except in their regular order. "Oh, your ladyship, your ladyship, take me, take me. God is good. Take me, take me," mumbled a toothless collection of wrinkles in white grave-clothes.

"I know the palace well. I know the Turkish queen. I showed the Prince of Wales all Fatehpur Sikri." And then guides grew thick and thicker around us, rising from the very flagstones. They whined in procession after us across the court, and it was easy to make compact with our guide, who was almost exploding with spasms of stuttering wrath at the interlopers. He was to lead us in the straight and direct path of the "Murray book," and receive bakshish in proportion to his success in keeping his rivals away and in omitting his "ladyships."

As we wandered in admiration through the sun-warmed courts, sheltered from the biting blast, our benumbed senses revived, and we warmed to real enthusiasm over this "romance in stone," over all the exquisite fantasies, the veritable *maisons bijoux* Akbar had built for his favorite wives. The Great Mogul was as eclectic and as far-reaching in his consort collecting as in his religion, and we were shown the house of his Turkish queen Miriam; that of his Christian Portuguese wife; the house of Birbal, his Hindu wife, and a great zenana. Of the same order of lavish ornamentation is the wonderful council-chamber with its central pillar, all these structures carved over every inch of surface with the finest and most intricate ornament, geometrical patterns, and traceries. Outside, inside, over all the walls and ceilings spreads the revel of ornament, and the windows hold perforated stone and marble screens as fine as woven reed-work. This was the real India of the imagination, the setting for "The Naulahka," every part of the carved labyrinth a scene for melodrama. There was one great five-story pavilion, strangely like Akbar's tomb in design, each pillared and open hall of fairy lightness, with a row of fantastic bell-cupolas on top. There the zenana women took the air, and near by was Akbar's great pachisi-board inlaid in a court pavement, where he played the game with his vizier, using slave-girls for pawns, and the successful one keeping the beauties he won. On the seat overlooking this checker-board, Akbar doubtless flourished his famous bon-bon box, with its harmless delights in one compartment, perfumed poison in the other. After having dealt death to many courtiers deliberately, he accidentally took the wrong sugar-plum himself one day, and ended his life in the most satisfactory, retributive, story-book way.

Our guide finally led us through the inlaid gate to the court of the mosque, and was about to launch full-lunged on his ancestors of honorable burial when our eyes fell upon the little white marble tomb of Selim Chisti, the hermit saint and local genius, whose prophecies led Akbar to build this palace and city on the arid plain. The saint's tomb is the most exquisite thing of its kind in India, a tiny marble jewel-box, hardly larger than an elephant's howdah, a filigree reliquary, with fine lattice walls, fantastic brackets, and a domed roof shining in the sunlight. The ebony doors admit one to the tomb, where ostrich eggs hang and ebony panels are inlaid with mother-of-pearl. One looks through the marble screens, as fine as basketry, at the Indian sky, as

MAUSOLEUM OF SELIM CHISTI, FATEHPUR SIKRI.

clearly blue as sapphire. We forgot the inlaid arches and the tiled facings of the mosque, which is a copy of the mosque at Mecca, and turned only to look again and again at the tiny white tomb shining like a frost creation in the empty stone court, the reality infinitely more satisfactory than even Vereshchagin's painting had led us to expect. In front of this little prettiness the great gate of Victory opens to the plain and the ruined city, a broad staircase leading down to the rubbish-strewn common. We went through the great domed arch, the doors studded with votive nail-heads and horseshoes, and from the foot of the staircase had the intended view of this gate which Fergusson calls "noble beyond that of any portal attached to any mosque in India, perhaps in the whole world." Across the front of this gate Akbar inlaid the famous inscription: "Isa [Jesus], on whom be peace, said: 'The world is a bridge, pass over it, but build no house on it. The world endures but an hour, spend it in devotion.'" There is a great green, oval well, with a parapet and arched chambers surrounding it, close beside the steps and the high, battlemented walls. Despite the keen and wintry air, lean men and boys, shivering in a few flutters of cotton drapery, offered to jump the eighty feet from the battlements into the well. While we demurred, covered with goose-flesh at the mere idea, there was a shout from above, a brown figure shot out into the air, whirling his arms frantically to keep the body upright, and dropped feet foremost into the pool. The green scum closed over him, and before we could recover breath the black head swam to the steps, wound on a dry sheet, and came, all green and shivering, to claim a rupee for the feat. He dashed instantly out of sight, reappeared on the battlements, and made a second plummet drop into the well. Only the fact that those two dearly earned rupees assured him food for the day could ease one's conscience for aiding and abetting such inhuman sport. Two Scotch tourists, who had watched the cold plunger from the head of the steps, refused to pay a rupee apiece, or even one anna, to the "poor man with family to feed." We could hear them say that they had not engaged the man to jump, the ladies had arranged that. "But you saw me. You watched me. You all looked at me," howled the jumper, following them. And the Scotchmen said: "Those Americans can just pay more, then. We won't give you an anna. *Jao!*"

After the arctic drive back to Agra, we had time only for a cup of scalding tea before hurrying to the Taj to witness the most wonderful sunset of all, an amber afterglow illuminating every inner curve and recess and dispelling all shadows, the light seeming to radiate from the glowing marble, to emanate from the white surface itself. As if that six-mile pilgrimage, added to our forty-four-mile drive of the day, were not enough, the clear sparkle of the stars and the nipping air of that night suggested a different Taj, and after dinner we rattled down the Strand Road to see by moonlight such a glitteringly white, splendidly snowy frost-palace as we had not dreamed of finding in India.

We essayed a rainy day of rest, taking our ease

at our inn, myself in a superior, sunless, fireless, cheerless room, which was but a long, whitewashed vault with a carefully curtained door opening on a brick portico. Drafts that were small gales blew through, making reading, writing, or anything but sneezing impossible. The peddlers marked us for their own that day, and every few moments there was a tap on the glass door, a brown hand was thrust in with some object for sale; and a plaintive "mem-sahib" or "ladyship" distracted one. "Please buy. Please buy. I am poor man," rang in my ears all day, and the transfer of packs from the bricks outside to the dirty matting within was accomplished imperceptibly. I was first aware of some pleading, whining creature with a shop spread on the floor around him—silver, jewelry, embroideries, shawls, beetle-winged gauzes, gay pulkharries, and souvenir spoons. Every day a huge damascened fork or trident was offered me as I passed in or out,—whether a dagger or an elephant goad I could not say. "Oh, yes, your ladyship," said the oily one in answer, "this is toast-fork. Very nice. Very comfortable thing for traveling. Please buy. I am poor man." But he and his tribe were ordered to begone, and as the toast-master shuffled out with his bundle he paused at the threshold to slip into his Mohammedan shoes, using the big fork for a shoe-horn. "Very useful. See, your ladyship," he said, adjusting the second shoe with the combination toasting-fork. "Silputs [slippers] help on, also."

When the sky cleared in the late afternoon we betook ourselves to the fort to await the rose-red sunset that the humid atmosphere promised. The old chuprassy welcomed us to the Jasmine Tower, and gave us wicker stools that we might comfortably watch the white bubbles beyond the green foreground flame to rose-red and then fade away, effaced in the gray mists that rolled up the river, presage of the deluge rain that followed. The keeper brought torches and led us down to the labyrinth of dark chambers and vaults that underlie the zenana and the Grape Garden. Six thousand people found refuge in the fort during the Mutiny, and then all this underground world was explored, with its oubliettes and long passages reaching to the moats and the water-gate. The rooms we saw were the prisons for zenana offenders, and by dumb show and much mixed language we were informed that it was Akbar's wives who suffered most often here by torture and the rope, the sack, and the drop down the echoing well. No screams could be heard in the sunny Grape Garden, nor in the beautiful audience-hall; and, after Akbar's career of domestic tyranny, it was fitting that his son, Jahangir, should be ruled by his Persian wife, Nur Jahan, and that Shah Jahan, the grandson, should worship in life, and after her death, Mumtaz-i-Mahal.

CHAPTER XVI

DELHI

IT was in the regular order of discomfort that we should leave Agra late at night and reach Delhi at four o'clock in the morning; the last straw lay in the fact that we departed in a pouring rain and made the midnight change at Tundla Junction in a cloud-burst. Fires had warmed the rooms (which we reached by a roof or terrace) when we arrived at the much commended Delhi hotcl, and we fell asleep to dream of Madura noondays until an unusual hour of the morning. Then we found that the rooms had no windows, so that when the doors were closed and the fire-places heaped with wood, we had easily enjoyed the climate of the tropics. That hotel, named for a great viceroy, was by far the worst, the most forlorn, run-down, and dilapidated of any we found up-country. The drawing-room was a muddle of broken furniture, of dusty and disorderly draperies, the dining-room infragrant and time-stained, and the manager—there are no landlords or innkeepers in British realms any more—a listless, depressed, poor white creature, a definite failure in life, who roamed the portico in pajamas and long ulster, smoking a German student pipe. We removed forthwith to another hotel, that had once been a splendid official residence. Our rooms opened by long windows upon a cement terrace flush with the battlements of the city walls, and from that high parapet we looked down upon the Jumna and green wooded spaces where the jackals howled all night and wherein are laid some of the scenes of "On the Face of the Waters." The entrance portico of the mansion was used as a dining-room, the great stone arches partly closed at night by bamboo blinds, ventilated curtains that swayed and swung in the drafts and breezes which blew over us as we dined there, practically out of doors, on those cold January nights, with the humidity great and the thermometer registering 38 to 40 degrees.

"It is a land of misery," cried a great American litterateur who was doing India with a rapidity unequaled by any personally conducted tourist. "All I want to do is to get out of it; to get away; to get something an American stomach is used to eating; to get some Apollinaris instead of this hygienic soda; to get warm again. If I get within one hundred miles of any place, I will say I have seen it. I don't want any more architecture at this price." And this tirade was in the same key and vein indulged in by all the coughing, sneezing, rheumatic, and neuralgic tourists. All were cross, half ill, and thoroughly homesick in this chill land of supposed tropic splendors.

When the sour mists or the frost hazes of those

Delhi mornings had cleared away, we had sunshine that mellowed grumblers to amiability, and they basked in the hot beams of noonday; but gloom settled on them with the damp chill of sunset, and there were the same depressed and depressing groups huddled before the few hissing twigs in the fireplaces of the chill white caves of rooms. Then the jackals came under our windows and laughed and shrieked hysterically, as well they might, at calling such a tour pleasure travel.

The old capital of the Moguls has great charm in sunshine, and Delhi's main thoroughfare, the Chandni Chauk (Silver Square), was the most brilliant and spectacular place we had seen. All native life was crowded into that street, which is a continuous market-place for a mile, with rainbow crowds of people streaming up and down, buying and selling everything from crown diamonds and jeweled jade to sheepskins and raw meat. The street has run with blood many times, and has been strewn and stacked with corpses. Nadir Shah put one hundred thousand to death, Timur had done worse, and the Mahrattas were the worst of all; so that the butchery after the Mutiny siege of Delhi was but another regrettable incident in its history. At the far end of the street towers the red sandstone gateway of Shah Jahan's fort, and driving in under this portal fit for kings and triumphal armies, we found sepoys lounging on charpoys by the guard-house door, tunics unbuttoned, turbans awry and at loose ends, and Moslem shoes hanging from one bare toe —the *sans gêne* of the race undisturbed by the noble environment or the contrasting presence of the tramping sentry on duty, turbaned and accoutred to perfection, spindle legs wound with smooth puttees, and the enormous English shoes blacked to a drill-sergeant's dream. Such loungers at the guard-house door are on view at every show fort and palace in India, incongruous, disillusioning, but thereby the real thing. Incongruity is the regular order in India, splendor and shabbiness, dirt and riches, luxury and squalor always going together. We were free to roam the courts and garden spaces of the palace unhindered, from Shah Jahan's open audience-hall, or music-room, with its panels of Florentine mosaic on black marble ground, to that inner throne-room, the most splendid in the world. This peerless Diwan-i-Khas, one mass of rich decoration from the inlaid floor to the golden ceiling, was worthy setting for the Peacock Throne. The renegade Frenchman or Italian who planned the palaces of Shah Jahan, and the skilled workmen brought from all the centers of Mohammedan luxury, made the Delhi palace equal in decorative details to the Agra palace and the Taj. "If there is on earth an Eden of bliss, it is this, it is this, it is this," was appropriately inlaid in Persian letters in this throne-room, whose square columns, arches, spandrils, frieze, and moldings are decorated with exquisite pietra dura. A small dais shows where stood the Peacock Throne, that low, square chair completely sheathed in rubies, pearls, diamonds, emeralds, and other stones, the Koh-i-nur one of the peacock's eyes, and a life-sized parrot cut from a single emerald its crowning ornament. That fabled emerald parrot, like the so-called emerald Buddha at Bangkok, was undoubtedly nothing but a very fine and clear piece of *fei tsui* jade, but it went with all the other loot that Nadir Shah carried away in 1739—loot the value of which amounted to thirty-eight million pounds, and which was scattered by the Kurds when he was murdered. India was drained of its riches then, for no good end. After Nadir Shah had gone his way with the Peacock and nine other jeweled thrones, this palace suffered neglect as well as sacking. When Lord Auckland's sisters saw it in 1838, the old King of Delhi sat in a neglected garden, his own dirty soldiers lounged on dirty charpoys in the beautiful inlaid bath-rooms, and the precious inlays were being stolen, bit by bit, from the rooms of the princes. One regrets the destruction that followed the Mutiny, when the zenana and whole labyrinths of guest-rooms were torn away to make space for barracks. Sir James Fergusson has dealt with these destroying British barbarians very thoroughly in "Indian and Eastern Architecture" (Vol. II, p. 208), and hands on to immortality the name of Sir John Jones, who tore up the platform of the Peacock Throne and divided it into sections which he sold as table-tops, the pair now in the India Museum at London having fetched him five hundred pounds.

The audience-halls, the baths, and the rooms around the Diwan-i-Khas were repaired and restored at great expense in preparation for the Prince of Wales's visit in 1876, and close watchfulness has maintained them in that condition. One can only wish that for completeness' sake a glass copy of the Peacock Throne might be installed in the original's place. Tourists would gladly contribute their annas to that worthy end.

The Jama Masjid, the largest and certainly the most imposing mosque in India, lifts its minarets across a great park where troops of great apes race madly, alert for the pious Hindus, whom one often sees ostentatiously feeding them inferior boiled rice, "to acquire merit." The great gateway of the mosque, high on a terraced platform, is second only to Akbar's Gate of Victory, and, opening formerly only for the Mogul emperor, swings widely now when the Viceroy visits it. On Friday mornings ten and twelve thousand people worship there; in festival times four times as many assemble. The priests are friendly, and in one of the lesser minarets show one richly illuminated copies of the Koran, Mohammed's slipper filled with jasmine blossoms, and finally one henna-red hair from the beard of the Prophet. There is a busy market around the steps of the great gateway on certain days, when grotesque two-story camel-wagons bring in country produce; dealers in poultry hold one side of the terrace steps and bird-fanciers the other. We had eaten mutton-chops from Tuticorin northward, but had never seen a live sheep until we heard its familiar voice by Jama Masjid's steps. But what flocks of goats we had seen in pastures, on country roads and city streets! "It is poultry," said the bearer as we regarded the fat-tailed sheep with curiosity, his application of

KUTAB MINAR.

the word "poultry" meaning tame or domestic as distinguished from "jungle," which defines a wild fowl or animal. "Yes, the peacock is poultry," he answered quickly, but when we inquired about the elephants and camels standing round he hesitated. "Yes. Certainly. The elephant once was jungle, and the camble too; but now they both are poultry."

The little Jain temple and the Black Temple of the Hindus are sanctuaries of other Delhi sects, but we forgot conventional sights and the rivalry of religions when we met a wedding procession in the labyrinth of streets in that quarter. The horses wore gold, silver, and jeweled bridles, head-stalls and necklaces to match, and gold-embroidered cloths and trappings. The bridegroom's brother was a dazzling, kincob-clad person, jeweled to distraction, with wreaths and tassels of jasmine covering him from crown to waist, and the bridegroom was twice as splendid. The populace gaped and ran after the cavalcade, and half-naked beggars flocked with extended palms. "Jao! Jao!" said the bridegroom's brother in a voice to make a policeman tremble; and swish! came his jeweled whip on the bare shoulders of one insistent petitioner. With a yelp of pain and a spiritless whine, the beggar slunk away.

Delhi remains the center of all Indian art industries. The most skilful jewelers and gem-cutters, painters, carvers, embroiderers, and craftsmen whose creations could tempt the purse or minister to the luxury of the greater and lesser Moguls, have gathered there for centuries, and trade habits are but slowly broken. Along Chandni Chauk plump merchants in snow-white clothes and tiny jeweler's turbans invite one to their white, washed, felt-floored inner rooms; and there, treading cat-like in stockinged feet, they unroll gold and silver embroideries, Kashmir shawls, and "camble's-hair" stuffs, and cover the last inches of floor space with jewels. Necklaces, girdles, and a queen's ornaments are drawn from battered boxes, scraps of paper, cotton cloth, or old flannel. Nothing seems quite as incongruous in this land of the misfit and the incongruous as the way in which the jewels of a raja are produced from old biscuit-tins, pickle-bottles, and marmalade-jars. One buys the gems of a temple goddess, and they are laid in grimy cotton-wool and packed in rusty little tin boxes of a crudity inconceivable. While on the claim the Klondike miner considers the makeshift of a baking-powder box, as a safe deposit for his nuggets and dust, as a huge joke; but the Hindu jeweler does it with no sense of the unfitness of things, of relative propriety in splendor. "Memsahib does not like tin box? Very well. See!" and the ruby necklace was wrapped in a bit of newspaper, and put in a broken pasteboard box that had held a druggist's prescription. When they have covered the floor with their most valuable stuffs, the shopmen walk over them without compunction, pull them here and there, and throw them in heaps into the corners. When this happens several times a day, and the traps are bundled to and from the hotels night and morning, it is small wonder that everything offered one is mussy, wrinkled, and shop-worn. Despite the lures and promises of the toy turban tribe, no important pieces of carved or jeweled jade were seen. To them any green stone was jade, and under that name they brought out serpentine, bowenite, and chloro-melanite—anything soft and easily worked that would look as well. Three generations of one family are no longer employed in carving one jade bowl, as in Mogul times. Art is fleeting now, and the lapidaries want quick sales and as large returns as the tourist's enlightenment permits.

One may handle these Delhi jewels by the hour and not see a flawless stone, a spherical pearl, or any string of pearls matched perfectly in size, shape, skin, or luster; and one moves in and breathes such an atmosphere of jewels in Delhi that he soon regards precious stones as the usual, serious accompaniment of daily life. A prosaic tourist, never given to such weaknesses, soon finds himself hanging and haggling over jewels, buying unset stones and gewgaws to indiscretion. From the earliest breakfast hour to the last home-coming at dusk, and until the train bears him away from the station platform, open jewel-boxes and rows of necklaces spread on cloths or shawl-ends are put before him. Some insinuating Lal This or Lal That, with caste-marked brow and tiny turban, is always salaaming and begging him to buy his blue *ferozees* (turquoises), or necklaces of the nine lucky stones. A tap at the door, and it opens to show a brown face and a tassel of necklaces swinging from a brown hand; and in time the victim is hypnotized by the glittering objects. There is bitter trade rivalry among the jewelers and their touts, and one cannot visit the shop or buy of one of the Lals without being denounced and upbraided for partiality by all the other Lals. "Please come my shop. Please buy my shop. I am only honest man. I am poor man," said one oily tongue, putting his fingers to his mouth in dumb show of rice-eating. "Yes, yes," we said to the importunate as we drove away from the hotel, and a fierce-eyed, viperish-looking Hindu made a flying leap to the other step of the carriage and hissed: "Don't go his shop. He is bad man. He cheat. He lie. His ferozees are all glass, chalk. I speak true. I am honest man. I have true stones. I am poor man. Please buy my shop." An emphatic "Jao!" made him drop away from the carriage step. Winding up his loose end of red shawl, he went back to the door-step and squatted there in apparent fraternity with the wicked rival—both blood-brothers in lying and cheating, both waiting for fresh prey, the tourist the righteous victim for such swindlers in all countries.

After much looking and comparing, a friend of that Indian winter bought a ruby necklace, and as she stowed it away in her inside strong pocket her particular Lal said, "Please, ladyship, do not show any one here in Delhi. Let no man know that I have sold, that you have bought my 'niklass.' Those bad fellows at hotel do something if they know I sell." We strolled for an hour along the Chandni Chauk, when we were met by our servant with a closed carriage and drove to the Ridge. As the horses slowed down for the long hill climb, the box was opened for a look at the new purchase. Hardly had the owner wound it over her hand, when the kincob turban and viper countenance of the rival jeweler was thrust in the open window. There was an "Ah" of such venomous rage that we screamed in alarm. The head vanished, and this sleuth-hound of jewelers, who had shadowed us all day and clung to the back of the carriage, was seen speeding like a deer back to the city.

"Oh, I found Delhi so sad, so depressing. All those scenes of the Mutiny, you know—the Kashmir Gate and the Ridge, don't you know. It was so terrible that I was really glad to get away," said an English visitor. The ruby collar and the detective jeweler had put us beyond any depression incident to the visit to the Ridge, familiar as is its history when one has read Lord Roberts's "Forty-one Years in India" and Mrs. Steele's "On the Face of the Waters." At Delhi, too, one feels that there have been too many sieges and reliefs in these later days for the events of 1857 to be dinned into one quite so endlessly. Newspaper readers are all strategical experts now, and they balance and measure the horrors and heroisms of the siege of Delhi against the modern ones; match the storming of the Kashmir Gate with the glorious storming of the South Gate of Tientsin and of the East Gate of Peking by the Japanese in the China campaign of 1900.

From the Ridge one looks down upon the great plain where the annual camp of exercise, or the great military manœuvers, are held each year. The great durbar or Delhi meeting of 1877 was held on this same plain, when Lord Lytton proclaimed the Queen of England as Empress of India in the presence of all the feudatory princes and an assemblage of more than one hundred thousand people. The plain was the scene also of the greater durbar of 1903, when Lord Curzon proclaimed King Edward VII of England as Emperor of India, with a pageantry and splendor unapproached in modern times,—the most magnificent state ceremony that has ever been seen.

CHAPTER XVII

OLD DELHI

ONE gets the full sense of antiquity in driving south from Delhi for eleven miles over a plain strewn with the ruins of seven earlier cities that preceded this modern Delhi, or Shah Jahanabad. Dwellings have crumbled away, but forts and tombs have withstood the ages, and there is a very feast of graveyards all the way to the Kutab minar. Hoariest of all the memorials is the carved stone column of Asoka (240 B.C.), inscribed with the Buddha's precepts against the taking of life, and which stands in Tughlak's ruined fort at Firozabad. At ruined Indrapat are the remains of the lovely inlaid mosque and the tall tower from which the emperor Humayum fell while studying the stars; and near by is the splendid red sandstone mausoleum erected for him by his widow and his son Akbar. A century after its erection, this domed tomb of Humayum furnished the model for the Taj Mahal, and one quickly notes the main points of resemblance between this massive red building and the white dream at Agra. Humayum's tomb stands upon the same sort of high platform, but lacks the slender minarets at the corners. The red building and its white marble dome are larger than the more delicately modeled, the more ornate, poetic, and feminine structure at Agra. The last scene of the Mutiny was played here when Hobson's men overtook Bahadur Shah, the fugitive Delhi king, and returned the next day for the princes, shot them, and exposed their bodies in the blood-soaked, corpse-strewn Chandni Chauk. Bahadur Shah lived in exile at Rangoon for forty years, and his son, childless and born in exile, a harmless nonentity, was permitted to return to India for the durbar of 1903.

At Humayum's tomb we left the tree-bordered Muttra road, where camel-wagons and strings of donkeys moved phantom-like through the dusty frost haze: the air so very sharp that one wondered how pipul- and tamarind-trees could retain their foliage. The revel of death and ruins, the feast of tombs and mortuary architecture, continued for miles, the names of the honored dead conveying no idea of personality, having no association of individuality to one, all this past so vague and unfamiliar that one moralizes, like Omar, on the vanity of man. One at last identifies four tombs—that of Akbar's brother, that of the Chisti saint, that of a Persian poet and that of the unhappy emperor Mohammed Shah, last occupant of the Peacock Throne so thoroughly despoiled by Nadir Shah. The saint, who was something of a juggler and miracle-worker, a Mohammedan mahatma, rests in a little white jewel-box of marble, whose red awnings give a comforting color-note to the chill court. The saint built a well guaranteed not to drown any one who leaped into it, and a lean boy in a tattered sheet begged us to see him jump. "One rupee—only one rupee, memsahib. *Ek rupia.*" He fell, anna by anna, to half that price. We shivered in furs to think of a cold plunge in that icy air and keen wind, and finally bargained, in the presence of the priest, to give him six annas if he would go home, put on more clothes, and not jump that day. One crazy foreigner more or less, with notions crazier than the last one, could not disturb a molla; but as it was past his prophesying what we might not pay six annas for, in the course of our crass philanthropy, he himself conducted us about and to the tomb of Khusrau, " the sweet-singing parrot of India, memsahib." Khusrau was a Turk, but his Persian verses were so beautiful that Sadi made a pilgrimage from Persia to pay homage, and to this day all the gild of Delhi musicians and dancers remember him with garlands and bouquets. In this group of tombs is that of Jahanira, the daughter of Shah Jahan and Mumtaz-i-Mahal, who is a very real personage. Her years of devotion to her blind and captive father, her long life of piety and goodness, dying unmarried at the age of sixty-seven, warranted her burial in the Taj Mahal, or the Jama Masjid at Agra, built especially for her, rather than with that mixed but interesting company in the suburbs of Delhi.

The most beautiful tomb of them all is that of Mirza Jahangir, Akbar's son,—a platform of white marble supporting a white marble screen, with heavy doors of marble carved in low relief, likewise the lintels, cornice, and base—a dream of decoration, a symphony in white. Near by is another arrangement in white marble in low relief and latticework surrounding unhappy Mohammed, once the wearer of the Koh-i-nur and occupant of the Peacock Throne, who concealed the great diamond in his turban and then was courteously invited to change turbans by Nadir Shah. If ever death had beautiful and artistic recompense, "it is here, it is here, it is here," surely. Remembering the monstrosities of monuments and mausoleums in our Western graveyards, the broken columns, cremation urns, and misapplied Greek vase shapes that make our cemeteries places of horror, one wishes that committees on American public monuments and memorials might study these Indian tombs. Akbar's brother has also a marble sarcophagus carved in finest lacework, that rests under a great open pavilion, a marble canopy supported by sixty-four carved columns. While we stood enthusiastic by this exquisite tomb, comparing it with the domed sentry-box by the Hudson where lies America's greatest soldier, a piercing wail arose. A lone turban on a near roof was waving a yak-tail in air as the voice wailed so dismally. Soon black specks in the furthest sky defined themselves as hurrying bird-shapes, hovered like gigantic butterflies directly between us and the zenith sun, and whirled in prismatic beauty to our feet, a homing flock of pigeons. Like foot-soldiers, these winged creatures obeyed the voice and signals of their keeper, went through their evolutions, and caught the grain thrown in air. Afterward we recognized the pigeon-

DETAIL OF KUTAB MINAR.

keeper's frequent cry from Delhi roofs, and watched obedient flocks circle and wheel at the will of invisible owners.

After five miles of temples, tombs, and graves we had had our fill of mortuary constructions, and, to the consternation of the bearer, refused to descend for Safdar Jang's tomb. "What, memsahib! Not see Safdar Jang? Everybody must see. Very nice tomb. Three-story place, that tomb. Gentries always go see that tomb." But we were obdurate. Safdar Jang was only the unlucky vizier of an inconspicuous Somebody Shah, and Fergusson had said that the mausoleum would "not bear close inspection."

All this time we were conscious of a slender, dark lance lifted against the sky-line. It was what we had come so far to see—the Kutab minar, one of the seven great sights of India, and certainly the most beautiful tower in the world. It grew as we advanced, until each angle, balcony, and band of lettering on its three red sandstone sections declared itself, and the flat, white marble sections at the summit were merged in inconspicuous perspective. This remarkable Kutab is emphatically such a departure from all the round or square towers ever seen that one has no wish to consider how it might have looked if constructed of one material throughout, or if the bands of ornament, the balconies, and the honeycomb work had been omitted. It is so richly decorated, it is itself so decorative, that at moments it seems as if it were only the fancy of a season, a mere World's Fair fantasy in staff or stucco, instead of a solidly built tower that has stood there for a thousand years, enduring earthquakes and sieges, and restorations by the later Moguls. One has to mount the roof of the mosque and see the great shaft at the level of its lowest bands of ornament to realize its size and the beauty and sharpness of those bold letters. One willingly traverses rubbish-heaps to do homage to the builder, Kutab-uddin, the Pathan ruler, who rose from slavery to the throne, and who, before the completion of his Tower of Victory, was laid away. One feels a personal loss and deprivation, too, that Ala-uddin, two centuries later, did not finish his great minaret, which would have repeated the Kutab on larger lines, and mounted five hundred feet in air,—twice the height of the Kutab,—the entire surface faced with carved stones. Viewing the Kutab at close range and from afar, one remembers pityingly the campaniles and giraldas, obelisks, spires, and pinnacles of the West. They used to do this thing so much better in India.

The Kutab is so entirely the thing at Old Delhi, that one lags in enthusiasm over the mosque, with its ruined arches and its hundred carved columns, spoil of Buddhist and Jain temples that the Pathans destroyed. To-day interest in the mosque court centers in the wrought-iron column, whose Sanskrit inscription dates back to the first century of our era. Native tourists flock to it as the great sight, and believe that if one reaches around the column backward and touches his hands together, good luck will follow him. The tomb of Altamsh, who built the mosque, and the one remaining gate of the court declare the scale of ornamentation that once covered all these crumbled walls and arches. Every inch of the roofless tomb is covered with carved ornament,—inscriptions, traceries, arabesques, and geometrical designs—the most ornamented mausoleum in India.

In the chilly, whitewashed vaults of the rest-house in the shadow of the Kutab, with dusty chicks to exclude any pernicious sunshine, we shivered over the cold, cold tiffin we had brought with us. Not hot bouillion nor hot chocolate could mitigate the death chill of that interior, or our interiors, and we hastened to drive with the wind four miles to the tomb of Tughlak. That massive, fortress-like place, of characteristic Egyptian solidity, was in extreme contrast to the highly ornamented tombs we had been seeing all day. The sloping walls and the entire absence of ornament came as a surprise, but the Pathan emperor has the ideal warrior's tomb. A crumbling wall half screens the ruins of his deserted capital of Tughlakabad, within which Tughlak's fortress is as Egyptian as his suburban tomb.

Some street-dancers pleaded with us at the hotel door, followed around and tapped on our windows, and we relented and moved the tea-table to the terrace, where it was really warmer than in the house. The two women, in cheap cottons and cheap jewelry, posed and whirled to a monotonous measure beaten on a skin drum. One woman gracefully carried a tiny child on her hip, or set it down on the cold flags, where it played contentedly with its fingers. Both dancers wore voluminous accordion-plaited skirts of red cotton, with yellow head-sheets patterned in red, and they were covered, as with breastplates, by many silver-coin necklaces. One dancer was a tall, sinuous creature, with a markedly Jewish or Egyptian face, who did the serpentine dance of Cairo cafés, and bent backward to pick up a rupee from the ground with her eyelids. Every step was marked by the jingle and clash of her bracelets and anklets, and this serpent of old Jumna, after one lively measure, paused and spread out her crinkled draperies in great butterfly-wings behind her in a "Loie Fuller pose" as old as Delhi. We had lamps and more lamps brought, eyes and turbans uncounted gathered in the dusk, and, inspired by native approval and tourist rupees, the skirt dance went on through many figures.

We sent runners to find them the next morning. We wanted them to dance at noon, that we might turn a battery of kodaks upon them. "Those are very poor, common dancers," said the bearer, scornfully. "I will get very splendid nautches, in silk and kincob saris and very splendid jewels, in 'niklasses' and 'griddles' of rubies and pearls." But we wanted only those same dancers in their cheap clothes and silver necklaces and girdles; and it took insistence to get them. They came; and in the sunlight their silver and glass, brass and lac jewelry were as gems, and our enthusiasm was greater than that of the night before. They danced their best, held their poses interminably for the time exposures, and we reeled film away so recklessly that the hotel manager said: "Oh, madam, if you have so many plates to spare, won't you take my baby?"

STREET DANCERS, DELHI.

CHAPTER XVIII

LAHORE

EVEN the Delhi bullocks were blanketed the day we left for Lahore and the farther, colder Northwest. We had bought more and more razais as we went up-country, until the *bichauna*, or rolls of traveling bedding, would barely pass through a car door, and, finally, yards of heavy pashmina cloth to wind around us in makeshift Indian fashion. The memorial Mutiny cross, standing high on the Ridge, was the last seen of Delhi; and there followed a few wayside stations with shivering platform groups, an uninteresting sunset over a dusty, barren plain; dinner at Saharanpur, and merciful darkness, while we jolted on until five o'clock in the morning.

It was dark night when we were whirled through Lahore's frosty streets, to find warm rooms with real coal fires in open grates. We reappeared with the latest British breakfasters at the long table d'hôte, and in the city of his youth we found a whole table full of Kipling characters—English army people and civil servants. We could almost call them all by name, and life at that hotel was a continuous dramatization of stories known by heart. What a company they were! And how they denied their maker, or portrait-painter, when we said Kipling to them! There was the major's wife, fat, brune, and long past forty, wrinkles drawn in lines of pearl powder around her eyes and under her chin. She wore a youthful sailor-hat, a frizzed front, and a Bath bun, and had all the kittenish ways of sweet sixteen. Her most devoted cavalier, in a cloud of attentive subalterns, was a callow blond, young enough to be her grandson; and if there had been no one else in the hotel, we should have had entertainment enough in the kitten-play of this elderly charmer. When not making eyes and simpering at her courtiers, she queened it over the "leftenants'" and captains' wives, and was inclined to snub a commissioner's daughter. She looked us over critically through a lorgnette, just as we had stared at the tigers and chetahs at the Zoo, and put to us those direct British questions that the rural Yankee cannot match. Having disclosed our relationships, our nationality, our past and future itinerary, and explained the other tourists as far as we knew them, we reversed the situation in Li Hung Chang fashion, and interviewed the interviewer. It always touches the sensitive nerve and presses the button of Anglo-Indian loquacity to mention Kipling, and away went the major's lady like a steeplechaser when we said that Lahore only meant Kipling to us. "No one in India reads Kipling," she said impressively. "We do not esteem him at all. He does not tell the truth about anything. Why, he was a very common, low sort of person here. He only associated with the 'Tommies,' as you see by his books—all full of things about the sergeants' and the soldiers' wives and their class. Of course, as he never associated with ladies, or went with the nice chaps of the regiments, how could he know anything about society, about Government House, or the Simla sets? Why, in that ridiculous story—" and she told me in detail how he had it all wrong about the Gadsbys, the Hauksbees, and others; for she knew some people who were in Simla that year, and it was this way, etc., etc. In fact, all those ancient and historic scandals were degrees worse than Kipling makes them out; for the Anglo-Indians allow no imagination to the novelist, every tale must be identified with some real event in their own experience. As to whether Kipling truly delineated native character—"Dear me, how should I know anything about the nasty creatures! As if we paid any attention to them! Government has schools and does altogether too much for them, anyhow." And then the memsahib, who of course did not speak Hindustani, who never came in contact with native women of any but the servant class, and who fitted exactly into the situation that Mrs. Steele upbraids, denounced that champion of the native people. It was quite like the creoles of New Orleans and Mr. Cable; but having heard Macaulay berated, Max Müller scoffed at, and Sir William Hunter denounced, it was taken with many grains of salt.

More interesting than anything inside the Lahore Museum is the fine old bronze cannon before its door—the Sikhs cherished Zamzamah, a national trophy glorified to them by history and legend, and immortalized to all English-speaking people as the gun bestrode by Kim the Rishti, when the Lama first appeared to him. The rich collections in the "wonder-house" were assembled and arranged by the elder Kipling, the white-bearded curator whom the Lama met there. Its unique treasures are the Greco-Buddhist sculptures which General Cunningham found on the site of the ancient Gandhara (modern Peshawar), capital of the Scythian empire when Buddhism was the state religion—majestic statues of Gautama as priest and prince, and bas-reliefs as exquisite as the Alexander sarcophagus. The arts of later India are well shown, and fine old carved and inlaid doors, panels, balconies, window latticings, and house-fronts serve as models for the students of the art school which J. L. Kipling founded and directed to such successful degree before he left India. Copies of these old carvings are sold at prices that torment the American, who, after paying their cost and transportation, nearly must pay for them over again at his home custom-house, in order to protect steam furniture-factories. Silver, brass- and copper-work, lacquers, potteries, textiles, and embroideries from the Panjab are gathered there, and the model of the Koh-i-nur has pathetic interest in Lahore, its last home. In January the stone walls and stone floors of the museum create an ice-edged atmosphere more benumbing than the death-dealing chill of the Lateran galleries in Rome, and one soon flees from it.

The tomb of Anarkali, given first place in the guide-book, and warranted the most interesting thing in Lahore, drew us to the domed white building, in turn occupied as the English civilian church and as local offices. Anarkali, pretty "Pomegranate Blossom," was one of Akbar's wives, and, being seen to smile when Akbar's son, Jahangir, entered the harem, was buried alive. Akbar held the trial after the execution, and must have had a very bad conscience, judging from the beauty of the little mausoleum and the white marble sarcophagus, covered every inch with the finest ornament and lettering in relief. It is a thing to be kept under glass and shown as the chief treasure of a museum; but British officialdom has shoved it aside, out from under the center of its dome, to an alcove where we pursued it around desks and braziers and wooden chairs, a babu in woolen neck-comforter obligingly lifting a heap of papers that we might see all the sculptured surface. Throughout Lahore splendid Moslem tombs were turned to practical use after British occupation. Even Government House was adapted from the tomb of Akbar's cousin, with additions to meet later requirements. When such desecration began, the angry Mohammedans foretold death within a year to all such vandals, and when any prophet's reputation was at stake he took care that poison, as a last resort, should verify his forecast. The Bengali babus perched on high stools around the mausoleum were amused at our indignant comments. Nothing could please them more than any affronts to Mohammedan prejudices or sensibilities, and the hatred between the men of the two religions is something one slowly realizes. The Mohammedan despises the Hindu and his sacred cow, and loves to kill and eat the peacock, while, in return, the Hindu delights in defiling Mohammedan precincts with the loathed dog and pig; and in Lahore the Sikhs are against both religions and have long scores to settle. In "On the City Walls," Kipling shows the turmoil accompanying any religious festival. The Mohammedan deeply hates the babu, but until the recent establishment of the Aligarh College had made no effort to put forward Mohammedan youth as rival to the glib Bengali in preparing for public service.

The street crowds of Lahore were more picturesque even than those of Delhi. A different type of man had appeared overnight, or rather the occasional whiskered giants seen on the Chandni Chauk were here universal—more beard, more turban, yards and yards more cloth in the baggy trousers and shoulder shawls. The long coats of the Persians, the flaring, crossed Chinese coat of Turkestan and Tibet appeared, and there were stray Afghans, too, picturesque and ferocious giants, wearing peaked turbans, sheepskin coats, and striped shoulder shawls. When we had left the orderly civil lines and had gone through the city gates, we entered the land of the Arabian Nights, more of color, incident, and picturesqueness to be seen in the bazaars of Lahore than anywhere else in India. Queer, ramshackle houses towered along the narrow streets, some frescoed in colors, their fronts broken by balconies, loggias, bay-windows, and latticings of dark, carved

THE ROOFS AND BALCONIES OF LAHORE.

wood, with flat roofs and parapets at every elevation —roofs that Kim ran over, roofs where the women gasped in "The City of Dreadful Night"; for, although Lahore is so far north, it is one of the hottest places in summer,—Meean Mir cantonment the acknowledged "oven of India," where epidemics always rage their worst.

All Lahore was muffled and bundled in cotton clothes and brilliant chuddas, and all sought the sun that crisp, frosty morning, until the streets held a living, moving rainbow mass and every shop-front seemed set for color effect. Women in gay head-sheets and children in satin jackets sunned themselves in window-frames of dark-brown fretted woodwork; and Mohammedan women in white cloaks falling full from round crown-pieces, with latticed holes for the eyes, wandered in the brilliant company, giving it still more the air of a fancy-dress ball. The carnival crowds, moving against such fantastic background, made one listen for slow music to accompany this stately spectacular march. It seemed as though the Lahore bazaars were but painted wings, drops, and flies, the crowds one well-drilled theatrical troupe—a continuous performance kept up for our benefit. All the industries were picturesque, every shop decorative, and we stood fascinated, to watch the baker reaching down into the deep mud oven with a hooked wire and bringing out pancake loaves of bread; the dyer stirring his vats, wringing out lengths of cloth and festooning them over the front of his shop; the printer, next door, stamping block patterns on turban ends, and the Kashmiri men and boys, cross-legged in alcoves, embroidering gold turban ends or fine shawl borders. One Kashmiri in purple satin jacket and a yellow turban worked with gold wire, while a small boy in a sleeveless red jacket and a woman in a headsheet of vivid pink looked on. Heaps of oranges and pale bananas, red Kashmiri apples, and green Kabul grapes made set color studies on every fruit-stand. The dried-sweetmeat shops were as rich in combinations of browns and tawny orange, and the curry-shops were as satisfying with their strands of red peppers and baskets of red, white, yellow, brown, and greenish meal. Candy-sellers crouched in the open with trays of sticky sweets, beseeching us to keep our shadows away. Having thus defiled a tray of *gujack,* we bought it and found many idlers willing to eat the defiled sesame brittle, made of sesame seeds, sorghum syrup, seedless raisins, almond meal, and crescents of thin cocoanut strips, the rich "fudge" rolled out in a thin pancake over a foot in diameter. Silk-shops, brass- and pottery-shops, gem-cutters' and shoemakers' dens, were all decorative and interesting. The tea-shops, with steaming samovars, were significant of the dreaded Russian advance and influence. The red beans of New England and pop-corn had a familiar look even in such strange environment.

After a revel in this living picturesqueness we went ruefully back to conventional sight-seeing and did the Jama Masjid, with its superb inlaid arches, and saw the relics of the Prophet. We saw Runjeet Singh's tomb, its carved doors and gay mirror and plaster interior, where Sikh priests shouted from the sacred books, waved peacock feathers, and threw jasmine garlands over us. We saw also Akbar's fort and palace—tawdry and flat after the splendors of Delhi; our fancy arrested by the inlaid hall known as the Naulahka, name also of a quarter of the outer city of Lahore. When the Sikhs captured Lahore they wreaked themselves on these halls of Jahangir and Shah Jahan, and the British barrack-builder has done the rest. The Scotch corporal who showed us through dwelt mostly on some finely damascened and grained guns, chain-mail, swords, and Sikh knives in the armory. In one pavilion the fantastic mirror and plaster walls were crying aloud at some hideous European carpets and furniture—the rankest of "Tottenham Court Road furniture." Small wonder that the Viceroy exhorted the Indian princes to patronize their own craftsmen when it came to palace furnishings. This pavilion commands a fine view out over the parapet of the city wall to the park below, with the blue windings of the Ravi beyond distant trees; but the best-remembered palace sight was a Sikh sergeant's wife, who was a walking jewel-show, covered from crown to ringed toe with such an array of ornaments as one might expect an emperor's favorite to wear. We expressed our thanks for the pleasure of seeing her, to the amusement of the Scot and the pride of the Sikh proprietor of the jeweled jade.

After a hasty tiffin with the Kipling crowd, who were full bent on the regimental tea and polo-match of the afternoon, we took a hastier look at the unusual animals of the "lion and tiger museum," where the most remarkable sight was a monkey holding a looking-glass that it might see to pick its teeth and prick its throat with a dangerous-looking darning-needle. We hastened back to the native city, and from the time we left the "Europe shops" and the avenue of trees with shabby tram-cars jingling by and penetrated the city gate, we moved in an ideal East, an Arabian Nights' revel of Mohammedan picturesqueness. The half-mile bazaar between Vazir Khan's and the Golden Mosque is the heart of Lahore, all the people and trades of the Panjab being exhibited there. In that narrow lane between the balconied houses, where every window flaunted some flaming turban or shawl, and each alcove shop was set for theatrical effect and overflowed to the street, there moved the same brilliantly costumed company of the morning. All picturesqueness and color centered in greatest intensity at the gateway of the Vazir Khan Mosque, single figures and groups in tableaux tempting the kodak, until we feared we should have no more film left after Lahore. Before that glorious portal, its façade a dream of soft old Persian tiles, there congregated barbers, beggars, peddlers, money-changers, letter-writers, and smithies, prostrate bullocks, venders of fat-tailed sheep, donkeys loaded with vegetables, hawkers, idlers, and busy people of every kind. "Remove thy heart from the gardens of the world, and know that this building is the true abode of man," is written in slender letters on the blue and green Persian tiles of the mosque front; and

SCHOOL-BOYS IN THE VAZIR KHAN MOSQUE, LAHORE.

AFGHAN FALCONER, PESHAWAR.

a legion of beggars have taken the Vazir at his word, lounging on the steps and in sunny corners all day, and sleeping at night in the quiet court overlooked by two minarets. Professional menders sit patching rags as though waiting for kodaks to come that way, and a balcony off the cloister overlooks the busy street, exactly as an opera-box commands less spectacular effects.

There was a sound like the chirp of many birds, and a school-teacher led three hundred small boys into the court. Each youngster put his books, coat, shoes, and turban-cloth in a heap, and knelt by the tank to bathe hands and feet before prayer. The teacher patrolled the lines with a stick, trouncing a laggard here and thrashing a boy there into the line and order of piety. When the unruly and restless flock were purified, a leader among them gave a call, and all filed in under the arches and prostrated themselves on the inlaid floor, facing westward to Mecca. One small turban explained to us that they came there every day to "pray to God," and the pious scamp showed me on the last leaf of his school-book: "In the name of God, the Most Merciful, this is my book. The property of Hassan Khan. Do not steal."

When we had seen the three gilded bubble domes of the Golden Mosque reflected in the tank of its white court, and the Hindus going through their purification rites at the temple by the bo-tree, the bearer was for carrying us back through the Delhi Gate to the silver-shops and Europe shops and the shops for Kashmir work and Bokhara silks, to hunt for green slippers with seed-pearl toes, for Peshawar shoes woven of strips of leather on models used by Alexander the Great's shoemaker—to hunt for Yarkand jade and Ladak turquoises, but our interest in such shops was gone. "Drive back," we said; and, repassing the mosque, we threaded again all those brilliant bazaars, were blocked in a narrow lane by a funeral, and came out finally on a common by the fort, where men and boys were flying kites. A crowd was jeering and cheering the fliers, and one bearded parent soundly boxed his son's ears when he bungled in launching his paper shield. "Drive back," and we worked slowly again to the Delhi Gate, where the crowds had even increased. Once more we threaded the brilliant labyrinth and saw the kite-fliers reel in their chargers. A spectacular sunset fired the sky, and when for the fifth time we traversed the narrow lanes, they were lanes of twinkling enchantment, every window and alcove carrying its kerosene-lamp and torches flaring by the Vazir Khan. The frosty air was laden with the bazaar's mixed smell of raw sugar, incense, spices, grease, and wood smoke, and only a dinner-company of Kipling's own could have drawn us away.

It was almost a surprise the next morning to find the streets, the shops, the crowds, the tiled front of the mosque all there, to find Lahore bazaars solid realities, and not dreams. We saw Shalimar Gardens, the triple-terraced home of the nightingale, once an imperial pleasure-ground, arranged like one seen in dreams, but now a rather dusty, dreary place of formal flower-beds, fountains, marble cascades, and canals, that becomes a palace garden of enchantment when illuminated for viceregal functions. More interesting was the drive to the Ravi and across a bridge of boats, where the passage of bullock-carts and trains of donkeys was regulated by the bridge-keeper's drum-beats. We found Jahangir's tomb deep down in a square marble terrace in another formal garden, where orange-trees hung full of fruit and flower-beds were masses of bloom. This son of Akbar, the reputed Christian, who at least wore a rosary and was so bad a Moslem that he drank to inebriety, spent his summers in the Vale of Kashmir with his clever Persian wife, Nur Jahan,—Nur Mahal, the Harem's Pride, told of in "Lalla Rookh," and who seems a very real personage. He is laid away in an octagonal chamber deep down in a solid square terrace, in such a cenotaph as rivals that of Anarkali. Instead of white relief carving, Jahangir's sarcophagus is inlaid, quite the most beautiful piece of pietra dura that I had seen. Flowers and arabesques are inlaid with large pieces of amethyst, lapis, jade, and carnelian, and the ninety-nine names of Allah in fine black marble letters surround the sarcophagus. Runjeet Singh despoiled the tomb of its upper pavilions and marble pavement, but the British have repaved and restored the terrace—and viceregal tea-tables are now spread directly over the body of Jahangir, and all is as gay as when he made it a feast-place before his death.

CHAPTER XIX

THE END OF THE INDIAN EMPIRE

IT was a damp and dreary, a raw and chilly afternoon when we drove away from Kipling's people and waited for an hour in that drafty, echoing fortress—the Lahore railway station. The Northern Railway across the Panjab, being a government line, is subject to delays and alterations of schedule to suit special needs, and the red carpets at hand for the arrival of the "L. G." of the Panjab on the following afternoon promised greater delays had we deferred our start. As all first-class cars are run at a loss on Indian railways, we could not complain at the usual forlorn conveyance; but the rattling window-panes of blue or violet glass, admitting the chill, actinic light, made the shabby car drearier and dingier than usual, and seemed to add degrees of cold to the air. The bleak and stony yellow plain, like the sage-brush and alkali wastes of Nevada, looked snow-covered through these tinted glasses, and the cold, blue, depressing light finally suggested the experiments made with invalids, lunatics, and plants at the time of the blue-glass craze and cure of so long ago. It was impossible to read in the jolting carriage, and we could only draw rugs and razais about us and watch the drear landscape roll by as the trucks thundered over the dusty roadbed. The groups on station platforms grew more pinched and more uncomfortable-looking, with cotton clothes more and more voluminous in cut, and streaming with more and more loose ends of extra drapery, as we ran on through the frosty, hazy glow of a sudden yellow sunset that, glorifying the white peaks of Kashmir, faded quickly to a green and a hyacinthine sky, and then to the blackness of winter night.

The one weary lamp in the carriage did not give light enough for us to read and lay to heart the several framed ordinances which the government railway holds up to travelers. Evidently there is a "dog question" in British India equal to the "cow question" in the Hindu and Mohammedan circles. "His Excellency the Governor-General in Council" had first to rule:

DOGS IN CARRIAGES

PASSENGERS will not be allowed to take any dog into a passenger carriage, except with the permission of the Station Master at the starting station, and also with the consent of their fellow passengers, and then only on payment of a double fare for each dog, subject to the condition that it shall be removed if subsequently objected to, no refund being given. This rule does not apply to dogs conveyed in reserved compartments, or carriages, or in private special trains. The number of dogs to be taken into a reserved compartment must not exceed three.

And again it was intimated to the public in the formal phrase of a viceregal ball- or dinner-card, by a secretary, who said:

> I am directed to state that His Excellency the Governor-General in Council considers it desirable in the interest of the travelling public to rule that in future no person shall be allowed to take any dog into a passenger carriage, except with the consent of the Station Master at starting station and also with the concurrence of the fellow passengers.

At sunrise the next morning we saw the blue range of the Hindu Kush with a sprinkling of snow on its sharp crest-lines, and the same dreary, dry, stony plain around us, broken only by a few clay bluffs and the gullied watercourses of the rainy season. The air was thin, sharp, and frosty as we lowered the rattling blue window-panes for a look at the forlorn adobe village on the banks, and the great fortified bridge across the Indus at Attock—Attock! the ford and crossing-place of every invader and conqueror from the North since Aryan times; where every one of them camped and fought,—Egyptian, Persian, Greek, Scythian, Afghan, and Mogul, down to Nadir Shah. When the train had trailed slowly across the high iron girders and passed through another great fortress bridge-tower, it turned sharply and ran along the bank, giving us a view of the great picturesque front of Akbar's fort on the opposite bluff. Except for that imposing battlemented castle and fortified bridge, the muddy river, the banks, the stony plain, and the blue mountain-range showing so clearly in the thin, dry air, might as well have been the country of the upper Missouri; but this plain between the Indus and the Safed Koh has been a world's battle-ground for more than two thousand years, and history is written on top of history like records on a palimpsest. Here at the Indus has always been the virtual frontier of India, the river drawing a natural line from the Himalayas down to the Persian Gulf; but, once advancing here to a valley and there to a range, the frontier has crept westward and northward, and is still ever-moving, changing, and elusive.

At Khairabad station, facing Attock, the early morning tea-table was ready on the platform, and muffled figures bore trays of steaming cups to the car windows, while benumbed travelers surrounded the tall samovar. The wildest lot of turbaned and disheveled folk, some in sheepskin coats and some wound over and looped up with unmanageable yards and yards of loose cotton clothing and loaded down with strange saddle-bags, bundles, water-jars, and hubble-bubble pipes, were already waiting when the train drew up. When the third-class passengers, who had been packed to standing-room all night, were bundled out and added to this waiting crowd while a fresh train was made up, there was spectacle indeed, local color too, and such an uproar as threatened the demolition of the Indian Empire—or at least the sacking of the train and the razing of Khairabad station. The whole traveling public had changed overnight to the fierce Afghan type, which had been so picturesque when first seen in the bazaars of Lahore; and the vehement giants, turbaned and bearded to exaggeration, ramped up and down the platform with bare feet thrust in loose, clattering Mohammedan shoes, shouldering and hustling one another in no gentle way. Despite the clamor and the crowding, as so many desperate tribesmen stormed and carried each third-class carriage and filled every cubic inch of its space with their own superfluous size and belongings, the train finally drew away, leaving the platform full of left-over passengers—"huge, black-haired, scowling sons of Ben-i-Israel," who raged aloud in their wrath, until one felt sure the station-master must barricade himself and the great guns of Attock thunder across the river before the uproar would subside. These tall, hairy, and noisy creatures, with peaked Afghan caps within their striped turban-cloths, were far removed from the soft and supple Hindus we had left in the South, unlike even the bearded Sikhs at Lahore. We had journeyed overnight to another country, had come again to a blue-eyed people, to the pale Aryans of the Northwest, to a race of weather-beaten and ruddy-cheeked mountaineers, to the Pathans of Kipling's tales—tales so true, pictures so clearly painted, that one recognizes these hairy giants as fascinating old acquaintances, characters in fiction come to life.

Crossing more of the same dreary, yellow plain, and nearing the mountain barrier, the train at last ran by the mud walls of a mud city in a mud plain, —Peshawar, Akbar's "frontier city," the extreme northern outpost of the Indian Empire; nineteen hundred miles from Cape Comorin and two hundred and seventy-eight miles from Lahore—the latter distance covered by fast-mail train in seventeen hours. The storied mud walls of the city were like adobe pueblos, and the same dry and treeless plain, dry, thin atmosphere, and glaring white sunlight of the American Southwest blinded us as we drove from the end of the track at the cantonment station to the drooping roses and poinsettias in the dusty gardens of the dak bangla.

By previous correspondence with the commissioner at Peshawar—and here let me bear testimony to the unfailing courtesy, the endless kindness, the considerate interest which every English official in India accords to the winter wanderers—through the kindness of this unknown northern commissioner we had been fully informed of the preparations necessary for a visit to the Khyber, and by dint of many telegrams everything was in train for our arrival. The khansamah at the bangla served his tiffin on the moment, and soon the babu of the political agent was there with the permits to travel the Khyber Pass as far as Ali Masjid on the following caravan day, and with an order for the detail of sowars of Khyber Rifles to act as escort. Straightway we judged horses and made bargains with splendidly whiskered old Hassan Khan at his hospital of broken vehicles in the bazaar, and quoted to him the while the commissioner's warning that the only danger in the Khyber Pass would be from the chance of an unbroken pony being put in harness. The turbaned one, with his hand on his heart, assured us that we should have the most safe and stately barouche and pair to convey us to Jamrud, at the entrance of the pass, at sunrise, and that he would speed us on thence toward Afghanistan and the elusive, illusive, ever-moving frontier in light dog-carts of the variety known to the natives as the "tum-tum" (tandem). All this for sixteen rupees, "and what your ladyship may please."

As "that narrow sword-cut in the hills" was open and guarded only on Tuesdays and Fridays, the two caravan days of each week, there was stir in Peshawar city and cantonment that day. Long caravan trains of camels and donkeys were then filing out and across the dusty plain to pass the night in the fortified serai below Jamrud fort, ready for a sunrise start through the defile to Lundi Khana at the Afghan end, where no white traveler goes, save by very special arrangement with civil and military authorities.

Peshawar, once an Afghan city in fact, still bears all its Persian and Central Asian characteristics; and this flat-roofed city within its great mud walls is also a metropolis, a little Paris for all Central Asia, whither flock Afghans and turbaned folk from over the border to shop and spend their money, to luxuriate and dissipate in all the ways of Orient and Occident there combined, and to hatch fresh conspiracies against Pax Britannica. One must read his Kipling to enjoy Peshawar, and must see Peshawar and its people fully to enjoy Kipling. All through " The Man Who Would be King," "The Drums of the Fore and Aft," "The Man Who Was," "The Lost Regiment," and "Wee Willie

Winkie," and in the "Ballad of the King's Jest," are pictures and glimpses of Peshawar, the Pathans and the hills, that flash upon one's memory at every turn. With Peshawar, too, are associated all the great names of Anglo-Indian history of the past half-century,—Lawrence, Edwards, Nicholson, and both the Robertses.

The great cantonment at the end of the track is one of the chief military stations of the empire, and while it rejoices in a crisp, electric air worthy of a sanatorium in midwinter, its climate for the rest of the year gives it an evil name. It is another of the many "ovens of India," where the thermometer rises to 102° and 110° every summer, and where the gray, beclouded, breathless dog-days during the rains aggravate men to madness.

After all the other bazaars of India, after the Chandni Chauk of Delhi and the brilliant, theatrical, spectacular streets of Lahore, the bazaars of Peshawar were captivating out of all reason, and held us fascinated until dusk, when lamps and lanterns threw strange illumination upon all the picturesque people known to the Middle East. There was not so much color as at Lahore, perhaps; but the fiercely bearded ones, with their tremendous turbans, long *chogas*, or caftans, and gay vests, were so many hundreds of Vereshchagin's models turned loose, and kodak film was reeled away by the yard as long as the spool would turn. It was too striking, too theatrical, and too spectacular to be the every-day life at even the farthest end of the empire. Each little open alcove of a shop along the broad street leading in from the Edwards Gate in the city wall held its tableau, its Vereshchagin group already posed, every man of them six feet tall, fierce and stalwart. These "Pathan devils," "these Kabul-ly men," as our bearer called them, were as truculent, turbulent, and untamed a lot as one could wish to see, and our bearer fairly quaked when one of these swashbucklers brushed against him, or a hook-nosed, wolfish red-beard scowled at him and contemptuously discussed him with a brother of Kabul. The Jewish cast of features was unmistakable, and the turbans and garments were identical with those worn by Moses and the prophets —a biblical picture, truly. These hulking giants who strode about like conquerors, these picturesque cutthroats and splendid fighting animals, are supposed to be harmless, from having been relieved of their arms and weapons when they entered British territory, but no doubt every one of them had a yard-long, triangular Afghan knife concealed within his baggy garments. All wore peaked caps within the turban-cloth and some heavy, striped blankets thrown theatrically over one shoulder, but the crocheted Afghan of fancy-work fairs was nowhere to be seen—another disillusionment of travel. An unkempt old falconer with hooded bird on wrist, and just such a Scythian sort of barbarian next him as sculptors show in the train of Alexander the Great, were a pair that willingly posed for their portraits.

There was such richness, such conglomeration and embarrassment of picturesqueness on every hand, that one needed the all-compassing eyes of a fly to see it. Persia's nearness was attested by the graceful shapes of water-pots, bottles and bowls, the damascened metals and the blue-glazed pottery; and the Russian advance was there in visible, tangible form in the tall copper samovars that steamed and hissed in the frequent tea-shops—the hand of Russia seen in every such gathering-place, and the seeds of sedition lying in every bowl of tea.

Disputing passage with a deliberate ox loaded with twice its bulk of fodder-cane, we came through a deep arch in a wall to the circular Bokhara, or silk bazaar, and to a dazzling picture all light and life and color in the blazing, blinding sunlight of that early, cloudless afternoon. Dens of alcove shops surrounded the great open space, where leafless trees cast thin traceries of shadows over the bare earth, and scores of men sat in groups in the sun, twirling reels of green, yellow, rose, and purple silks, tossing glistening skeins of every hue as they came fresh from traders' packs or dyers' vats. Bales of woven silks and shimmering lengths of gay tissues were heaped and spread over the floors of the tiny shops; and sitting statuesque, or moving in and out among the whirling spindles, were Afghan and Bokhara silk merchants and brokers, who brightened the scene with their gold-threaded and -fringed turban-cloths, gold-embroidered and cloth-of-gold vests and waistcoats, and inner garments of gorgeous Bokhara shadow-silks. From "silken Samarkand," from Bokhara and Kabul, these men come every winter to this silk bazaar, and huge bales of raw silks and woven stuffs were being unloaded that afternoon from groaning camels that had trod softly down from the Khanates to kneel in the Peshawar oval—to be reloaded with Manchester piece-goods and tread slowly back again before hot weather.

There were picturesque money-changers, too, in this bazaar—bearded and turbaned old Persians, wrapped in long and richly furred garments, sitting somnolent and prosperous in the sunshine, with loose heaps of coins from all the border countries before them. One even wondered if the rupees and annas, the unknown coins with crescents and Persian texts, and the yet more insidious rubles and copecks were real,—if they were not stage accessories and part of the tableaux rather than the visible capital and assets of genuine Shylocks.

Color was rampant in the shoe bazaar, the long line of cobblers' lairs strewn and strung over with peaked slippers and great strips of brightest red, green, and yellow leathers, and hung in the sunlight to make a braver show. In all that leather bazaar we could not find a pair of the braided leather sandals or buskins that at southern railway stations are sold as Saharanpur or Kashmir shoes, farther north are called Lahore shoes, and in Lahore are called Peshawar shoes. The Pathan public very generally wore the same conventional Mohammedan heelless slippers, with the pointed and curling bows and high sterns of antique junks. Some few wore wood or rawhide sandals fastened by heavy thongs, the most primitive and archaic of foot-gear. There was a narrow strip of railed-off, sacred ground down the middle of this shoe bazaar, which held some venerated Moslem tombs, and scores of devout ones, ranging themselves before them, saluted the glowing west beyond which lay Mecca. They prostrated themselves on their bits of carpets, and prayed fervently, deaf to the hum of cobblers and idlers around them.

There were sweetmeat sellers and sugar-cane peddlers hawking their wares through all the bazaars; letter-writers plying their craft in the open; schools of small turbans rocking in studious circles around some pious teacher; and barbers, lawyers, peddlers, touts, and jugglers. And there were beggars, too! Such beggars! Such tattered and picturesque figures as never before diverted one,—Afghan and Bokhara beggars, shaggy and ragged beyond all the religious mendicants of India. Coats of a hundred patches hung in a hundred shreds from the frowzy, turbanless ones, and but half protected them from the keen mountain winds that blew through the bazaars at sunset. Many of these were Pathan "saints," who live in caves in the hills, lead revolts, and urge the murder of unbelievers. The more holy of these beggars cast glances of scorn and hatred at us Kafirs or unbelievers; "white pagans," they called us, to the perturbation of our bearer, who seemed to fear that some one of these Islam saints might brain him with his long pipe-stem, but with six annas and a yard of sugar-cane the maddest molla of them all was bought over to stand tamely before the kodak. A few of the holy men coaxed annas from the crowds with songs and story-telling,—even an infidel anna came not amiss,—while others had for sale furs, rugs, and bits of soft jade or heavily veined turquoise. Not this side of Samarkand had I expected to see men with rugs piled on their heads and shoulders, throwing them down at sight of a possible customer, and displaying there on the dusty ground what treasures or trash they possessed. Men with bales of furs and *poshtins,* or sheepskin coats, for sale, paraded the bazaars or lounged by gates and bridges. One scowling giant had for sale a dead peacock, a sacred Hindu bird, another showed a leopard-skin; and there were blue-eyed, woolly Persian cats on view, whose dispositions had been so crossed somewhere in transit that they would only spit, glare, and claw at any possible purchasers who ventured near.

The jewelers' dens had their gossiping groups, and the leisurely jewel merchants produced bags, tins, and bottles of seventh-rate pearls and talisman turquoises, cemented on sticks, all quoted at soaring prices. A woman in a gaily-embroidered red and yellow phulkari or Afghan head-sheet, who sat watching the hammering of a bracelet, was a moving exhibit of jewels, that furnished a feast to the eye when combined with her own beauty. But we were plainly no feast to her scornful eyes, and, after a critical inventory of our dusty traveling attire, her glances and shrugs sufficiently translated her remarks to the merchant of high prices and doubtful gems.

Even to that far end of the Indian Empire, the tout dogged one's steps with his monotonous plead-

THE MAD MOLLA, PESHAWAR.

ing: "Please come my shop! Please come my shop!" and our repeated "Jaos!" glanced harmlessly past his ear. To stop the whining pleas of the most persistent one we followed him down a side street, up a dark stairway, and on to a flat roof from which we reached inner rooms piled high with rugs and stuffs, where we might sit on floor cushions and toss glittering embroideries and rolls of shadowy-patterned Bokhara silks and sheeny stuffs from "silken Samarkand" to our hearts' content. In another shop men were busily ornamenting squares of dark cloth with showy Afghan waxwork. A pan of a white, waxy dough stood on a charcoal brazier beside each worker, who, laying a dab of the hot compound on the back of his hand as a palette, drew from it a long, viscous thread which he dropped in continuous arabesques and traceries over a faintly outlined pattern. This waxen relief was dusted over with silver, gold, or bronze powder before it cooled, and there resulted gaudy and tawdry curtains and table-covers, that in dusty, mildewed, and bedrabbled condition add to the fustiness and shabbiness of so many British-India hotel interiors.

There was a picturesque salt and corn bazaar in a vast open space, and the fragrance and the cheery music of popping corn drew us directly to the booth where, in a huge turban and tremendous trousers, the pop-corn man stirred the snapping kernels with a bunch of twigs in a great, shallow iron pan. The pan rested on the same rude mud oven and was furnished with the same layer of black sand as is used by hot-chestnut men in Peking and all North China.

Peshawar pop-corn was as edible under its Pushtu name as at the Chicago World's Fair, barring the grit of the black sand driven into every snowy kernel. Sweetmeat shops and peddlers' stands overflowed with gujack and kindred candies, thickly peppered with the dust of the streets.

The caravans bring down the white Kabul grapes which, packed in cotton in small, round wooden boxes, are sold at remotest railway stations all over India each winter; and such mountainous stores of pistachios, almonds, walnuts, raisins, figs, and fruits from fertile Afghan and Persian vales, as made one imagine a great horn of plenty had been tipped through the Khyber Pass and its contents spread over Peshawar plain. For twenty centuries at least the *povindahs*, or traveling merchants, have brought caravans down from Kabul, Bokhara, and Samarkand every autumn. They bring horses, wool, woolen stuffs, silks, dyes, gold thread, fruits, and precious stones, fighting and buying their way to British lines, where, leaving their arms, they are free and safe to wander at will to Delhi, Agra, and Calcutta, appearing even at Rangoon and Tuticorin each winter. The railway has changed something of their habits now, and all save the horse-dealers leave their animals to graze near Peshawar while they take train to the uttermost parts of the peninsula, and, returning when their wares are sold, lead their camels back to the cool plateaus and valleys of the north for the summer.

Kafila, or caravans, bringing more and more of Afghan wares, were defiling in through the city gates, and toward sundown the great square of the caravansary was full of groaning camels, and the loads of merchandise grew to mountain heights. A fountain and a sacred spot of prayer is reserved in the center of the serai, and there caravan-men and camel-drivers cleansed and prayed, their faces to the west, oblivious of all the acre of protesting beasts and wrangling men, screaming peddlers, chanting beggars, and even the shouts of a bear-leader, who danced and wrestled with his shaggy pet to the very edges of the prayer-carpets. The serai's inclosure, the Ghor Kattri, has always been holy ground. On this spot first stood the great vihara of Kanishka's time that was four hundred feet high and a quarter of a mile in circumference, chief fane when all this valley was head center of Buddhism. To it came Fahien and Hiouen Thsang, those Chinese pilgrims of the fifth and seventh centuries, who, crossing Tatary and Turkestan, came down through the Khyber Pass to visit the holy lands of the Buddhist faith. In their time, too, a great suburban stupa sheltered the golden begging-bowl of Sakya-Muni, "the holy grail of Eastern legends," which, brought here from Benares, was carried to Persia, and then is said to have been looted by a marauder and taken to Kandahar; and Mohammedans treasure the so-called Buddha's bowl —a great bronze or iron caldron. Peshawar once had its Bodhi-druma (Tree of Knowledge), descendant of the Bo-tree at Buddha-Gaya, planted by Kanishka, the Scythian ruler of the Panjab, according to one legend; it had already grown to a shelter sufficient for Buddha when he appeared to foretell the coming of Kanishka, according to another version. At any rate, it was a pipul-tree of uncommon size, and held in such esteem that the conquering Baber, the Bokharan, saw and described it when he came this way in 1505. All this Peshawar plain has yielded rich store of Buddhist relics, records, sculptures, and inscriptions, including the finest examples shown in the Lahore and Calcutta museums and in London.

The holy spot of Peshawar, in these modern times, is the jail, where so many hillside saints from the border have been put for stalking British sentries, sniping stragglers, and inciting the tribesmen to mischief and revolt in the name of the Prophet, that the great barred building is crowded at times with these vagabonds. As the abode of saints, the building has all the sacredness and vogue of a temple, and is a place of popular pilgrimage. Fanatic Mohammedans have even committed petty crimes in bazaar and cantonment for the sole purpose of gaining admission to this saints' abode and rest; and, with such crazy people to deal with, one may well admire the spectacle of England's humane and patient rule on the border.

From the top of the city wall near the old temple there was a fine view of the city, the hazy, lilac plain, and the snow-striped mountains just showing through the clouds of mingled dust and frost-haze on the Jamrud road. The rugged mountains rose and grew sharper in outline as the sun fell, one higher and whiter peak marking where the Khyber cleaves its way through to the Afghan plain of Jellalabad, only forty miles distant. But beyond the Safed Koh lies—Russia! And upon all that northwestern sky we saw projected the great shadow of the double eagle, rather than the Afghan symbol of the tree.

The gold and ruby mists of the plain soon faded to cold violet shadows and purple darkness, and the flat white roofs around us were indefinite when the great demonstration in the sky was over. The crisp autumn air grew momently sharper as we haggled through the gharry door for a last bargain in Bokhara silk, and drove, that January night, to the dark, cheerless, stone-floored dak bangla which stood a thousand feet above sea-level, north latitude thirty-four degrees, Fahrenheit many less.

CHAPTER XX

THROUGH KHYBER PASS WITH THE CARAVANS

ONE who reads much of British and Anglo-Indian print learns that the Indian Empire is not only bounded on the north by the Himalayas and their continuation, the Hindu Kush, but that running with these lofty boundaries are artificial, imaginary lines marking the administrative, the defensive, the strategic, political, geographic, actual, military, temporary, and prospective frontiers. Then, too, says Lord Curzon (London *Times*, December 20, 1894): "Our frontier must be, not hypothetical, fluctuating, adventitious, but definite, recognizable, scientific," adding yet more to the list of qualitative adjectives commonly applied to the word frontier—never meaning anything, however, but the northwest frontier, in Anglo-Indian speech. One might naturally wish to see the region of such an aggregation of frontiers, where boundaries run like contour-lines on a topographic map—the wavering, imaginary lines upon the earth's Asiatic surface, for which, and to which, literally, millions of lives have been sacrificed—expressions of an "idea" for which many more lives must be given.

One hears, too, the Russian advance daily discussed and harped upon all over India, until it becomes as real a fact as the Aryan migration or the Mogul invasion, and one wishes to see where the next great history-making incident will certainly occur—the theater where the greatest world-drama since Timur's time will be played. One becomes so familiar with this fixed idea of the Russians coming down through the Khyber Pass and snatching the great jewel of the British crown, that he can jest with British friends about all Anglo-India lying awake of nights, frightened by the Russian bogy, and can advise them to rent the Panjab to Russia outright, and so have it over with quickly, and enjoy sound sleep again. But the Briton takes his northwest frontier—his many frontiers—seriously, sees the Russian hand in every little border war, and finds no humor in the charge that every time he cries, "The Russian! The Russian!" as Afridis, Waziris, and Kafirs revolt, he is playing the part of the boy who too often cried, "The wolf! The wolf!"—albeit this boy claims to have found many incriminating documents and positive proof of the trail of the Muscovite wolf in the abandoned camps and villages of warring tribesmen.

It was bitterly cold that night in the government house of rest for travelers; and as the two opposite doors of our grand salon of a room gave directly upon garden and court, we had sweeps of icy air through it whenever a servant entered, and such currents across the floor from two-inch cracks below each door that we soon retreated to the high string-beds, and, wrapped in rugs and razais, longed for steam-heated and furnace-cheered America. The small pocket of a fireplace sheltered some hissing green twigs that smoldered and filled the room with smoke which refused to escape by a transom window sixteen feet up in the absurdly high, windward wall—which same north window was ropeless and wedged open to encourage further the icy drafts that encircled us. The khansamah, bearing the courses of the dinner, was swept in with a small gale each time, but we dined well on the usual Indian menu. The khansamah made a final entry on the wings of the wind, bearing proudly the proper British tart of conclusion. "But, missis—" he pleaded in injured tones when I too had said, "No, thanks." I had too often suffered in arguments with British pastry to hazard it in far places, but I relented to this courteous old soul and gave the heavy serving-spoon the swing and force of a golfer's club, when *pouff! pou-s-sh!* went a fountain spray of minute flakes of true puff-paste up into the air and down in showers all over the table. And we gathered them up—every last flimsy flakelet—and with praises consumed the khansamah's masterpiece, the very apotheosis of covered apple-pie, the most supremely perfect tart the British flag ever floated over—away off there in the shadow of the Hindu Kush, on the borderland of the heart of the world, close to the old Aryan home of the pie people's first ancestors.

"Pie, sir," said Henry Ward Beecher, "goes with

civilization; where there is no civilization, there is no pie." Hence Peshawar, etc.; and one more count may be added to the great total of what England has done for India.

In what seemed only the middle of that arctic night we heard our servant beating on the cook-house door with such an alarum as might herald the coming of the Russians; and after the misery of a candle-light breakfast we drove away in the frosty dawn, the sun rising behind us in a haze of pink and purple, lilac and burning crimson, as we made straight toward the mountain wall. The carriage-road to Jamrud fort runs for all the ten miles close beside the caravan track, on which were lines of slow-moving camels, enveloped in clouds of glorified golden dust—a fine, loose sort of powder, as light and dry and white as flour or snow, covering the broad caravan track five and six inches deep. Every one abroad was beating his arms and stamping his feet to keep warm, and we soon shrouded our heads in rugs as shelter from the icy wind and choking dust, and to hide from our sight the path of the projected railway which travelers now use to Jamrud.

At Jamrud fort, towering picturesquely at the edge of the plain, we gave up the spacious carriage and waited for guard-mount and the signal-shot to declare the Khyber open for the day. This last British outpost was apparently the frontier. We must then have been close to Afghanistan. But no. Lord Curzon had written (London *Times*, January 2, 1895), "Without exaggeration it may be said, that where Afghan territory commences, there

British territory ends, and that the true British frontier is not at Jamrud, but at Lundi Khana." Yet the political agent would not let us go even to that edge of India and look over; would only guarantee our safety to and let us drive as far as Ali Masjid, half-way to Lundi Khana. A merely hypothetical frontier that of Ali Masjid, and Jamrud nothing but the administrative frontier.

The native officer on duty at the Jamrud gates took our passes and presented the visitors' book, in which register it was written and underscored: "*Gentlemen* visiting Khyber Pass are requested not to give money to the sowars, as it is setting a dangerous precedent"—advice which seemed reasonable when my special military escort for the day appeared, climbed up promptly on the back seat of a tum-tum, and laid his Enfield rifle across his knee. We felt the need of arms ourselves when we saw that handsome, evil, reckless-looking young bandit playing knight-errant for the day, tidily dressed in brown khaki uniform, his fine turban-cloth fringed with gold, and his lean, Israelitish face lighted with the evil eye of generations of robber ancestors.

Low ridges before us rose to hills, and they to mountains, and three miles away at Kadam is the real entrance, the beginning of the pass that leads to Afghanistan and the mystic lands of Central Asia, through which a procession of conquerors have come. Out there have gone only the British, bent on punitive expeditions and to the questionable triumphs of what Sir Charles Dilke calls, "thrashing the Afghans into loving us."

No other mountain-pass in the world has had and retains such strategic importance and holds so many historic associations as this Khyber gateway to the Indian plain. In the thirty-three miles of its length it cuts through cliffs of shale and limestone rock, and from an elevation of sixteen hundred and seventy feet above the sea at Jamrud it rises to thirty-three hundred and seventy-three feet at Lundi Kotal, beyond Lundi Khana, and is never closed by snow in winter. One does not see snow-fields nor glaciers, nor the wild, stupendous scenery that such a pass in such a mountain-range should have. The winter is the season of greatest caravan trade and travel, since the original, woolly, two-humped Bactrian camel, native of the Pamirs, does not endure hot weather well, and, as in North China, can only travel at night in midsummer, while he performs his longest journeys in winter.

This mountainous borderland between India and Afghanistan is occupied by the independent tribes, who yield allegiance to neither emperor nor amir, who never have been nor will be brought thoroughly under subjection. Numbering over two hundred and fifty thousand, all Mohammedans, easily inflamed through religious fanaticism, and ready to respond to any *jehad,* or holy war, these independent border tribes are to be counted with on every occasion. The twenty thousand Afridis living in the immediate Peshawar frontier are the most turbulent, fanatical, irresponsible tribe of all, ever ripe for revolt, always scheming and conspiring, ready to attack the power that supports them with subsidies,—literally quarreling with their own bread and butter, or, what is more vital, with their own powder and shot. Loot, ambush, and murder, rick-burning and cattle-poisoning are daily or nightly amusements of these fire-worshipers turned fire-eaters, who have waylaid, harried, and hung on the rear of every body of troops that ever entered this defile—even turning Alexander the Great away from the Khyber, so that Bucephalus was forced to pick his steps to northward and eastward and bear his master down through the Michni Pass to the Peshawar plain. They have always lived by pillage and blackmail, taking a subsidy to guard and protect the British transport trains in the last Afghan war, and then plundering the baggage and commissariat trains every night, cutting off and sniping every straggler and deserter with as much zeal as they had shown in robbing Shere Ali's train. The stealing of arms and ammunition goes on all along the Peshawar border, neither Sepoys nor English soldiers proving any match for these accomplished thieves, descended from generations of freebooters and plunderers, dedicated to the craft by regular ceremonies at birth, and holding skill in that line as their greatest pride and boast. They have stolen the carbines of European guards sleeping on those arms in the guard-house, taking even the sword of the sentry as he rested it against the wall beside him; and they maintain a steady freemasonry of communication with the British troops through spies and confederates in the native regiments and deserters returned to their tribes. Any saint or akhoond or Mad Molla can inflame them and start them on a religious crusade against the infidel, and every little hill village has its saint or saint's tomb to make it a place of distinction and pious pilgrimage. It is even told of one clan of Afridis that, lacking such pious attraction in their village, they lured a saint their way, killed him, and set up a tomb worthy of neighborly envy.

"Nothing is finer than their physique, or worse than their morals," wrote Sir H. Edwards long ago; and Sir Richard Temple has said: "Now *these tribes are savages,* noble savages perhaps, and not without some tincture of virtue and generosity, but still absolutely barbarians, nevertheless. They have nothing approaching to government or civil institutions; they have, for the most part, no education; they have nominally a religion, but Mohammedanism as understood by them is no better, or perhaps is actually worse, than the creeds of the wildest races of the earth. In their eyes the one great commandment is blood for blood, and fire and sword for all infidels."

"We are content with discord, we are content with alarms, we are content with blood, but we will never be content with a master," said one of these turbulent turbans to Elphinstone; and the Amir was well rid of the lot when the Gandamak Treaty in 1879 declared these tribes independent, nominally under the political control of the British, who have vainly tried the policy of conciliation and subsidy varied with occasional thrashings. Only personal influence, and rough and ready, quick justice can avail with them. Colonel Warburton held them wonderfully in check for twenty years by a kindly, paternal rule, and their confidence in him justified the saying that his presence on the frontier was worth any ten garrisons. He retired when his age limit was reached, and on the heels of his departure came the revolt of the tribes and the closing of the Khyber. Colonel Warburton offered his services to return to India and try to pacify the tribes again, but they were declined, and the border war continued from July, 1897, to January, 1898, General Lockhart for months employing against these hill guerrillas a greater army than that which defeated Napoleon at Waterloo.

"The forward party" of Anglo-Indians argues that these border tribes are an inexhaustible recruiting-ground of the finest fighting material in the world, and that for the British not to avail themselves of it would be virtually giving Russia this almost ready-made army. Another faction argues that the tribesmen, once drilled and taught the tactics of war, will be more formidable enemies of the British than ever, more ready to revolt, to join Afghans or Russians. Lugubrious prophets declare that when the struggle comes the British must win the first battle in Afghanistan or lose all India —the Mohammedan Nizam of Hyderabad, with his great army, being arbiter of the destinies of India, in any serious disturbances that may arise with Mohammedans on the northwest frontier. One specialist even wrote out and tabulated his fears in a "confidential book" to his government, in which he figured out every detail of the probable Russian transport problems, their line of march, the points of attack, and their possible resistance. A copy of this confidential and reliable guide to the conquest of India was promptly obtained by the Russian government, translated and sent broadcast through the Russian army as a manual of tactics, a handy sort of military Murray for Muscovite use when the Czar is quite ready for another winter visit to India. Russia has now reached the Pamirs and the borders of Kashmir; Bokhara is hers, and Persia, virtually; exploring parties of Russian soldiers have twice crossed the Hindu Kush, surprised of course to find they were in India, within British lines; and Kipling has depicted the Russian spy in "The Man Who Was," in which the retiring Dirkovich says, "Au revoir!" and, pointing to the Khyber, adds, "That way is always open."

The conquest of India is the dream and the duty of all Russians, and having closely followed every other clause of advice in that remarkable and much-questioned paper known as the will of Peter the Great, they are not once forgetting this one:

> VIII. Bear in mind that the commerce of India is the commerce of the world, that he who can exclusively control it is the dictator of Europe; no occasion should therefore be lost to provoke war with Persia, to hasten its decay, to advance to the Persian Gulf, and then to endeavor to re-establish the ancient trade of the Levant through Syria.

While England has been pushing her frontiers northward for the good of the native, and to give the

Pathans good government, schools, hospitals, pure water, and sanitary redemption generally, Russia, the pure philanthropist, is pushing her frontiers southward with the sole object of evangelizing the Khanates and bringing these people out of spiritual darkness.

Through the efforts of Colonel Warburton, for twenty years the political agent at Peshawar (and a worthy successor of those other splendid examples of the British official, Lawrence, Edwards, and Nicholson, and those rare men of earlier border and Mutiny days), the marauding tribesmen were taken in firm hand when their independence was guaranteed. The Afridis themselves were made to guard and guarantee the safety of travelers in the Khyber, one of the most remarkable examples of setting a thief to catch a thief that was ever known. From 1879 to 1897 the government paid an annual subsidy of eighty thousand rupees to the Afridi and Shinwari clans on condition that they keep open and guard the caravan track through the pass, live in peace, and do not raid British territory. By tolls levied on each camel and vehicle passing Jamrud, the Indian government raised annually an amount sufficient to pay off part of the subsidy and maintain "Colonel Warburton's road," as the tribesmen call it. Following easy grades, this road could be as easily traversed by an artillery train as by light tum-tums; although, to avoid expensive cuttings and tunnels, the projected railway into Afghanistan will follow the track of Alexander the Great along the Kabul River and through the Michni Pass.

CARAVANS IN THE KHYBER PASS.

Colonel Warburton made levies of tribesmen, constituted them the Khyber Rifles, to police and guard the pass, and assigned them to six fortified posts between Jamrud and Lundi Kotal. A force of eight hundred infantry and thirty troopers were recruited from the wild robbers of the region and set to keeping off the other robbers. The infantry were paid nine rupees a month, the troopers twenty-six rupees, each man providing his own khaki uniform, and the trooper the keep of his own horse. Their commander, Colonel Islam Khan, who drilled and brought the corps to such efficiency and roused in these hill guerrillas the military pride that seemed to animate them when once inside the Queen's uniform, is a descendant of the former ruling Afghan family, and served with the British in the last Afghan war. On caravan days his sentries were stationed at every hundred yards along the pass, troopers patrolled it, and the Khyber was as safe as Broadway or Piccadilly,—safe until the sunset gun proclaimed the military day ended, and the Khyber sowars, dropping uniforms and rifles, became predatory tribesmen again, ready to loot a camel, cut a throat, steal the arms of any soldier, or make away with any stray man, horse, or camel found out after dark.

Bugle-calls and rifle-shots announced that the pass was open, the gates of the serai below Jamrud swung back, and some six hundred scornful and unhappy-looking camels, with great shags of fur on neck and legs, dragged their deliberate way out, and in single file went swaying along the road to Afghanistan. Each belled leader was led by a man on foot, and other camels were fastened one to another by long guide-ropes. Groups of shaggy caravan-men paused to pray by a wayside shrine at the outset of their journey, and then trudged on, they no better groomed, no more sociable or joyful than their camels.

Our bearer was in a panic of fright. "Yes, you must drive fast," he said, with chattering teeth and timorous looks over his shoulder. "I tell you true. I am your servant, not your enemy. These Kabul-ly men are all Russians, enemies of the country, bad and dangerous. They shoot—*bang!* They kill—*bang!* every time. They always rob. Hold fast your money. Let no one see your watch to-day. These Kabul-ly men are not men. They are animals—wild animals of the jungle. They fight, they cut, they shoot!—oh! oh!"

"But there is the sowar and his gun. We need not be afraid," I said.

"Yes," said the trembling Hindu, "that is just the danger. All these Pathans are devils. Sowar one day, robber next day. They take England's money; shoot and rob England's men. They are all Russians, enemies of the country. Just now the sowar is England's soldier. Four-o'clock gun goes *bang!* and he is wild man again, England's enemy."

The smooth, hard carriage-road wound farther in among the yellow hills, and the camel-train was soon far behind and out of sight. We were as an advance-guard, the first passengers of the day, and the riflemen sitting on the rocks and perched on hill crests every hundred yards exchanged greeting glances with the sowar that sent more cold chills down the inert Hindu spine. There were round stone towers and square mud towers of defense as thick as sentry-boxes, and the khaki clothes and turbans, toning in with the stones and barren ground, made many of the sentries invisible until we saw a gun-barrel move or a bayonet flash. It was a radiant, perfect, sunny day, the sky one vast pale turquoise, soft and pure and gently blue, and in among the hills the air was still, and only fresh enough to make the swift ride exhilarating. Around Kadam's mud hovels there were innumerable caves in the hills, where hermits had lived in meditation in Buddhist days, and where Mohammedan saints of unwashed and doubtful sanctity now spend lives of leisure, enjoying the climate and view, subsisting on villagers' offerings, and giving themselves to much mad exhortation, animadversion of England's rule, and mouthings of Allah il allah!

There the pass really begins—a narrow ravine which runs between steep heights. Battlemented walls and far fortresses on crests suggested all the frontiers we had come to see, but it was a deserted road. There was no procession of brigands coming down steep places at the back of the stage, as would have become the historic pass. The identical defile where rode Timur and Jenghiz Khan, Baber the Bokharan, and Nadir Shah with the Great Mogul's Koh-i-nur in his turban and ten jeweled peacock thrones following after him—really, at the beginning, this defile lacks the wild, melodramatic scenery appropriate to its history. It was not as striking, in the landscape way, as the Nankow Pass by the Great Wall of China. At every little upgrade my pony balked until the sais got down and led him by out-stretched bridle to the top of the hill. When I demurred at myself dismounting to walk up the next trifling hill, the gentle sais whined: "Gentlemen go Khyber Pass always walk up hills." The sowar lounged in splendid ease on the back seat of his tum-tum, dawdling his Enfield on his knee, and watching us from on high as we toiled up each gentle gradient after him.

"How about that sowar? If gentlemen always walk up hills in Khyber Pass, why does n't he get down and walk?"

"Oh! Sowar no gentleman," said the naïve one. But at the next hill a disgusted Khyberi, no gentleman that he was, dismounted and walked too.

At last Ali Majid's battlemented towers, crowning a pyramidal hill at the middle of the pass, came in range, most picturesque of many great fortresses of India, completing the wild landscape which, in turn, it commands. There the pass is narrowest, only fifteen yards from wall to wall, and a steep zigzag path leads up to the deep gateway of the old Afghan stronghold. From that aery there is a bird's-eye view down the narrow defile. The history of this Gibraltar is an unbroken record of attack, siege, defense, and slaughter—last captured, recaptured, and burned in 1897. Beyond Ali Masjid we might not go, and we could only look up the narrow rock corridor, soon closed to view by a jutting point, and imagine the Buddhist stupas and inscriptions we might not see—Samarkand four hundred and fifty miles away in air line, seven hundred and fifty by caravan road.

By noon, a far tinkling told that the camels were coming, and the caravans bound down from the fortified serai at Lundi Khana, where they had rested the night, reached Ali Masjid's gorge. The shaggy, swaying animals, with their shaggy keepers, made fitting pictures in that wild glen. Traces of vivid Bokhara waistcoats illuminated a few dingy figures, but for real, theatrical effect the troupe needed fresh costuming. Some of the caravan-men stood stock-still, rooted, transfixed, and stared at us; others feigned indifference; and others vented Pushtu curses.

Then tum-tums passed us, speeding on from Peshawar toward Kabul, and a two-horse trap, very nearly a buckboard, that was filled with prosperous Kabul merchants, ranks above common povindahs, all shapeless fur bundles topped with preposterous turbans. Gaily domed ekkas, like idols' cars, and filled with squatting figures, sped by; other ekkas, with curtains discreetly screening the traveling females, and drawn by ponies wearing blue bead necklaces, went on toward Kabul; and then came the tum-tum of a mission worker from Peshawar, who had essayed the task of reaching the Pathan heart, of subduing the wild Afridi villagers with Christian teaching. Some heroic-looking old men on spirited Kabul horses pranced by; a mounted Khyberi with pennoned lance made a picture as he cantered up;

and all the while the shaggy men afoot and the strings of camels went noiselessly on, their rocking, wavering, swaying motion, the slow, deliberate, methodical lifting and placing of the soft feet, exercising a sort of hypnotic charm.

"Why do these Kabul-ly men have such white faces and blue eyes like Englishmen?" we asked our servant, who quailed when any of them glared curiously at him.

"Oh, it is very cold at Kabul, and they eat so much white grapes and fruit. That makes them white men. Kabul-ly grapes are very dear, and poor Hindu cannot buy."

Then, nearly all the long way back to Jamrud, we were meeting and overtaking strings of camels—camels to right of us and camels to left of us, camels ahead and camels behind, that thrust their unpleasant heads, with their foaming lips and yellow teeth, altogether too near. Once when the sowar fended away a too-friendly camel with his rifle-barrel, there came such screams, groans, and shrieks from the insulted beast that we felt that all the vaunted dangers of the pass were understated, and that the camels were as dangerous as the Khyberis. The diamond hitch is not known in Afghanistan evidently, for the loads were balanced rather than girded on, and cinching seems never to have been applied to the camel's waist-line. The drivers were continually rearranging loads that had tilted over or worked loose, and bending their triple-jointed legs, gaunt beasts with elongated necks sat down and protested to the echoing cañon walls while their burdens were clumsily fastened again. Kodak film was reeled away regardless of the distance from the cantonment photographer's dark-room, and still the caravans came on, bringing silk, carpets, wool, furs, fruits, and sweetmeats from Kabul; while up from Peshawar came blocks of rock-salt, chests of Indian tea, and all of Birmingham's wares, together with an unending movement of British piece-goods, into the heart of the great continent.

As we came out to wide reaches between the decreasing hills, the road was all our own again, save for the lounging sentries here and there among the rocks. Soon we emerged on the plain, the hills closed behind us, and there was spread the view that has gladdened the heart and thrilled the pulses of every marauding conqueror from the north; but for us the land of romance and mystery lay behind us, among, beyond the frontiers. The real spice, the greatest element of danger, was gone, too, when the sowar swung himself down from the tum-tum and strolled off to his barracks with a scornful smile of good-by—a smile that grimly seemed to promise a less conventional meeting.

Once beyond Jamrud walls, our Hindu bearer recovered heart and spirits, and chattered and gesticulated almost joyfully with the sais all the dusty ride back to Peshawar, as one who had faced certain death and escaped it.

There was the same scramble by the wild mob on the Khairabad platform when we again sighted the great Attock fort and bridge across the Indus. There was uproar among as many mad Pathans as ever, and it seemed as though there must always be more Afghans than room for them on the railway. The Bengali station-master, who greeted us as old acquaintances when we returned safely to his theatrical platform and its wild war drama, stood by our window and talked, and heeded this riot and the mingled roars in Pushtu no more than the ripples of the Indus on the stones below. Six-foot ruffians, with rage and hate distorting their countenances, ramped the platform and flung themselves in heaps before each third-class door, each man with enough extra cloth flapping, bagging, flying loose and trailing after him to clothe two other men in European patterns. Each bawled and beat the air like a madman, screaming rage and defiance at the earlier occupants of compartments where not another foot nor elbow could be insinuated by the most determined of these hairy giants. And still the Bengali talked gently on, airily admitting that the Afghans were a very bad lot. "But Abdurrahman can manage them as no one else can. They all fear him. When he dies we will have the war."

"Tell me about the Khyber Pass. How did *you* get permission to go there? What did you go for?" bluntly asked a German cavalry officer when we had returned to table d'hôte circles at Lahore. He cross-examined me as to every civil, social, military, and geographic fact that might have come under my observation. "You wanted to see the live Pathans because Herr Kipling has written? and to see where Alexander came through?"

We charged the uhlan with wishing to see where

the next world contest will be fought, where the Russians are coming through.

"Umh-umh! Yes! I may want to see where *we* might want to come through ourselves."

"You! The Germans in India?"

"Certainly. Why not?"

"But will you come as the ally of the Sultan or the Czar?"

"Ally?" he repeated, in apparent amazement.

CHAPTER XXI

AMRITSAR

THERE was a combination hotel and dak bangla under one roof at Amritsar that was as amusing as anything in comic opera. We arrived at the dak bangla late at night, and moved to the hotel in the morning, by merely crossing the hall. Instead of being served in our own cold, white vault of a bedchamber in the bangla, we dined in the lofty, drafty banquet-hall of the hotel quite as comfortably as if in the train-shed of a railway station on a winter night. All the doors of the place were besieged by insistent touts who sang the same song, "Please come my shop. Please buy my shop," thrust greasy cards at us, clung to the carriage-steps, and outdid their tribesmen elsewhere.

Amritsar, as the holy city of the Sikhs, has an importance and a character distinct from all other places. It is as large a city as Delhi, and for ages has been a great trade-center, lying on the main caravan routes from Central Asia and Kashmir. The streets show a mixture of races, and for color and picturesqueness the bazaars equal those of Lahore. Nearly every man wore a chudda of either vivid red, green, or orange, and if we had remained another day I should have succumbed to the prevailing mode, assumed a bright-red shawl, and with it the theatrical pose and stride, the flap and fling of loose ends of drapery. The Sikhs, "the Swiss of Asia," were old friends, whom I had known before I knew the Panjab—the splendid statuesque, red-turbaned policemen of Shanghai and Hong Kong, "the red-top men" of such terror to Chinese malefactors. Originally Hindus, their Luther protested against caste and idolatry and denounced the corruption of the Brahmans; and, just before Columbus's voyage to America, he established his dissenting sect near Lahore. Akbar showed tolerance and granted them the sacred pool at Amritsar, but his successors persecuted them, tortured their leaders, and so aroused their national and military spirit that after many battles they established their independence in the middle of the eighteenth century. Their last great leader was Runjeet Singh, after whose death in 1839 they embroiled themselves with the English, were defeated at Gujerat in 1849, and the Koh-i-nur went with the Panjab to the victors, and now the pensioned descendants of their ruler live as country gentlemen and champion cricket-players in England, marrying with the English nobility. The Sikhs' loyalty during the Mutiny gave them a prestige still preserved, and these stalwart and interesting people are claimed by the Magyars as long-lost Aryan kinfolk, many common words and the common fashion of beards first suggesting the relationship. While the old men of the Sikhs bewail that their people are backsliding and drifting into Hinduism, a stranger sees that they are as anti-Hindu as anti-Mohammedan; that they pray to the east, refuse tobacco, indulge in spirits, eat pork, and button their coats to the right—if only because their opponents do otherwise. While they venerate the cow, they loathe the saffron color of the Hindu fakir and love the blue the Hindu hates. The Sikh never shaves or trims his hair or beard, parting the latter and twisting and tucking it behind his ears and under the turban. He always wears a sword, if only the miniature tulwar in his turban, and he terrorizes the timid babu, the limp Bengali, and the cowardly Kashmiri as he does the Chinese, and in general is the first man one meets in India.

The heart of the Sikh city and the soul of its people is the Golden Temple in the center of the sacred tank, the Pool of Immortality, and for beauty and impressiveness this Amritsar shrine is second only to the Taj Mahal. Marble terraces and balustrades surround the tank, and a marble causeway leads across the water to a graceful marble temple whose gilded walls, roof, dome, and cupolas, with vivid touches of red curtains, are reflected in the still pool. One gets the first view from a high terrace by the modern Gothic clock-tower, where the Sikh guards halt one until he has removed his shoes. A bearded giant exchanged our shoes for huge felt slippers that were damp and even wet, and led us around the white terrace. The palaces and gardens of Sikh nobles surround the tank, and the path is bordered

THE GOLDEN TEMPLE, AMRITSAR.

with venders of fruit, flowers, and turban ornaments. Processions of brilliantly clad people passed under the towered gate of the causeway and out over the path on the water; and, doubled in reflections, it all seemed too picturesque, too theatrical to be real. Only the north door of the temple is open to Europeans, but the bearded priests sitting in a gold and painted hall before a magnificently bound Granth, or sacred scriptures, over which the attendants waved brushes, received us kindly. Pigeons flew in and out the arched openings with their massive silver doors; the musicians pounded and blew; the priests sat chanting before the jeweled Granth, which is the object of adoration to the sect, and after we had made our offerings, threw jasmine wreaths over our shoulders and gave us fragrant oranges. The Sikh visitors worshipfully knelt, offering money, cowries, and flowers before the book, and, garlanded in return, were conducted with us to the upper chamber of the temple to see even richer wall decorations of mirrors and gilded fretwork. The place is so precious that it is swept and dusted only with peacock feathers. The silver doors of the temple stand open day and night, and the chanted services are continual, and on moonlight nights in summer this fairy floating temple must seem a dream. Only the chill of those wet felt slippers on that cold winter morning could have hurried us away from the enchanting place; but, sneezing and shivering violently, we fled, and although we spent two more days in Amritsar, we were content to view the temple from the terrace.

Gardens, forts, towers, other temples and palaces dwindled in interest by comparison with the bazaars and street crowds of Amritsar, and hours went by rapidly as we followed the narrow streets of this truly Persian and Central Asian city. In the caravansary by the city walls we saw such delightfully tattered and patched and lusty beggars from Yarkand and Bokhara as no fancy could picture. They are last in the train of pilgrims that come down from the north each winter, taking train at Amritsar and excursion steamer at Bombay for the pilgrimage to Mecca. These plump, red-cheeked, Tatar-faced beggars beat time on a triangle and sang an appealing verse or two, accompanying it with dramatic and graceful gestures; and they wished us long life, health, and wealth in return for our infidel annas. Other Yarkand men came out from the arches of the quadrangle, some blue-eyed and with faces absurdly Teutonic, their originally white skins tinged with sunburn and dirt until, like the Sikhs, they were a dark leather or ginger color. Some were horse-dealers, others had brought wool, silk, jade, turquoises, and agate for sale. All wore long, fur-bordered, wool or wadded coats, with real sleeves and seams in them, instead of the loose ends of cotton and pashmina cloth of the people of the Indian plains. One man in an old Russian military coat and top-boots looked the veritable stage secret-service man, and then we remembered that in this caravansary Kim slept and listened. But how we reveled in the streets and bazaars beyond! The quarter of the shoemakers, where gaudy Mohammedan slippers dangled in gorgeous strings and bunches, and leather-workers bent over rainbow tasks! The wool-shops, where Bokhara camels' wool and Kashmir and Rampur pashmina cloths overflowed from open sacks and bales! And yarn-shops, hung over with skeins of every color! Dye-shops, where turban lengths hung dripping with every brilliant fluid! Copper and brass and damascened metal shops, and shops for the sale of coarse carpets and dhurries, of skin bottles and earthen bowls,—all were fascinating. *The* shops, however, were the dens of shawl-shops, where pale, fine-featured Kashmiris sat embroidering shawl borders with silks and gold thread. The little Kashmiri boys, with their great eyes and long lashes, were charming creatures, fine products of an old race and an old civilization, purest Aryans of all these people; but the bearded Sikhs despise the Kashmiri only a little less than they despise the Bengali. The gentle, esthetic Kashmiri is not a fighting man, and there are thousands of pure and mixed Kashmir weavers and embroiderers long resident in Amritsar who still quail before the giant Sikhs.

We found the jewelers' row, where women who were themselves walking jewel-shops sat bargaining; and we found the gem-cutters' dens, where jade blocks from Yarkand and farther Turkestan were sawed, cut, and polished. Jewel-boxes, knife-handles, knife-blades, ear-rings, bracelets, slabs, and medallions for Delhi jewelers to inlay with precious stones, were all being evolved from the rough lumps of green stone by means of the primitive bow-string drill and emery-wheel driven by the foot. There was a sociable jade merchant of silky, persuasive manners, who lost much time trying to convince me that gray was green and that any soft stone, if it were even grayish-green, was jade, and that brown streaks and white clouds were desirable variations in the monotonous monochrome surface. After this prelude, he produced better pieces of this most fascinating and oldest lucky stone in the world. Bullock-carts crowded us to the wall and camel-trains brushed contemptuously through the narrow bazaars. One camel, loaded with baskets, scraped a destroying path through the tortuous lane, tearing down flimsy awnings and curtains, sweeping signs and trade samples along and tramping them under his spongy feet, while the shrieks of the despoiled tradesmen filled the air.

All the way touts dogged our steps. "Please come my shop. Please buy my shop," rang in my ear whenever I stopped to look or to point the camera. They followed us, pleading, if we walked; they leaped off and on the carriage-step if we drove; and "Jao!" had no significance to them save when emphasized by the bearer's stick. One persistent nagger drove us almost to frenzy with his lamentations and upbraidings whenever we stopped at a shop-front. We bade him "Jao!" and to stay "jao," but he was omnipresent, and to get rid of him we went to his shop. He had nothing but weather-worn rubbish; and while he ran to borrow stock from a neighbor we made our escape.

At the large carpet-factory ninety-seven looms

WINDOW AT GWALIOR.

were strung with cotton warp, and little Kashmiri boys, sitting elbow to elbow before them, tied in the wool threads, cut them with miniature scythes, and pressed down the stitches with wooden combs. A spectacled old Kashmiri, seated behind each curtain of warp-threads, read off the directions for the pattern from pages of Kashmir cipher, all understanding and following this ancient, conventional cipher by inherited association more easily than any of the clear, mechanical directions devised and used by the managers of jail carpet-works. Four small boys, with one old man to read the pattern to them, will make a fine, close, velvet-pile carpet, measuring eleven by thirteen feet, in two months and a half,—a carpet worth twenty-five dollars gold at Amritsar. The design is chosen, the materials allotted, and the contract let to the reader, who pays each boy three or four rupees a month. Conventional old Turkish and Persian designs are followed. They are first drawn in colors, traced on scaled paper, graded to the number of warp-threads, and the pattern written in Kashmir cipher. The small boys work mechanically, tying on two, four, or twenty stitches, as the reader calls to them, paying little heed to what is growing under their fingers, whether scroll, leaf, or stripe. "Two pink, three green, one red," chant the boys in monotones after the reader. The reader watches the pattern grow, and, detecting a false stitch, raps the offender with the stick he holds for the purpose. The carpets are valued both for the fineness of the stitches and the quality of the wool, the ordinary "fine old Persian, or Tabriz, rug" of Western auction-rooms costing eleven and twelve rupees a square yard in Amritsar; while a copy of a precious old wine-red Bokhara rug they were then weaving of fine pashmina or shawl wool was worth fifty rupees a square yard.

Each loom was a genre picture and a color study, with the spectacled Kashmiri in sober turban and jacket on one side, and on the other the row of long-lashed boys in brilliant garments, elbowing and shoving one another and tittering together, quite as all children behave in the presence of school visitors. No finished carpets could be seen or bought, since the looms were working overtime, a year behind their orders. New York buyers order largely each year, and large consignments go to London and Paris. There were shawls for sale, bales and bales of them, and stitched in silk threads at the end of each chudda was the number of warp-threads, by which their fineness and value are determined. They are kept in press between boards, and when one bought the silky fabric it was sewed in Kashmir wax-cloth and sealed in a clumsy tin box.

So very enchanting did we find these bazaars that we lingered another day and yet another, to feast on their picturesque setting and incidents each warm, Indian-summery afternoon. Then we hastened to the guard-house terrace overlooking the tank and the Golden Temple, and watched that building of beauty, whose reflection seemed to float upon the splendid sunset sky.

We hurried back to the bazaars again, to see the narrow, irregular lanes illuminated with every kind of poor, crude, clumsy lamp and lantern, tallow dip, rush-light, saucer of oil, and floating wick, fagot, and torch. Shadows hid the dirt and incongruities; each unique thing had its right value; and we haggled over blue-embroidered Yarkand felt rugs, over striped Ludhiana lungis or gold-shot cotton turban-cloths, over jade and blue ferozees and the shadowy Bokhara silks, far into the frosty darkness up to the late dinner-hour.

CHAPTER XXII

SIMLA

AMRITSAR'S railway platform—the same where Kim was put off the train for want of a ticket to Ambala, and by his wits was soon on board again—was most picturesque the noonday we started for Simla. A man in a blue coat with yellow cuffs and a red shawl thrown over his shoulder was only first figure in the crowd of red, blue, orange, and green-shawled creatures, in turbans of red, pink, orange, lemon, and salmon, in blue and gray Ludhiana lungis with gold-striped ends. An ash-smeared fakir crouched gibbering by the wall near the tank labeled, "Water for Mohammedans," and a high-caste Brahman protected water sacred to his co-religionists' use. A woman whose jewelry was but half concealed by a thin sari held an umbrella down over her face as she squatted on the concrete, and her owner threw a sheet over the umbrella and fiercely guarded the beehive tent. From this retreat, the woman peered forth, clashed and jangled her jewels to attract our attention, and made eager signs for us to come near that she might inspect us.

All afternoon we rode straight toward a long, blue horizon-line that grew, until at sunset, at Ambala, we had the great wall of the Himalayas plainly before us. We changed trains, and jolted over the thirty-five miles to Kalka in complete darkness. At nine o'clock we stumbled through a dark, deserted village to the so-called hotel, which was a little better than a stable only in that it had not yet been used for horses. We spread our bedding in chill, whitewashed, stone-floored rooms opening upon a stone porch; and once more in darkness followed a lantern through the streets to the post-office. There we agreed to pay the government of India, or the postmaster-general, seventy-five rupees for a "tonga phaëton," *i. e.*, a two-pony victoria, with sixteen relays of ponies, for the fifty-seven-mile drive up to Simla and return.

Wholly by our own energies we got the establishment astir the next morning at half-past six o'clock. The worst coffee in India was brought, with the usual smoky toast and repulsive butter-plate—this at perhaps the only hotel in India ever patronized by the official class, and which the smart, the luxury-loving and disdainful, must endure twice a year if they go to Simla. Western civilization in India, taking the hotel as its index, is at lowest ebb at Kalka.

Our tonga, or "fitton" in native colloquial, arrived at our door before sunrise, drawn by two bullocks. We mounted and were slowly dragged to the post-office, from which exact point the government had agreed to transport us. The two ponies were then affixed,—"as per contract," said the babu,—made fast by traces running to a tonga, or steel bar fastened yoke-wise to both girths. Away they went by leaps and bounds, and at a gallop, up hill, around corners, and along a country road through the foothills. Every three or four miles, the driver winded his horn, the ponies redoubled their efforts to run away, and we bounded into a tonga station, where the relay ponies stood waiting in harness. The steel bar was loosened and pinned to the girths of the new ponies, the traces and reins made fast, and we shot forth at the fixed gait of eight miles an hour.

It was a clear, cloudless day, with hoar-frost over the grass of the bare hillsides and on the rice-fields that in curving terraces filled every valley and ravine, rippling away in lines that seemed designed for ornament only. There were plantations of trees, but no forests—none of the jungles that one expects at the foot of such a mountain-range. In the distance clumps of intensely green *Pinus longifolia* waved their nine- and ten-inch-long needles as softly as bamboos. We mounted long inclines, whence we had a magnificent view of the hills and plains below, or looked up and across to the loops of the road above us. Sometimes we could watch the next relay station as we drove toward it, and with the glasses note the preparations for our arrival. Bullock-trains under guard of sepoys, low mail-tongas bringing convalescents down from the sanatoriums, and a few camel-trains passed by. The bearded Sikhs, the turbaned Pathans, and the handsome Kashmiris of Lahore and Amritsar streets had vanished, and in

THE HALL OF AUDIENCE, JEYPORE.

their places appeared a nondescript people in sober attire,—sturdy hill-men whose clothes and cheek-bones had the same Chinese suggestion as those of the hill-folk around Darjiling. At ten-thirty we shook off our razais and rugs and limped into the dak bangla at Solon, with fierce mountain appetites added to what naturally succeeded the imitation of a breakfast at Kalka. A courteous old khansamah, with a velvet manner and perfect decorum, ushered us to a dining-room where the chill of Himalayan summits lingered, and we soon had the table brought out to the sunny veranda. Twenty-seven miles of travel, and a lift of a few thousand feet in air, had raised the art of cookery far above its level at Kalka, and we breakfasted with enthusiasm.

While two plunging animals refused either to be led or backed up to the "fitton," the babu informed us that this was the best post-road in India; that it had the best carriages and best ponies; that the government pays one and two hundred rupees for the best Peshawar and Agra horses, and sells them cheap at the end of six or eight months, since only the best stock will do for or can stand the Simla travel. Across the valley we could see twenty horses sunning themselves before the next station, ready for the day's relays, and our early start gave us the choice of the successive stables. From Solon the road led steadily up over bare brown hills, marked by the path of landslides or the green of afforestation efforts, set with candlestick cacti and striped with an occasional patch of snow. All the boulders were painted over with and the pine groves stuck full of advertisements of a certain "Green Seal Whisky," the Himalayas as gaudy as a London omnibus or railway station. At last a turn revealed to us the snowy range, far away up against the sky, and then Simla's straggling crescent of houses was seen across a great chasm or valley. In seven hours and a half—just the time taken for the trifling trains to climb to Darjiling—we reached the Simla tonga station, seven thousand and eighty-five feet above the sea.

It was the place of the "Phantom Rickshaw," but what a material vehicle appeared to us! No wonder it is spelled with an unnecessary "c" and a barbarous "w," or with any alphabetical lumber that can be dragged in by Anglo-Indians. Nothing could be more ludicrous in a farce or burlesque in a Japanese theater than such a vehicle. Four thousand miles by road and centuries of intelligent development lie between the Tokio jinrikisha and the Simla "jinny rickshaw"—the one an airy seat on flying wheels; the other a solid, clumsy cart, a rattling, rumbling affair of cast-iron and thick planks, drawn by four shuffling coolies, who walk leaning against the long tongue or the back board of the undersized juggernaut.

A late tiffin awaited us in the ramshackle wooden hotel, which, patched, shabby, and unsightly, was in the hands of workmen getting ready for the opening of the season in March. The landlord was voluble and kind, for tourists never come to the hilltops in winter, and he gave us the best of the shabby old rooms—dark, sunless holes, with cheap furniture and fittings so long past their day that they might well be put in a museum of last-century crudities. Yet here fashion and arrogance abide from March to November, and the gayest social life goes on, despite the frightful thunder- and hail-storms—rains that are nearly water-spouts and cloud-bursts, and that continue for three months.

It was like turning the pages of "Plain Tales from the Hills" even to read the street signs as we lumbered about that crescent ridge of the summer capital. Jakko, the Mall, the Ladies' Mile, Elysium Hill, and all the rest were there, and we traveled the same road that Mr. Isaacs and the fair English girl rode together. There were the shops of jewelers,—in one of which Kim and the other boy counted the loose stones in trays,—shops of silk, silver, and curio merchants, of milliners and pastry-cooks, all boarded fast for the winter, and behind them the ramshackle buildings of the native bazaar dropped along the hillsides in crazy terraces. There were English villas and cottages, and nothing Oriental or truly Indian in the aspect of the place, and we had a stranger's feeling. Our slow-moving coolies were barefooted and barelegged, and when they stepped aside from the beaten track of slush to let bullock-trains pass, they often stood more than ankle deep in snow. As the setting sun played a fire-pageant over the line of snow-peaks, the chill mountain air penetrated our wraps and rugs, but the red-cheeked English girls in cotton shirt-waists strolled slowly home with their tennis rackets, as if it were a day in June. How we wished we might go with them; that they would ask us to follow on and have a cup of tea and meet Mrs. Hauksbee, the Gadsbys, and all the rest we knew so well! We wanted, too, to hear more about those long-past seasons when occult science and the new religion were setting Simla wild; when Mme. Blavatsky, the suspected Russian spy, was working her miracles, and great mahatmas and yogis were arriving from nowhere, with nothing in their hands, and letters dropped from the ceiling as commonly as from the postman's bag. A. P. Sinnett, the editor of the *Pioneer*, was leader in the occult movement, and by his "Esoteric Buddhism" and "Karma" theosophy spread to the Occident. We had glimpses of those days in "Mr. Isaacs," and Mr. Crawford's Ram Lal is to be taken seriously. The whole clumsy fraud had been exposed when Kipling came, and in "The Sending of Dana Da" we have an irreverent account of a specimen case. When all the claptrap and collusion, the mechanical devices and unblushing frauds had been exposed, laughter shook the Himalayan hills, and the rich natives, who had financed the apostles as furthering a crusade against Christianity and mission work, were left in tears. The London Society for Psychical Research sent their keenest investigator, and there was no mystery left—Isis was completely unveiled, and theosophy has since been a dead issue in Simla; and all its miracles were proved to be in line with Dana Da's sending of the kittens.

In February we walked the terraced promenade by the reservoir alone, and had the sunset view of the snowy range quite to ourselves. Three small

Anglo-Indians lingered by the cathedral door. We asked them the name of the large, white peak that rose above the long, snowy ridge. "I don't know the name. The snows—just the snows—is what we always call them," said one Wee Willie.

Even the landlord made a wry face when we said we had come to see Simla as a tribute to Kipling; that we should not have been satisfied to leave India without visiting this scene of so many of his stories. We assured the landlord—manager, rather—that we could not have appreciated nor understood India but for Kipling, nor Kipling but for India; that we now realized our debt to Kipling and the measure of his genius. The manager did not make vigorous protest, like all the other Anglo-Indians, for the wise man quarrels not with his bread and butter, and women who make pleasure-trips to Simla in February are not to be held accountable beyond the regular per diem rates in rupees.

The nights at Simla were something to benumb an arctic explorer, and it was a relief to rise in darkness and leave the tonga station long before the sunrise glow was seen beyond Jakko's heights. As we galloped away and down, the shadow of the Himalayas retreated from the tawny, hazy plain—a plain, as level and vast as the ocean, lying beneath the frost-haze. We had another sunny breakfast at Solon, and, timing our halts, we found two minutes by the watch sufficient to change ponies at any station. At ten minutes past two o'clock, seven hours after leaving Simla, we were at Kalka post-office, and a train soon carried us on to Ambala, where a four-hour wait was enlivened by the departure of a wedding-party from the cantonment. Ladies in laces and pale pink gowns brightened the dark train-shed and platforms as they threw slippers and rice. Silk-hatted men in frock-coats and pearl trousers covered the rails with torpedoes that gave joyful salute as the wheels rolled over them. A gorgeously turbaned person in a gold brocade dressing-gown and silver-toed, green leather slippers, and who ought to have been one of the hill rajas we forever read about, caught the eye completely. Sad to say, he was only the coachman of a polo-playing hill raja who had sent the bride and groom to the train in his state landau.

CHAPTER XXIII

ALWAR

THE superior tourist in India usually makes a point of his acquaintance with rulers of native states, generally harps on the fact unduly, and raises bitterness in the heart of the plain tourist and common sight-seer, who cannot refer casually to the rajas, diwans, residents, and political agents he knows. "I was the guest of the raja at So-and-So," "I was put up at the maharaja's bangla in Here-and-There," say such enviable beings. One listens with envy and deep humility if he does not know that a card from one's consul, even a courteously worded note from the tourist himself, will secure one the privilege of stopping at the government rest-house or raja's bangla in a native state —at a fixed price for his lodging and carriage. One makes the usual grand tour and sees the great sights of India without leaving British territory, although one third of the area and one fifth the population of India are under native rule. Hyderabad in the Deccan, where the Nizam rules twelve millions of people occupying a territory as large as Italy, Udaipur (spelled in seventy-two different ways), Jodhpur, Baroda, Indore, Alwar, Gwalior, and Kashmir are the native states the tourist finds most worth seeing. "I am only visiting native states on this trip," said one superior traveler. "I do not care for the beaten track." When we met him on the grand thoroughfare weeks later and asked as to his enjoyment of innermost India, he denounced native rulers in sweeping terms. "I arrived in —— the day the raja died in Calcutta, so there was nothing doing there, unless I waited a week to see a funeral. I presented my letter to the diwan at —— and he said: 'I am very sorry, but His Highness has been so intoxicated for the past fortnight that he has not seen any one. He is drinking a bottle of brandy and one of chartreuse a day, in addition to much champagne and Scotch and soda. I really cannot say when His Highness will be fit to receive visitors again.' At —— it rained cats and dogs, the bangla leaked, the bedding was wet, and the food bad, and I came away without presenting my letter. All India is off the beaten track."

We stopped at Alwar, in Rajputana, on our way back to Agra to keep our engagement with the February moon in the garden of the Taj. We reached Alwar station, as we had reached so many other places, between one and two o'clock in the morning. There was no carriage, no khansamah, nor any one from the maharaja's bangla to meet us—only sodden darkness and the platform of the small railway station. A tiny ekka was found, and in some way we, with the luggage and bearer, managed to get in the absurd little cab, and a mite of a pony managed

THE OLD CITY OF AMBER, FROM THE TOP OF THE DESERTED PALACE.

to pull us to the bangla. A sleepy khansamah made us comfortable for the rest of the night.

A relay of messengers, and finally a victoria with men in blue palace livery, came from the diwan, or prime minister of the tiny empire, at nine in the morning. We were driven to his house, and went through many anterooms to a cool, dark inner drawing-room, where a portly personage in a mixed Oriental and European costume of white flannel received us with great cordiality. His little daughter, in a woolen hood and many calico coats, but with only jingling anklets to keep her little bare brown feet and legs warm, was brought in and duly admired, and then he presented one Soorajbux, the learned librarian of the high school, who was detailed as our cicerone for the day. He took us first to the modern palace, a suburban villa full of European furniture and notions, where the young raja spent his occasional vacations from the Mayo College at Ajmir. Among the incongruities in the raja's study was a framed chromolithograph of Wood's single-apron binder at work in an American wheat-field. There were inclined planes as well as staircases that the ruler might ride to his bedchamber if he wished, and a beautiful durbar hall with carved window-lattices. From the upper windows we looked down upon a sunken garden, once a sacred tank, where fern- and orchid-houses overflowed with beautiful plants; and by avenues of bo- and banian-trees we reached the garden of the lions, tigers, and bears, home also of wonderful red, blue, and yellow parrots who uttered long Rajput sentences.

We drove rapidly back to the city and through the bazaars, where women in gaily embroidered phulkaris set with looking-glasses seemed to have walked away in those long-favored decorations of British drawing-rooms. We saw the stables, the five hundred horses, the forty elephants tramping and swinging their trunks in idleness "for the honor and glory of the raja," and then made another dash through city streets, with the populace saluting the palace equipage. In one court of the palace, an elephant in state trappings and a body-guard of soldiers waited before the temple where the raja's mother was praying. In the next court, the bearded keeper of the library waited for us in highly impatient mood. He had been waiting for hours, by the diwan's command, and, with much communing in his beard, he produced the books which are Alwar's pride—a beautifully illuminated Koran, a gorgeous Gulistan whose medallions, letters, and borders would excite a Western bibliophile, many Persian books illuminated by the best old Delhi painters,—and showed us one room full of sacred Vedas.

We were taken on to farther courts and through many marble halls to the banquet-hall, where the long dining-table was of solid silver. The water ran gurgling in silver channels down its length, and jeweled birds in gold and silver cages warbled over this precious garden-bed. There was a beautiful white-marble durbar hall with carved balconies and lattices, and a glittering Shish Mahal adjoining it, all a dazzle of mirrors and colored glass. It further overlooked a great tank or lake surrounded by marble terraces, balustrades, and pavilions, with a rugged mountain fortress crowning the perpendicular rock mass beyond the tank. It was a fairyland sight by day, and when illuminated for viceregal fêtes must transcend all Indian fantasies. A picturesque old turban claimed us and led the way to the armory, where room after room was filled with weapons with murderous and agonizing edges and points; their handles jeweled, carved, inlaid, and damascened; the blades wonderfully tempered, mottled and grained, often chased and inlaid with verses. One sword-blade had a shallow runnel near the hilt, in which a dozen loose pearls ran up and down in the gummy ooze of oil left by the zealous cleaners. Sword-hilts set with pearls, rubies, and diamonds; jade hilts jeweled all over; and hilts of Jeypore enamel were the delight of the gleeful, proud old armorer, who had a dramatic way of drawing a blade, giving it a flourish in air, and presenting it suddenly level with one's eyes for close inspection. We had finally to tear ourselves away from the array of more and more terrible weapons his minions brought from some inexhaustible storehouse—spears, daggers, elephant-goads, battle-axes, and chopping-knives of terrible ingenuity. The jewels of Alwar, the emerald cup, and the precious cabochon fringes would take pages to themselves, rivaling as they do the collections of temples.

We were hurried out to the white court overlooked by the zenana windows to see the return of the maharani,—such a spectacular scene that it was a pity the central figure in it was so curtained and veiled as not to be able to see it herself. Lancers on horseback, state elephants and color-bearers, first appeared in the white archway and, with the troops, ranged themselves around the dazzling court. Silver palanquins with red silk curtains held the royal ladies, and three hundred women attendants muffled in red, yellow, and white draperies chanted as they walked beside them. It was such a brilliant pageant that we could hardly believe it the ordinary weekday proceeding. To prove how much more splendid Alwar rulers could be on gala occasions, they showed us a two-story red and gold elephant carriage in which fifty people ride in state processions, and storehouses full of jeweled elephant trappings.

Then we saw the chetahs, or hunting leopards, huge spotted yellow cats, blindfolded and wearing funny little leather caps, and tied head, tail, and legs to a cage or skeleton stall. They stood inert as wooden cats, and would neither growl, snap, nor even wink when the keepers tried to rouse them, two men lifting a chetah and setting it down as they might lift and move a four-legged table. In the jail yard and workshops the law breakers were contentedly weaving carpets, dhurries, and cloth, making paper, grinding corn, and otherwise making themselves useful. The leader, a red-handed murderer, chanted the carpet pattern, and his fellow-criminals bawled loudly in response, tying "one green, three white, two blue" automatically. There are already hereditary criminals in these modern, comfortable jails, and the jail caste is fast becoming a definite order.

THE DESERTED PALACE, FROM THE LAKE, AMBER.

Soorajbux took us to his high-school building, showed us his illuminated Persian books, and asked many naïve questions about the outer world. "The Japanese—are they at all like the Hindus? Of what religious caste are they? Are they civilized like us?" And we left Soorajbux exclaiming: "What! they are the most refined and artistic people in the world! Their art a revelation to and the despair of all Europe! They are more esthetic than the English! How very wonderful! Do the English know it?"

In the afternoon the courteous old diwan returned our visit, his yellow turban and suite sending the bangla staff into such agitation that we barely made the station and train in time as a fierce thunder-storm came on. We dined and waited a few hours at Bandikui Junction, and then took train for Agra, arriving at half-past three in the morning; for, no matter from which direction the traveler comes, it seems impossible ever to reach Agra at a rational hour. We stopped this time at the hotel where the German professor had enjoyed the grilled mutton-chops, and a notice on the wall of my room requested: "Visitors will please not beat the servants, but report them to the manager, who will punish them."

We revisited the Taj on a gray, cloudy morning, the moist air heavy with the fragrance of flowers. We sat again on the balcony of the Jasmine Tower at the fort and watched a murky sunlight play upon the distant white bubbles of the Taj, and then took an afternoon train for Gwalior. The whole timetable of the Indian Midland Railway was put out of joint and our train made an hour late by the lamp dropping through the roof of our compartment. Guards and station-masters at three stopping-places chattered and gave frenzied orders, and while a small lamp was in some way tied into the large socket, nothing could bring a man of sufficiently ignoble caste to wipe the oil and broken glass from the floor.

CHAPTER XXIV

GWALIOR

AFTER any experience with the ordinary dak bangla and the up-country hotels, the Mussaffirkhana, the maharaja's rest-house at Gwalior, is a dream of luxury. Used only to dirty carpets and dhurries, or ancient reed mattings laid on cement or mud floors, we rubbed our eyes at sight of the shining white stairway, at the clean, soft-piled carpets of the beautiful white villa, and more at the great-windowed bedrooms that were actually furnished. There were real bureaus and real beds—complete beds with springs, mattresses, pillows, sheets, blankets, and spreads! We sat down in amaze, and the sense of wonder was exhausted when we found every lock, hinge, knob, and fastening of the doors and windows in working order and the whole place spotlessly clean. Such sights had not been seen since Colombo. Below-stairs the pretty drawing-room and dining-room were as well kept and modern. The Mussaffirkhana was the greatest surprise in India, the enlightened maharaja a special providence to hardship-worn tourists fortunate enough to be permitted to inhabit that abode of bliss, a literal rest-house and a temple of cleanliness and order. Naturally we dreamed of American hotels and other high products of our civilization, and happily waked to find the Mussaffirkhana not a dream but luxurious reality. After the chota hazri, as daintily perfect as the little breakfast of a Paris hotel, we drove about the well-kept town in a palace carriage, a perfectly appointed victoria. The streets were lined with white houses, whose tracery windows and ornamental balconies were worthy an art museum. The street crowds were most brilliant, and more yellow was worn in Gwalior than elsewhere, along with the endless variety of Mahratta turbans, which surpass in number and originality those of any other people. The very imposing coachman snapped his whip and the blooded horses sped away like the wind, straight down the middle of each street, the sais yelping shrill warnings, the crowds parting automatically and saluting the palace livery. We saw the beautiful unfinished temple to Sindhia's mother, for which the stone-cutters were chipping out as fine traceries and latticings as any in Delhi or Agra, and then returned for the serious British breakfast, at a table fragrant with roses and mignonette. It was radiant, mild, ideal spring weather, and after all our sufferings from cold we basked with delight in the open air, faring forth again to the foot of the rock-fortress which rises like Gibraltar from the plain. A splendid elephant in red-velvet trappings stood waving its trunk as we drove up, and at the word of command sank upon its hind legs in a deep courtesy, stretched out its great body, slowly bent its fore

THE HALL OF MIRRORS.

legs and sank to the ground, and we climbed up a ladder to the dos-à-dos car or saddle on its back. With earthquake heaves, a rock this way and a lurch that way, it stood erect and lumbered up the steep, flagged path, through six defensive gateways, to the blue-tiled walls of the "painted palace" at the edge of the rock. We penetrated its deserted courts all carved with flat traceries and arabesques and set with enameled tilings and stone latticings, and from the flat roof had an unlimited view over the level yellow plain more than three hundred feet below.

Again our stately transport knelt, we climbed to the red-velvet jaunting-car on its back, and it paced across the flat, table-topped mesa to the half-ruined Jain temples, where conquering Moguls wreaked their fanatic zeal, chipping and mutilating the myriad tiny figures in the bas-reliefs with which walls and columns were covered, and further effacing them with coats of chunam and whitewash. The wealth of intricate ornament lavished on these temples would be incomprehensible were there not the perfect Jain temples at Mount Abu to show what the shrines of Gwalior rock once were in less degree. While we lingered at that angle of the rock's parapet to look down upon the city below us, the yellow-turbaned mahout made his elephant do tricks like any poodle. It picked up and threw stones, waved its spotted ears and trunk as commanded, and nosed up the tiniest coins from grass or gravel and gave them to the mahout. It lumbered after us over the grass as tamely as a kitten, its great soft feet shuffling with a strange barefoot tread as it followed us to a pyramidal temple ruin very similar to the Buddhist ruins in Java. The same indefatigable Major Keith who rescued and preserved the old carved and tiled palace worked over this temple, too, restoring the gateway and replacing as far as possible every carved fragment. We remounted, and the mahout guided the monster down the road and then close beside the parapet, goaded it until it was as close to the coping as possible, and then bade us look down and see the rock-sculptures that adorn the perpendicular face of a ravine of the rock. With three hundred feet of space below our feet, the breathing of the elephant seeming enough to burst the girths that bound the car to it, and its lurches as it shifted its weight from one foot to the other enough to propel us into the air, we cared nothing for bas-reliefs and images. A tank far below, and the winding white Lashkar road, seemed to sway in air and rise toward us, and we clutched the car-frame in agony and begged only to be taken down to the safe level of the plain again, to horses and wheeled vehicles. We could easily believe that much elephant-riding makes one mad, and that the motion and the heat of the elephant's body affect the spine and shorten the life of a mahout. After the jerking and jolting of its downhill progress we gladly left the gentle giantess in the red-velvet cloak salaaming and putting its trunk to its forehead in thanks, in ridiculous parody of the slim little mahout beside it.

We were allowed to peep into the court of the Jama Masjid without unshoeing, and went then to see the splendid and impressive tomb of Mohammed Ghaus, a Moslem saint of Akbar's time, who rests in an immense domed hall shut in by sandstone lattices of exquisite and intricate design. Next came the tomb of Tansen, a musician, sheltered by a tamarind-tree whose leaves, if chewed prayerfully, will secure one a sweet voice. The dancing-girls come to worship at this tomb, and tree after tree has been stripped of leaves and killed, so that seedling descendants are kept at hand to replace them.

"Memsahib," said the bearer, excitedly, "there will be fight this day with lion, unicorn, and elephant. Will memsahib see?" Learning that the unicorn was a rhinoceros, we were ready to see the fray which is the national pastime, as in Akbar's day. A British major from Rawal Pindi cantonment, showing India by winter to a visiting niece and nephew, and staying at the Mussaffirkhana, implored us so earnestly not to go that we deferred to his advice—and have regretted it ever since, wondering how much of local color and national character we missed in not seeing Sindhia's subjects at their favorite sport, to which bull-fighting must be child's play.

The bazaars were brilliant enough when crowded with white-clad Mahratta men in their fantastic turbans, and Mahratta women in full, bunchy skirts of every hue, swinging and tilting past, clashing and jangling their anklets; but when a part of the raja's body-guard, preceding the maharani on her way to worship, paraded down a street of white houses, the stage pageant was complete. Horsemen in gay uniform and gorgeous turbans, with fluttering pennons; horses in bright saddle-cloths, yellow bridles and trimmings; a state elephant in red velvet and gold trappings, with cloth-of-gold curtains to its gilded howdah; and a troop of women surrounding the gilded palanquin, made up a very spectacular church parade. It was all so splendidly theatrical, so really Oriental, as at Alwar, that we said: "This is the last touch, the perfect climax. Let us go quickly, before the curtain falls, the people put on their every-day clothes, and we are disillusioned. Let Gwalior remain in memory with all the bloom of the first overpowering impression." We would not wait two days on the chance of meeting Sindhia himself when he should return from a hunting-trip, and we took train for Agra—arriving at midnight, of course.

We had a quiet Sunday to revisit tombs in appropriate observance of the day, and to sit again on the Jasmine Tower and watch the sunset play over the Taj Mahal. There was an unmistakable Sabbath atmosphere to the view, although the dhobiemen were swinging, pounding, and spreading out acres of cloths to dry on the flats below the fort, and twittering parrakeets flashed in and out of the creviced wall, and fluttered over the dry moat where Akbar's elephants and unicorns fought for his entertainment. A sudden impulse seized us as the pageant began, and we hurried to the gharry, implored the sais to make all speed, and running through the garden of the Taj, settled ourselves once more in the upper story of the western minaret overhanging the river.

The great white temple was richly yellow in the last beams of the sun, with blue shadows in every recess. Softly rolling white clouds across the Jumna took on rose-lights and were reflected in the river. The Taj flushed rose-pink, and before the golden burst of the afterglow had faded the February moon rose full, round, blood-red in the east. The vision was complete. Fifteen times had we entered the garden of the Taj, and each time the spell of the Taj was stronger.

The next day dragged through with odds and ends of sight-seeing until sunset. We dutifully did the jail, the most populous in India, where often a thousand prisoners are kept, and carpet-weaving is the chief of many industries. Great efforts have been made, by following the best old designs and using only vegetable dyes, to attain a high standard and keep the Agra carpets first in the foreign market. Thirteen rupees a square yard is the average price, and over five thousand yards are woven a year, the jail earning 90,000 rupees a year by its industries. Agra criminals long furnished the best jail carpets in India, but good conduct reduced the time of some and Jubilee benevolence released others of the best long-sentence weavers, and the Agra carpets declined for a time. That afternoon we stayed by the Jasmine Tower and watched the white bubbles on the horizon flush rose-red for a brief moment against a misty gray sky. Then white mists rolled up from the river, and rain-clouds gathered and hid the Taj Mahal forever from our view.

CHAPTER XXV

JEYPORE

AT Agra we were midway in the peninsula—eight hundred and forty-one miles from Calcutta, and eight hundred and forty-eight miles from Bombay. It was very cold, and rain was falling in sheets when we started, late at night, to ride the one hundred and forty-nine miles to Jeypore, and during the night it grew colder. Clouds of dust came through the loose, rattling carriage-windows, and when we shook off our razais at daylight, near Jeypore, there was a small dust-storm in our compartment.

The pompous, fat proprietor of the Hotel Kaiser-i-Hind was strutting the platform in a solferino plush coat, waving a telegram and shouting for "Eliza! Eliza!"—meaning the person who had sent the message. His rival, the proprietor of the dak bangla, fawned at our elbow, beseeching us to come to his house instead, and there was wordy war between the two across me, charge and counter-charge. "I will furnish elephant for Amber, no charge!" shouted one. "Oh, memsahib! memsahib!" hissed the other, "that elephant no good elephant, not got teeth." "Mine is first-class family hotel," roared the solferino villain. "Oh, his is dirty, rotten hotel," wailed the other. "Please come my house, please come my house, I am poor man," bawled the bangla-keeper, as the big solferino banged the carriage-door on his trophies and climbed the box to guard us from being kidnapped on the way.

The dining-room of the Kaiser-i-Hind was in the cellar-like ground floor, and an outside staircase led to the cement terrace or roof on which the bedrooms opened—lofty rooms, with many doors and long windows to admit air in the hot weather when the hotel is empty, and fireplaces the size of a crumb-tray to warm them on the frosty nights when the place is filled with shivering, sneezing tourists. Two dozen times the solferino one asked me if I wanted a guide for Jeypore, and as many times he received the decisive "No." Two babus were breakfasting in the general room, quite like Europeans, and speedily opened conversation. No discouragements could check their volubility, and we watched to see what game was premeditated. "I am not common man," said the larger turban. "I am prince. I am Nawab of Behar. Go! fetch me those letters from the duke," he said to his companion, who returned with a greasy note, worn like a beggar's certificate. The secretary of the Duke of Connaught had written to "His Highness Mer Abdul-asal Alum Khan, Nawab of Behar," to express condolences on the death of the Nawab's wife. Then this doubtful Nawab, eating in the public room of an inn with casteless unbelievers, told us that his family owned the Esplanade Hotel in Bombay, and that he spent much time there. He offered to telegraph to his brother-ruler of Indore, or to any native state we might wish to visit. He would even take us around Jeypore and show us the sights, since he had nothing else to do that day. He would take us to the shops—and then all suspicions crystallized without this democratic raja adding: "I will take you to the best shops. I am not common man after commission." This latest form of tout, the princely one of the table d'hôte, was such an amusing climax to our touting experiences that we could hardly keep serious countenances before the clumsy confidence-man and his accomplice. His tongue ran on and on, in sheer joy in its running. "I want not commissions on what you buy. I want not money in this world—only friends, and weeping when I am dead." We could not tell how much conspiracy there was between this pair and the solferino landlord, who had been so persistent about our taking a guide; but the solferino one handed the Nawab into a carriage with a great flourish just as our "fitton" drew up. "You are going to the museum?" asked the Nawab. "So are we"; and he was whirled away without escort or outriders. He stood on the museum steps dumbly staring when our carriage went past him toward the city gates, and when we did return to the museum, two hours later, the Nawab was waiting and showed the strain of that long suspense. The pair followed us from case to case for a while, profuse in praises of what we looked at longest, voluble until we put direct questions to them about the methods and processes of manufacture of some of the old art objects. "I can find you shop to make you copy of anything you see here," repeated the bogus Nawab several times plaintively. To end the farce, which had then been played long enough, we confided loudly to each other in prearranged dialogue that we had not an anna left for shopping in Jeypore—only our railway tickets and rupees enough to get to Bombay. The Nawab melted away without adieu and was seen no more.

This art museum, housed in a beautiful palace in a park, is filled with the choicest examples of old pottery, brass, enamel, gold- and silver-work, carving, weaving, embroidery, jewelry, and everything else on which Indian fancy and genius lavished decoration in the past. At the art school in the city replicas of many of the museum objects were for sale, and others could be commanded. The class of young brass-beaters sat in the cellar-like entrance of the school, beating out Saracenic traceries as borders of large brass trays sunk in beds of pitch; and a dyer and his wife next door walked up and down, stretching between them to dry the rainbow-striped cotton head-sheets which are a specialty of Jeypore. Everywhere in this "rose-red city, half as old as time," the street groups were so theatrically picturesque that we forgot everything in watching them. The city is new, architecturally, and its two long, straight streets, crossing at right angles by the palace walls, cause all picturesqueness to converge there. The crowds were so brilliant and fantastic that one remembers Jeypore as some pageant in grand opera, the bazaars more spectacular than even those of Lahore. At noon, we saw the broad main street crowded from curb to curb with men in white clothes, with gay turbans and shawls,—a crowd that swayed and surged and moved until the long expanse of turbans was like a tulip-bed in the wind. It was the climax of all Indian street scenes, and such a kaleidoscopic play of color as could only be seen there on the day telegraphic bulletins are received from the government opium auctions, which fix the price of the drug for the month.

At the great Four Corners there is a monumental fountain, and there elephants continually pace by, camel-trains pass and repass, and pigeons descend in clouds if one tosses a few grains in air. Sheeted women, with jingling anklets and full-swinging skirts, come to the corner of the jewelers' bazaar to buy their glass, brass, lacquer, and more precious bangles and nose-rings. There were wedding processions passing the fountain all that sunny day, which had been declared the lucky one of the month. Many cortèges were preceded by elephants in rich velvet and bullion trappings, their faces, trunks, and ears elaborately painted. Jeweled bridegrooms went by in velvet-lined palkis hung from silver yokes, and from time to time the processions halted, a canvas was spread on the ground for the company to sit on, and nautch-girls—middle-aged colored women in bunchy accordion skirts and full panoply of jewels—gave a deliberate song-and-dance interlude. These mature sirens literally "trod" their slow-footed measures in clumsy, dusty leather shoes that a hod-carrier might wear. Each family circle wel-

INTERIOR OF JAIN TEMPLE, MOUNT ABU.

comed us to the company of wedding guests, and we assisted at several such interludes. There was the palace to see—a modern, tawdry, semi-European affair of much plaster-work, mirrors, and gilding. The carpets were rolled up in the throne-room of the beautiful Audience Hall, the furniture covered with brown holland, and the state treasurer, cross-legged between two accountants, occupied it for the day while he paid off the palace servants. We were led down the long marble paths of the formal garden to see—a billiard-room. But we saw, on the way, the myriad-bay-windowed walls of the zenana, which greatly resembled the street fronts of San Francisco hotels. We saw the palace stables and two aged elephants eating grass; and later in the day went to "the lion and tiger museum" to see two real, live unicorns. "See," said our bearer, "with how very loose skins these unicorns are," as he led us to the rhinoceroses' cage.

There were the regular, cut-and-dried tourists' shops filled with crudely made weapons, rough brasses and potteries, for which gullible folk pay twice the London price; and one such proprietor met us at the door with his visitors' book and insisted that we should read the praises of himself, his wares, and the Indian tiffin he serves good patrons, written but the day before by some young travelers from New York. He dilated upon the virtues of Americans, and showed us the boxes and boxes of trumpery stuff bought by those tourists; and it was great comfort to us, the worthy poor, that we were not as the millionaires are—to be taken in by Brummagem goods and cast-iron sword-blades at double the Broadway prices.

At another shop of archaic weapons that had but yesterday come from the foundry, we bought an elephant-goad for peace and sociability's sake, and sat for an hour to watch the panorama of the main street. The bearded proprietor bubbled away at his hooka and pointed out the Jeypore celebrities as they went by—the prime minister, the chief magistrate, the political resident,—even the treasurer going in state, with an artillery escort, to pay visits. A group of Brahmans bringing sacred Ganges water from Benares had military escort, too, and a military band; and there was an air of religious state to all the great ekkas drawn by noble white bullocks, the kincob curtains but half concealing the rainbow-wrapped women within. Noble graybeards pranced by on Arab horses, and five wedding processions, with jeweled nautch-girls in gold-gauze dresses, passed before us, the wise old elephants looking very bored with all this fuss and folderol over the marriage of small boys. A customer came and bought some big brasses; a minion ran off and found a dilapidated box for a few annas, and they patched and mended it on the spot. Then the proprietor swept a glance over the crowded thoroughfare and let forth wails like a muezzin on a minaret. A woman, bent under a great bundle of forage, stepped aside, dropped her small haystack on the shelf-like floor of the shop, and the packer's material was bought from her, a simple, direct, and primitive proceeding that delighted me.

Such scorching sunshine and piercing winds were never experienced together as in Jeypore. One needed an umbrella as protection from the sun and fur wraps as protection from the wind at the same time. We tiffined in the icy dining-room and took coffee on the scorching terrace, where merchants of arms gathered daily to display their ancient weapons —cast-iron stuff made to order in England to furnish the "cozy corners" of Christendom, to hang on the walls, and to prop up the divan draperies of so-called Oriental rooms.

It was on one of the most brilliantly sunny and piercingly cold days that we drove across the city and out to the flat country beyond, where abandoned gardens, crumbling tombs, lone minarets, and domes lined the road, and alligators basked by neglected tanks where green scum floated. As we drove into a courtyard, a weary old elephant with a painted face sadly in need of retouching saluted us with foot and trunk. It knelt, and we climbed to a rickety charpoy, or string-bed frame, covered with doubtful razais. After the noble beast at Gwalior, with its splendid trappings and comfortable jaunting-car, this ill-pacing, moth-eaten, tourist elephant of the Raja of Jeypore was a disappointment; and after it had lurched and lumbered along a few miles that we might have done more comfortably in the carriage, our disgust was unbounded. We were disenchanted before the creature began the steep ascent to the deserted palace of Amber, delighted that the elephant is fast being relegated to the background, a creature for shows and ceremonials only, the railway and the automobile displacing it as a means of travel, and American overhead machinery crowding it out of timber-yards; and the Delhi durbar of 1903 very probably the last great parade of state elephants.

All the way out from the city the road had been streaming with people in brilliant clothes and the kaleidoscopic street crowds of Jeypore continued far into the country. Troops of Rajputs in green, white, and yellow clothes, on foot, in bullock-carts, sitting by the roadside, and going in and out of temples, enlivened the way, and, as we mounted the side of the mesa, we could see this brilliant ribbon of road stretching away through the level of the abandoned city of Amber. The lurching elephant gave us momently finer and wider views out over the plain of ruins, and finally lumbered into a court of the fortress palace and knelt for us thankfully to dismount. In the little temple to Kali, at the palace entrance, the floor was still red with the blood of the goat just sacrificed, and we had heathendom fresh and hot there at the maharaja's door. Guidebooks and sentimental tourists have said so much in praise of Amber that we had keyed our expectations too high. Also, one must land at Bombay and see Amber before seeing Agra, Fatehpur Sikri, Delhi, and the rest to value it so highly. The tinsel looking-glasses and plaster rooms at Amber were wearisome. We had seen too many before. The pavilions, the baths, and the gardens seemed small and contracted, and even the pomegranate-trees grew in pots. Best of all in the palace was the high balcony, where we enjoyed a picnic tiffin and a view out over the lake and the plain of ruins and tombs. The elephant took us slowly down hill with the greatest possible discomfort, the mahout goading it until drops of blood stood on its neck, and we rejoiced that there was no more elephant-riding in prospect that season.

We were delighted to get back to the fantastic, pink-plaster streets of Jeypore and join in its theatrical pageantry, throw wheat to the pigeons in air, join arrested wedding processions, and watch the sedate old dancers in brogans tramp their slow measures and sing their nasal songs. The street juggler looped the torpid python around his body and held the head before him to be photographed, as if the coiling creature were only a garden-hose with fangs in the nozle. The streets fairly blazed with color in the last red and yellow rays of sunset; brilliant turbans and head-sheets were moving languidly in every direction around the four-corners' fountain; pigeons whirled in clouds and trotted beside us by hundreds; flocks of noisy crows flew to settle for the night in trees just outside the city wall; and when we reluctantly drove away the frost-haze was silvered by moonlight, and Jeypore remains a brilliant picture—too spectacular and color-satisfying to be real, too good to be true, a certain feeling possessing one that the scenery was rolled up that night and the troupe went home or on to the next town. In the cold hotel we slowly congealed, enthusiasm declined, and we joyfully quoted Lord Curzon's opinion: "The rose-red city over which Sir Edwin Arnold has poured the copious cataract of a truly Telegraphese vocabulary, struck me when I was in India as a pretentious plaster fraud.'' In memory one reverts to Sir Edwin Arnold's view, sees only the fantastic pink palace fronts, the brilliant turbans, the wedding processions, and the jeweled women switching their red and yellow skirts in the sunshine; and of all places in India, I should like best to be put down for an hour in the streets of Jeypore, when the midwinter sun is shining, the opium-market is lively, and the astrologers have declared it a propitious day for weddings.

CHAPTER XXVI

MOUNT ABU AND AHMEDABAD

WE were jolted from midnight until the next noon, to cover the two hundred and seventy-four miles of railway between Jeypore and Abu Roads, our bearer standing in his crowded car for all but three hours of that time. At Abu Roads we met again the long-tongued Anglo-Indian "jinny rickshaw." There were six coolies to each cart; two leaned against the cross-beam of the ridiculously long tongue as they slowly walked; two more leaned against the back of the vehicle; and the two reliefs rested as they lounged along the flat country road; all six dragging their clumsy shoes in the dust and enveloping us in a cloud for the six miles of level carriage-road. Running was not in their thoughts as, with frequent rests, they slowly crossed the plain and, at a snail's pace, crawled up the easy grades of the mountain road. Even ox-teams overtook us. We passed only the wretched hovels of the people, mere pig-sties of bamboo and mud beneath bamboo-trees, each with its banana-patch, and our shouting coolies made all who came to the doors to stare, kneel and salute us. We rested once by a tragic black pool shaded by two enormous banian-trees, where Scotch whisky and soda was insistently offered us by a black keeper of a refreshment booth. The temple domes on the mountain-top showed in sky-line; the golden plain shimmered far below us; and in six and a half hours we accomplished the sixteen miles. We dragged along beside a lake in the late sunset as bullock-carts filled with rosy English children came from a picnic. There were rice-fields on the mountain top, flooded by primitive Persian water-wheels, wonderfully green and thriving crops, and groups of palms in every vista. Violets bloomed by the dak bangla's door-steps, where a fine old khansamah greeted us and gave us tea with Goanese guava jelly on crisp toast in a warm room.

Mount Abu is the headquarters of the resident who rules the seventeen Rajput principalities, and from him we secured a permit to visit the Jain temples. The Jains are the last of the Buddhists left in India and their creed is still closely akin to that Gautama devised for his people, although their observance of caste is contrary to the fundamental principle of Buddhism. A Rajput officer in European coat, draped dhotee, and a sword as his badge of race and rank, with a red-coated chuprassy from the Residency, escorted us the next morning the two miles to the Dilwarra shrines. The guard at the temple gate hurriedly wound himself into his kamarband, set his turban straight, and, shouldering his carbine, paced the flags energetically while we waited for the permits to be examined.

CEILING OF JAIN TEMPLE, MOUNT ABU.

Another red coat and yellow turban came, and the three guided us around the two Jain temples, which are the most elaborately carved and decorated shrines in India. They were built in the eleventh and twelfth centuries, and the marble was brought from quarries twelve miles away and carved to frost- and lace-like fineness.

Marble cloisters whose alcove chapels contain seated images of the *tirthankars,* or Jain saints, surround an inner court holding the elaborately constructed and decorated central shrine and altar. One marvels as much at the perfect preservation as at the minute, lavish ornamentation; and for the preservation the Rajputs have to thank the English. In the central domical halls of both temples the columns, arches, struts, trusses, beams, central panels, and altar-fronts are covered with myriads of tiny figures and bands of conventional ornament in full and low relief, a marble filigree-work surpassing anything to be seen elsewhere. Scenes from the lives of the saints frame the niches holding their images; wonderful rosettes and pendentives enrich the ceilings; and saints by the meter band the columns and walls until one feels hypnotized by the myriad repetitions. Leaf forms suggest the Greek acanthus, while the Buddhist swastika, elephant, lotus, and Hansa goose appear, and a whole grammar of Indian ornament can be traced in those halls, where the white saints sit absorbed in eternal meditation. At the first temple fifty-five saints sit in as many cells around the court, and a coolie was dusting the images as indifferently as if they were but common furniture, flicking at them with a doubtful rag, and whacking them again in a way to make one wonder what a European could do to shock religious sentiment and make the Jains hedge a visitor's entrance with permits and guards. It is expressly enjoined that Europeans shall remove their hats and not step on the platforms of the shrines or within the image-cells.

The second temple is the older one and simpler in some respects; but the pillared hall of the main shrine is loftier, its serpentine brackets and struts even more lavishly ornamented, its dome and pendentives more exquisite. We went back and wondered again at all the extravagance of carving in the first temple. Certainly these two Jain shrines are the climax of Indian decoration and ornamental construction, miracles and masterpieces of patient art.

The night on the frosty mountain top aggravated colds dating back to the wet felt slippers at Amritsar temple, and it was a delight to get down to Abu Roads and the dry, hot plain again. The station-master let us go at once to the waiting car that was attached to the train in the middle of the night. The down mail jolted us into Ahmedabad before daylight, where another kind station-master let us remain in the shunted car until breakfast-time. At the end of the station platform an ornamental minaret rose above the trees, first harbinger of the day of architectural feasts. Had Ahmedabad not been one of the exceptionally unique and interesting cities of India, I could not have maintained enthusiasm to explore its mosques while burning with the fever of influenza. The air was soft and warm as late spring in the earliest morning, and the sun had a desert scorch at noon at that end of February. By dreary lanes and ruined gates in broken walls, we reached the beautiful mosques whose carved sandstone columns and walls recall those of Fatehpur Sikri. Rani Sipri's mosque, the Queen's mosque, the tombs of Mohammed Chisti and Muhafiz Khan each seemed the perfection of beauty in line and carved ornament, the minarets, arches, and walls covered with such a wealth of arabesques and traceries as vied with the white wonders on Mount Abu. At the Queen's mosque a band of Moslems bore in a sheeted figure bound to a charpoy covered with a rich cloth and garlands of marigolds. All the mourners bathed at the tank, united in standing prayer, lifted the charpoy, and bore it off to the graveyard.

We drove into a dreary, rubbish-strewn common, and, through a breach in an old wall, reached the court behind Sidi Said's desecrated mosque of the palace to look from the outside upon the two famous tracery windows, best known and most beautiful work of that kind in India. Nothing in marble traceries elsewhere approaches them. We drove to Hathi Singh's Jain temple, whose saints in niches and elaborately carved ornament in white marble are in the style of the Mount Abu shrines, and then we went to see the great tanks and green wells surrounded by marble galleries, where luxury-loving rulers sought coolness during the great heat.

The streets of Ahmedabad are dazzling and kaleidoscopic to one beginning his India at Bombay; but Ahmedabad, once "the handsomest town in Hindustan, perhaps in all the world," is a dull second after Jeypore. There were new models in turbans to be seen, and the picturesque pigeon-cotes erected by humane Jains are other novelties peculiar to this one city; for the Jains observe the strictest Buddhist tenets against destroying life, provide refuges and hospitals for animals, strain all the water they use, and step aside to spare the lowliest insect.

The vegetable, brass, and pottery bazaars, strung down the middle of a wide street, were centers of life and uproar; but the local guide bore us off to the workshop of a carpet-weaver,—poor show after Amritsar, Lahore, and Agra's factories,—and to the gate of the chief wood-carver who executes American orders for interior decorations. There was holiday or bankruptcy on for that day, but much searching and pounding on mute doors at last produced a lank Moslem with a key, who opened a great room containing a table, a book of designs, and four carved chairs, tagged with price-marks five times those of the Lahore Art School. We searched the brass bazaars and all the brass-shops for the pierced screens that a winter-touring M. P. lauds as a local specialty. In clouds of warm dust we drove here and there, hunting the famous kincob-shops, walking through archways to alleys and ill-smelling courts and cul-de-sacs, where small dealers had bundles of creased samples of tawdry, wall-papery brocades. Others

TRACERY WINDOW, AHMEDABAD.

shook squares of tinselly stuffs from upper windows, and shouted, "Fifteen rupees!" for each damaged remnant. The smells of those byways were invitation to and promise of any pestilence, and in one damp, fetid corner that we retreated from abruptly even the glib guide seemed to smell a thing or two. "Phew! the drains! the drains! What a very bad municipal!" and we never wondered that the native states show such a great decrease of population during the last five years of the century, while the bubonic plague raged.

At the busy clothes bazaar, tinsel caps and orange jackets for little boys were the bargains of the day that crowds were competing for, and more and more peddlers were opening rainbow packs and preparing for an evening bazaar. We had done our duty by the sights and shows of Ahmedabad; we had had our fill of local color and smells; and we drove back to rest at the comfortable station. Our guide and the bearer were bewildered, and the latter tearful at our wasting two hours on foot in the bazaar, and losing that much time in the use of the horses taken at so much for all day. "But, memsahib," he whimpered, "if you pay six rupees a day for a carriage, you must use all day. You *must* see all. There are many nice tombs yet. You must see more. You must not stop now. These horses just stand around, while you walk two hours, and now you stop for tea, and no more use. It is too expenseful."

When the Bombay mail rumbled in, we found our reserved compartment, spread our razais, and lay down, and all at once had a strange, dizzy, floating sensation, as if hypnotized or drugged. The train was moving, but without jar, jolt, or thumps. The carriage rolled smoothly, as if on springs, and we sat up and stared out and at each other to fathom the mystery. At last, on our seventeenth night, and after many days spent on Indian railway trains, we had met the mythical "bogie-car"! The car-spring was a reality.

CHAPTER XXVII

THE CAVES OF ELLORA AND KARLI

WE touched the Western world at Bombay only for a day, and quickly took train again, spreading our razais for an all-night ride of one hundred and seventy-eight miles to Nandgaon. No bogie-car, no sort of spring or buffer, softened the thumps of the hard-cushioned couches, and the occupant of the upper berth, feeling a draft when she had climbed to her swinging shelf, unhooded the lamp and found that the side wall of the car consisted of wire netting only in its upper portion. Her bedding was removed to the floor, and as there was no way to check this generous ventilation, chill drafts swept the compartment as the train ran through damp fields and dark spaces, and the dust of the road-bed covered us an inch deep by morning. The feeble lamp flickered out soon after midnight, and it took vigorous shouting at two dark stations before we could get the station-master and his note-book to investigate, report, and reilluminate with a broken-down lamp that went out as soon as we left his station. As everywhere in India, there were steaming tea-kettles on the platforms and cups of tea at one's window at every halt; and we thawed and packed in the darkness in time to dismount at Nandgaon at six o'clock. More tea, with some toast and bananas, constituted breakfast, and we got away in two small tongas, each with a pair of tiny, galloping ponies. It was not the tonga of the Simla road, but the original native vehicle which has lent its name to everything on wheels. "The tonga is a low, two-wheeled, dachshund of a cart, with the build of a gun-carriage," is Steevens's happy description of it. The road led across an uninteresting, level, unfenced, dry plain, with detached hills showing on the horizon. We stopped every seven miles to change ponies, and we changed tongas, visited back and forth from one cart to the other, rode backward as the passenger is supposed to ride, sat on the front seat with the driver, and did everything to beguile the tedium and discomfort of that all-day ride of fifty-six miles. The sun grew warmer, and it was almost hot at noon, the country more and more uninteresting, with few villages, few travelers, and no incidents to distract us after an indifferent tiffin at a way-station. At three in the afternoon, we reached the foot of the ghat in whose perpendicular face the great cave-temples have been excavated. The rock-cut temples at Mahabalipur had been but preparation for the great series of caves at Ellora, where the face of a steep hillside has been burrowed into, great chambers hollowed out, and porticoes, galleries, staircases, and passages cut in the solid rock and covered with splendid bas-relief sculpture on the most elaborate scale. The line of rock-temples extends for a mile

ROCK-CUT TEMPLE, AT ELLORA.

and a quarter along the front of the cliff, Buddhists, Jains, and Brahmans having in turn cut their shrines in the everlasting hills, accomplishing this stupendous work in the sixth, eighth, and later centuries. For more than two hours we rambled along the face of the cliffs, in and out, up and down the different stages and galleries of the thirty-four rock-cut shrines; and, fatigued as we were, hastened with breathless interest from one to another of the many surprises.

All that we had seen of rock-sculptures and monolith temples elsewhere paled before this great display, and all the monuments of patient toil and infinite labor in the world seemed nothing compared to the Kailas at Ellora. First, the great sunken court, measuring one hundred and fifty-four by two hundred and seventy-six feet, was hewn out of the solid trap-rock of the hillside, leaving the rock mass of the temple wholly detached in a cloistered court like a colossal boulder, save as a rock bridge once connected the upper story of the temple with the upper row of galleried chambers surrounding three sides of the court. One enters from the plain by an ornamental gateway in the cliff front, a rock screen closing the front of the court. Colossal elephants and lamp-posts stand on either side of the open *mandapam*, or pavilion, containing the sacred bull; and beyond rises the monolithic Dravidian temple to Shiva, ninety feet in height, hollowed into vestibule, chamber, and image-cells, all lavishly carved. Time and earthquakes have weathered and broken away bits of the great monument, and Moslem zealots strove to destroy the carved figures, but one hardly notes these defects in presence of this greatest wonder of the Indian world, absolutely unique among architectural monuments. Patches of ocher and shreds of flower garlands remained from the last festival, the only suggestion of human touch or occupancy. One seemed to feel the presence of magic forces there, as if the Kailas had been turned to stone by some enchantment. It dazed one to consider that one mind could have conceived such a stupendous monument as this ex-voto of an eighth-century raja—his material expression of gratitude at his restoration to health by the neighboring springs.

The three-story Brahmanical temples were the next most amazing spectacle: gallery over gallery hewn in the cliff front and connected by curious arched passages and tunnels of later date, as in the Do Tal (two-story) and the Tin Tal (three-story) temples. The Das Avatar's main hall is cut one hundred and forty-three feet into the rock, forty-six massive pillars connecting the roof and floor. One Buddhist cave with a double gallery in the screen front, and an upper window opening to the plain, has a ribbed roof, and from so closely following the lines of the early chaitya halls of wooden construction, it is known as the Carpenter's Cave. There is a carved dagoba in the apse of its long hall, where the seated figure of Buddha and attendant figures in air are in the spirit of the best period of Buddhist art. There are storied viharas or monasteries near it, which, like this great chaitya, follow closely the forms of wooden construction. The Dehwarra, adjoining the Carpenter's Cave, measures one hundred and ten by seventy feet, two rows of massive rock pillars joining the floor and roof. In the Jain caves beyond, cross-legged tirthankars sit in meditation in carved cells, archaic prototypes of the fairy marble alcoves on Mount Abu.

Sated with wonders, we were carried up the steep hill to the Nizam's dak bangla, where brass bedsteads with wire springs and double hair mattresses were as great a surprise as the architectural wonders that had stunned us. With great consideration, we omitted from the khansamah's menu all dishes requiring long preparation, in order that we might dine as soon as possible and go to those mattresses the earlier. At the end of two hours of calling and waiting on the "Very well, madam," we crossed the dark lawn to the cook-house door to make a final demand for food of some kind. White figures and turbans flitted about in the lighted interior, making an admirable picture within the frame of the door, and we stood in darkness, silently appreciating it, and wondering if it would be attainable by kodak in daylight. We saw the cook strain the soup into the tureen through the end of the dish-cloth he had used and flung on his arm while we watched, and then we cried aloud. Cook, khansamah, and bearer all leaped aside, soup and dish-rag dropped to the floor, and they retreated to far corners of the cook-house mumbling and wailing: "Oh, memsahib! Please, memsahib!" etc. I had long revolted at the taste and smell of the ordinary gray soup served everywhere, and reckless flights of the imagination in trying to describe the flavoring were borne out by that scene. A very meek and deprecatory khansamah served that dinner of plain chops and potatoes with the inevitable cauliflower, cringing as he offered any dish, backing away quickly at each sound, and keeping one eye fearfully turned upon us and the door of escape as he moved about.

Early the next morning we returned to the temples, climbed the steps, and passed through the rock screen or gateway of the Kailas, fearing lest it be a dream of the night. We sought vainly for some vantage-point in the contracted court where a camera could cover the whole mass of the Kailas. From the galleried chambers surrounding the court we saw the central temple best, and by a pitch-dark stairway we happened into an upper chamber where the finest bas-reliefs at Ellora covered the walls, and the ornamental capitals of the columns were pierced and chiseled out in the free and bold designs of a wood-carver. Even there the hand of Alamgir and his fanatics had fallen, and the tiny figures and the ornaments were defaced. The caves are still places of pilgrimage, and at the great festivals of Shiva crowds troop through the Kailas, and the images are smeared with ocher and hung with garlands. The tread of these thousands of bare feet for centuries has given that peculiar, greasy polish to the stone floors that no other treatment bestows. In the rainy season, waterfalls stream over the front of the cliff, the courts and halls are flooded, and the path that runs along the cliff from cave to cave is a moat defending the temples from the plain.

It was an ideally fresh and fragrant morning when we started down from the grassy plateau to the plain, but it grew hot as the tongas bumped along the tedious way. As we reached a more cultivated stretch of country, sago- and cocoa-palms rustled their dusty fronds in the rising breeze that soon brought with it a rain-cloud and a cold mist that pierced to the marrow. The rain came in blinding sheets, swept through the tongas, and for two hours trickled down on us and our rolls of bedding. We arrived at the station in time to be partially dried over pans of charcoal as we ate a hurried dinner. The train rumbled in toward nine o'clock, and we rode as far as Kalyan, where we waited from four to seven o'clock, when the Poona train picked us up. We had the first new car we had seen, a shining, highly varnished contrast to the ancient, unswept, unwashed cars in which we had been jolted over India. Peacock-blue glass in the windows gave an unearthly look to the red, scorched landscapes we rode through in ascending the Bhor Ghat. By twenty-one tunnels and many loops and zigzags we rose two thousand feet in seventeen miles, the train halting at several reversing stations, where the engine switched past to join the other end of the train. We had eagle views out and down to rocky cañons as bare, dry, and roughly sculptured by the elements as any in our arid regions of the Southwest, even the familiar cactus of Arizona deserts flourishing in the wastes of rock and sand.

From Lonauli station a very trim dog-cart carried us through a model settlement toward the open fields. Our guide to the caves of Karli was Dhoond Dhu, a cheerful little barelegged turban of thirteen, who spoke good English with the chirpy voice of a young robin, and made every point tell by the appeal of his deep, dark eyes. He fought valiantly to make a good bargain for us with the chair-bearers at work in a cactus-strewn field, when the cart had stopped at the end of wheel tracks in a plowed ground. They were decrepit chairs with makeshift poles tied to them—carrying-chairs only, as one decrepit leg and then another fell out if one attempted to sit in them while they rested on the ground. The path led steeply along the side of a hill that became a precipice in places, the chairs creaking and momently threatening collapse. We remembered our bogus Nawab at Jeypore when three fraudulent priests assumed to do the honors of the great Buddhist cave at Karli. Blackened columns and a lofty entrance recessed in the rock are an imposing preparation for the great chaitya hall, a chamber one hundred and twenty-four feet long, forty-two feet wide, and forty-six feet high. A row of ornamental columns rises on either side to the ribbed teak roof, and at the far end, in the nave, a massive dagoba, despoiled of its bas-reliefs, images, and ornaments, is claimed as their sacred emblem by the Shivaites who have so long held the place. Dating from the beginning of the Christian era or earlier, this cave shows the first and purest form of Buddhist temples, and is the largest and finest cave-temple of its kind in India.

THE GREAT CAVE-TEMPLE, KARLI.

Steps lead to adjoining viharas, three-story caves where the square cells with sculptured walls allowed room only for the stone shelf or string-bed of the anchorite.

Workmen dawdled with pick and crowbar, clearing away rubbish at the entrance, and the discomfited priests lounged there, chatting, when we came back from the viharas. Black rain-clouds were rolling up, and we started down the rocky path, leaving Dhoond Dhu to stir up and drive the chair-coolies. Then a great cry arose as priests, workmen, and coolies ran howling: "Prissint! Prissint! Mem-sahib!" rubbing their itching palms across their faces and extending them beseechingly. They shoved one another aside, wrangled fiercely, and seemed ready to do violence to the small guide. It was not the place in which to have an argument with even one bad man, and the dozen big beggars could easily have pitched us over the precipice, or shut us up in farther caves, without killing, until we were ready to pay ransom. But one has such contempt for the Hindu that fear or the possibility of danger never suggested itself until we were well away and thought what that number of Afghans or Macedonians might have done. To stop the clatter and warn off the bogus priest who had snatched Dhoond Dhu roughly by the shoulder, I lifted my umbrella and took but one step forward, when the pack ran back to the cave entrance, and the chair-coolies threw themselves flat and crawled to their poles, imploring mercy. We had to lean against the rock wall while we laughed at the farcical dénouement, Dhoond Dhu shaking the last turban fold loose with his child-like spasms of glee.

On reaching Lonauli early in the afternoon, we had asked the station-master to have a compartment reserved on the midnight train to Bombay. "Certingly, memsahib, certingly. I will wire to Poona." At six o'clock we had no answer—because no wire had been sent. At seven the condition continued, the station-master was still absent, and the assistant would not send a telegram "because there *iss* no rule for *thatt.*" We sent a telegram and asked the assistant to sell us the tickets then, that we might sleep in the waiting-room until the train came at five minutes after midnight. "No, no," said the babu; "the 12:05 *iss* one of to-morrow's trains. I cannot sell you ticket now and mix my accounts for two days so terribly. I should lose some money, and I am poor man."

It was a hot, close night, and the scorching air came in waves from the bare cliffs of the Bhor Ghat as the train curved and reversed and crept from one twinkling light and group of lights to another down the two thousand feet to the plain. With our arrival at Bombay at six in the morning, we had spent our twentieth night on Indian railway trains in three months of travel, in that first winter; and gladly we bade farewell to the red razais.

CHAPTER XXVIII

BOMBAY

AFTER two months "up-country," Bombay seemed a European city, a Western metropolis; and that hotel which strikes such dismay and disgust to the heart of the tourist coming from Europe seemed to us a very palace of comfort; that hotel whose corridors are strewn with servants and their rolls of bedding, their pots, pipes, and traps,—servants who gabble and smoke, eat and sleep, dress and undress, each before his employer's door, as unconcernedly as in their own serais; that hotel of hard and hillocky beds, which all one's winter accumulation of razais cannot soften; that hotel whose partition walls stop two feet from the ceiling, where every room has an outer balcony and an inner dark bath-room whose primitive plumbing puts the American in fear for his life. By contrast with up-country hotels it was the home of comfort, and at last we understood how people could talk of the "luxury of Indian travel." All things are comparative, and one's ideas of splendor depend on what has gone before. Even the Madras and Calcutta hotels would have seemed splendid after a round of inns and banglas.

The soft, sea air, the warm days and mild nights were balm to us, after the dry scorch and frostbites up-country. The sight of Gothic architecture was a revelation after having reached the edge of satiety among Hindu, Jain, Mogul, Pathan, and Dravidian masterpieces. Street-cars, European shop-windows and houses were objects of interest; and to drive over sprinkled roads beside the soft-sounding sea, where bands played and fashion walked; to drink tea on club-house porches,—all this was too exciting.

We were invited to a Parsi wedding on our first day, and drove across the native city, around the curve of the Back Bay, and up the slopes of Malabar Hill to the villa of the bride's family. A procession of Parsi ladies, wrapped in saris of delicate silks, and preceded by a band, entered the gates before us and joined the group of Parsi women in gold-bordered saris who made the drawing-room blaze with their jewels. The bride was quiet and subdued, the groom self-possessed to the point of flippancy when he came in from the assemblage of Parsi men in the garden, all attired in white ceremonial dress and queer black hats. Bands played, and the ceremony by the priest was very long and full of symbolism. The bride, at one point, held a cocoanut and clasped the hand of the groom, while the priest delivered a long exhortation and showered them with rice, fruit, and flowers. The bride was invested with the jeweled necklaces and other gifts of the groom, sprinkled with rose-water, and touched with attar of roses in the strangely mixed Parsi and Hindu ceremony that has come about during the long residence of the fire-worshiping Parsis in India. The conventional menu of a London wedding breakfast, with champagne and ices, was served to the company of Anglo-Indian officials, foreign consuls and merchants, a Portuguese bishop, and some Japanese naval officers and American visitors. The Parsi ladies and children were served in the large marquees on the lawn, where ceremonial dishes were added to the foreign dainties. Each had a palm-leaf for a plate, and a vegetarian repast was partaken of without knives or forks. Each visitor was garlanded with tuberoses and sprinkled with rose-water when he left, but the gilded *pan*, or betel-nut part of Hindu ceremony, was omitted.

A few days later we attended a second Parsi wedding, where still more of the old ceremonial was observed. There was the same garden company of men in white ceremonial dress, and a drawing-room full of Parsi ladies covered with jewels and draped in silks of every delicate color. The bride seemed not to like the way in which her veil was pulled and rumpled by clumsy hands, and sweetmeats thrust in her mouth, and with some emphasis unwound her sari herself and wrapped around her the silver-bordered one given by the groom's mother. The bride and groom sat in chairs facing each other, and the priest wound around and bound them together with the symbolical white cord, and then bound them further with the groom's kamarband. A veil was held between them at the next stage, and finally they ate rice from the same dish, the groom feeding the bride with his fingers. There was a pantomime of her washing the groom's feet with milk, and his purse was given the bride, that she might spend it on a feast for the poor. The ceremony was full of meaning and deep significance to the beautiful, dark-eyed Parsi women and to the serious, priestly looking men, but it would take many pages to convey the full meaning of the customs brought from Persia so many centuries ago.

There were stock sights to be seen in Bombay, and we took the red Murray book and did them; but it was not exciting after the up-country sights and people. First, to the twin Towers of Silence, with the friezes of living vultures on their cornices, where the Parsis, who do not believe in defiling the earth, expose the bodies of their dead to the elements and the birds of the air. Nothing could be more gruesome and repellent than the rows of huge, motionless birds awaiting their prey. There were chill, sepulchral halls where ceremonies are held by the mourners, and from the parapet of the high garden one has a fine view down over the Back Bay and the city, and across the harbor to the mainland shores.

In all the many accounts I have read of these Towers of Silence, the narrators always looked down the winding road and saw a procession of white-clad mourners approaching with a body, and gruesomely told how the vultures saw it too, and flapped their wings. We looked and looked in vain, the first travelers to miss that regulation spectacle. When we boasted our exemption to a resident of Bombay, he said wearily: "But of course you will go home and say you saw a funeral winding up.

"PLEASE BUY MY NIKLASS."

They all do. Four travelers whom I had taken there have published minute and thrilling accounts of how the procession wound up and up, and how the vultures flapped their wings, although I had seen nothing of the kind."

Guide-book in hand, and Sir Edwin Arnold's caves of Elephanta fresh in mind, we rose with the dawn one morning and sped away by steam-launch across the harbor to the cave-temples of Shiva that date before the twelfth century. We landed at a pier of detached concrete blocks, and made our way by leaps to land, where the old sergeant who guards the place described every temple, every bas-relief, every group and image, so minutely that we ought never to forget a detail of those rock-sculptures, many of them of such beauty that we echoed the sergeant's anger at the Portuguese for firing cannon into the caves to destroy the idolatrous work. We tiptoed here and there, kept away from the darker corners, looked suspiciously at every rock and bush and tuft of grass, remembering Sir Edwin Arnold's tales of the deadly cobras on Elephanta; but the sergeant insisted that there were no snakes, that he had never seen one. It only remained for him to tell us, as he did, that he never had fever, for our last illusion to vanish. If we were not to be bitten by cobras and filled with fever germs by visiting Elephanta, what more was it than a pleasure excursion and boating picnic? What glory in daring it? What credit for anything more than one morning's hire of a steam-launch? We did the museum, the art school, the hospital for animals, the markets, and the serais where Mohammedan pilgrims stop on their way to and from Mecca. At the large serai we met the three tuneful Bokhara beggars we had seen in the serai at Amritsar. They were still red-cheeked and cheerful, still wrapped in their north-country wadded clothes on that warm morning, and they showed proudly their Cook coupon ticket for the pilgrim-ship and further journey to Mecca. For the rest, Bombay was a European city; the hotel life, the teas, the drives, all of the West only. It was hardly India to us, save as Delhi jewelers salaamed in recognition and sang to us beseechingly: "Please buy my niklass. Please take that griddle."

We had but a few days to wait for the ship to Ismailia,—hot days, when the thermometer stood at 90° for hours; a haze hung over the ocean, and the evening drives to the Breach of Kandy and Malabar Hill were none too refreshing. All Bombay turned out of doors at sunset, to drive, to walk at the edge of the ocean, to linger by the band-stands long after dark. The groups of white-clad Mohammedans gathered together to pray and to listen to the Koran, and the groups of Parsis playing cards by electric light as they sat on the grass by the Queen's statue, were the sharpest pictures in memory after Bombay and the mainland hills had faded on the horizon, and one turned gratefully toward lands where it is not always afternoon.

"Did you enjoy India?" my friends continued to ask me, with unhappy choice of words; and, to be literal, the answer could only be negative.

"What impressed you most?" To that it was easy to answer: "What England has done for India; the incalculable debt all that continent of diverse peoples owes for the just, intelligent, humane rule of the Great White Queen and her son; for the treasure of noble lives poured into the peninsula for a century, for the burdens the white man has borne." If all the people should gather daily, like the multitudes praying on the Ganges bank at Benares, salaam toward England, and chant their acknowledgments, it would be fitting; but one discovers an ingratitude of dependencies degrees blacker than that of republics.

INDEX

INDEX